SOLVING 9-11

The Deception that Changed the World

CHRISTOPHER BOLLYN

This book is dedicated to the people who
were killed on 9-11 and those who have suffered
and perished in the aftermath as a result of the evil
deception about what happened that day.

The individual is handicapped by coming face-to-face with a conspiracy so monstrous he cannot believe it exists. The American mind simply has not come to a realization of the evil which has been introduced into our midst. It rejects even the assumption that human creatures could espouse a philosophy which must ultimately destroy all that is good and decent.

J. Edgar Hoover, Director of the FBI, *Elks Magazine*, August 1956

Contents

F ear not the path of truth
for the lack of people walking on it.

Robert F. Kennedy

Preface

9-11 is an unsolved crime of terrorism and mass murder. In its name wars have been waged, governments overthrown, and an untold number of lives sacrificed. The crime itself, however, which was exploited to usher in the "War on Terror" with its Draconian security laws, remains unsolved. Ten years after the terror attacks that changed the world, we still do not know what really happened at Shanksville, what hit the Pentagon, or why three skyscrapers collapsed on 9-11.

The unanswered questions about the events of September 11, 2001, have not even been addressed by the government officials entrusted with the responsibility to investigate crimes of terrorism and prosecute those behind them. No trial was held in the decade after 9-11 to determine who is responsible for the terror atrocity that killed thousands. It is now very unlikely that there ever will be. The politicians and news media who should be demanding answers and accountability are not even interested in discussing the subject. How can that be?

To understand why the government and media avoid any serious discussion of 9-11, we need to realize that the terror attacks that changed America were an elaborately planned criminal deception that was not meant to be solved. The "false-flag" terror attacks were designed and carried out with the intention that the public would be deceived with a false explanation blaming the atrocity on Osama Bin Laden and Al Qaida in order to get popular support for the pre-planned "War on Terror" and the invasion of Afghanistan. The U.S.

military had, in fact, invaded Afghanistan and ousted the Taliban regime before the fires beneath the rubble of the World Trade Center had even been extinguished.

That 9-11 was not meant to be solved is evident from the fact that rather than conducting a proper criminal investigation, the federal authorities responsible for prosecuting crimes of terrorism allowed the steel from the Twin Towers, the most crucial evidence from the crime scene, to be destroyed before it could be examined by experts. Other important pieces of evidence, such as the numbered parts from the aircraft, were thrown out like garbage rather than being identified. The outrageous failure by the Department of Justice to protect and properly examine the evidence has resulted in the federal investigation of 9-11 being rightfully labeled a "non-investigation".

The relatives of the victims and those who had hoped that the truth would be found through litigation in the U.S. judicial system have been greatly disappointed that there has been no trial for any of the families of those killed or the alleged perpetrators of the crime. With all the wrongful death cases having been settled out of court it is extremely unlikely that there will ever be a trial to determine who is really responsible for the worst act of terrorism to occur on American soil.

As a journalist, I began writing about 9-11 shortly after the attacks and quickly realized that the truth was being buried beneath a false story pushed by the U.S. administration and compliant media. It was clear that there was a concerted effort to promote a politically expedient explanation and avoid the evidence and questions that contradicted that account. There was no real effort on the part of the government or the media to actually solve the crime. Although the Bush-Cheney administration did finally appoint a commission and several engineering studies, these were all fundamentally flawed in that they were strictly limited in their scope, denied access to the evidence, and began their investigations by accepting the unproven version as true.

By the summer of 2006, after nearly five years of research and writing about 9-11, it was evident that a form of Thermite had been used to demolish the Twin Towers. This was confirmed by the large amount of molten metal found in the rubble and dust and by the abundance of nanoparticles discovered in the smoke that rose from the burning pile at Ground Zero. Shortly after visiting the two scientists whose research confirmed the existence of Thermite at the World Trade Center, I was attacked at my home outside Chicago by heavily-armed undercover police, arrested, and *later* charged with assaulting them. Innocent of the false charges, I pled not guilty and the case went to trial.

Although I had discovered evidence showing that the police had conspired to harm me, the judge did not allow it or my expert witness to be presented in court. Video evidence from the police vehicles that would have proven my innocence was destroyed by the police in violation of their own regulations and my formal legal request. The police then openly lied on the stand and presented both false evidence and the fabricated testimony of a witness to the court. With my evidence having been rejected and the police lies accepted by the court, the state won its case against me. Realizing that I was at the mercy of a very corrupt and criminal system that would do anything to silence me, I took my family to Europe in June 2007 before sentencing.

Determined to find and expose those who were really behind the terror atrocity, I began writing *Solving 9-11: The Deception that Changed the World* in September 2007. Having written hundreds of articles about different aspects of the crime, I wanted to present my hypothesis in a coherent and easily readable format. Much of the information in this book is derived from the many investigative articles I have written about 9-11, which are published in a second volume. I recommend reading the companion volume to this book with the collection of my original 9-11 articles to understand how my thesis of Israeli and Zionist involvement in 9-11 developed.

Solving 9-11 and my research articles that support it are the work of one man. I wrote this book as a service to the American public and mankind because I could not remain indifferent and watch in silence as the lies about 9-11 were used to wage wars of aggression and transform America into a police state.

My hypothesis that 9-11 was an act of false-flag terrorism carried out by Israeli military intelligence and Zionist fifth columnists has not been accepted by many in the so-called 9-11 truth movement because it breaks a cultural taboo regarding how Israel and Jews are viewed in America. There are many Zionist apologists who believe that Israel can do no wrong. It needs to be understood that Zionism is a political ideology, not a religion. Although the more belligerent Zionist faction is very well funded and organized and has a highly-advanced military at its disposal, it does not represent all Jews. If it is true that Israelis and Zionist partisans are indeed behind 9-11, it does not mean that all Jews are guilty by association. The only people who deserve to be condemned are the criminals behind the terror atrocity and those who have helped to conceal the truth about what really happened. The purpose of this book is to find and expose the real culprits so that the American people and mankind can be liberated from the lies about 9-11, for to submit to such evil deception is to be enslaved by it.

Christopher Bollyn
March 6, 2012

There is a much larger group behind these [9-11 attacks] which is the international banking cartel which controls trillions of dollars and which has an interest in controlling countries in the Middle East which are not under their control.

Professor Steven E. Jones on RadioWest with Doug Fabrizio, September 5, 2006

The Truth Marches On

By Glen Stanish

September 11, 2001, like December 7, 1941, is a day that will live in infamy. The post 9-11 period is one of the saddest times in American history. It has, however, provided the American people a slow and painful awakening of sorts.

As a pilot for American Airlines, the attacks of 9-11 hit very close to home. I was in the middle of a four-day trip on a layover in downtown Fort Worth on 9-11. Like many Americans, I woke up to the news of the devastating attacks. And, like most Americans, for a brief period after the attacks I was in a state of shock and awe.

Very shortly after the attacks we were informed by our elected leaders and the media that we had been attacked by Osama Bin Laden and Al Qaida because they didn't like our freedoms. Simple enough, but lacking a plausible political motive. For those who think a bit further than what we are told and deeper about the causes of war - greed in a word - this explanation was hard to accept. It was as if President George W. Bush had given us a square peg, and no matter how hard we tried, we could not make it fit into the proverbial round hole. I suspect that the author of this book, Christopher Bollyn, may have experienced this same thought process.

My own personal discovery of the truth of September the 11th began with Bollyn. I had been a subscriber of *American Free Press,* a weekly newspaper he wrote for. I had enjoyed reading Bollyn's articles over the years, appreciating his thorough research, open and honest candor, and writing style. In one of his articles he wrote about a visit to Shanksville, Pennsylvania, where he interviewed several eyewitnesses of the alleged United Airlines crash of Flight 93. He described in detail how many people, including the mayor of Shanksville, reported having never seen any wreckage of a Boeing 757 airliner. Witnesses stated they saw no smoke or fire, no airframe pieces, no real evidence of an airliner crash, and things along these lines. The coroner on the scene said there were no bodies or body parts to be seen. While reading these statements and descriptions, I could not reconcile them with the usual scenes of large airliner crashes and disasters that I was familiar with.

As an airline pilot, during our initial and annual training we are required by the Federal Aviation Administration (FAA) to complete a course called Crew Resource Management. This is the study of airline accidents and incidents in which we, as flight crew members, are asked what we could have done to prevent a particular accident. This course typically involves reviewing cockpit and air traffic control recordings, flight data recordings, and the documented scenes of the accidents. I have studied many airline accidents over the course of my career.

It was difficult for me to accept the reports from Shanksville about the lack of any wreckage of Flight 93 because large pieces of the aircraft are normally found. There are the remains of the virtually indestructible engine cores, landing gear, and tail sections, to name just a few of the larger parts that would be found in the debris field. Other wreckage that one would expect to find from a Boeing 757 airframe would be the plug-type entry and service doors, cargo doors, over wing exits, sections of fuselage and passenger seats, hydraulic tanks and pumps, and flight controls such as spoiler panels, flaps, slats, rudders, and elevators. Wreckage from inside the cabin that would have survived would include the emergency exit slides, the emergency inflatable rafts, life preserver jackets, and other emergency equipment, galley carts, lavatories, coffee pots, ovens, in-flight magazines, and catalogues. Luggage, freight, and mail would also be recovered from the immediate vicinity. These are the things eyewitnesses and first responders normally observe after a Boeing 757 collides with terrain. Temporary morgues are usually set up in nearby facilities where recovered bodies and body parts are taken and identified.

After reading Bollyn's article, and experiencing the difficulty of reconciling these reports with my experience, I contacted him, and thus began my personal friendship with the author. Bollyn has continued to report breakthrough material and information about the erroneous and deceptive nature of the official 9-11 reports. He has bravely pressed forward with determination, working with scientists, professors, and other qualified professionals to show that the three World Trade Center buildings that collapsed on 9-11 were brought down by explosives in controlled demolitions. He has enlightened many to the intrigues of "false-flag" operations used as pretexts for war by powerful, corrupt, and covetous politicians and bloodthirsty heads of state.

This he has done in the face of heavy resistance by those who would prefer to keep the American people in the dark, namely the mainstream press and other special interest groups. But like a small candle in a dark room, the light shines through.

The 9-11 truth movement, as it is known, owes much to the work of Bollyn. Since his first writings about the subject, virtually thousands of scientists, professors, architects, engineers, pilots, politicians, firefighters, religious leaders, lawyers, and others with expertise and qualifications have organized to have their voices heard and refute the official explanation of the attacks of 9-11. These are our attempts to petition the government for a redress of grievances, as it were. Yet some still ask why would the U.S. government attack its own people or cover up for those who did on 9-11?

And this is where some of Bollyn's most important work leads. To answer difficult questions like these, observers of history and geopolitics should consider the policies that have shifted, been postponed, cancelled, or otherwise bent as a result of the attacks of 9-11. As most observers will attest, there is a major unresolved political issue in the Middle East, one whose developments have been very much affected by 9-11 and one that has divided the U.S. political house, leaving it unable to clearly define and implement its policies. This unresolved political issue is the establishment of an independent and democratic Palestinian state, co-existing with Israel with peace and justice for all.

What is our national policy concerning an independent and democratic Palestinian state? Is it fluid, undefined, and changing course over time or is it solid, stable, and complete, just waiting for the ideal time to be implemented? Or, perhaps, there is more than one policy? Is there one policy for the public, which is never implemented, and another secret policy that is carried out in opposition to and in defiance of the stated public policy?

As former President Jimmy Carter wrote in his book *Palestine: Peace Not Apartheid:*

The unwavering official policy of the United States

since Israel became a state has been that its borders, unless modified through negotiations, must coincide with the armistice lines prevailing from 1949 until 1967...

The unanimously adopted UN Resolution 242 specifies the withdrawal of Israeli armed forces from occupied territories... these include the Golan Heights, Gaza, the Sinai, and the West Bank, including Jerusalem...

U.S. policy was that Israeli settlements in the West Bank and Gaza were 'illegal and obstacles to peace'... also, as a member of the International Quartet that includes Russia, the United Nations, and the European Union, America supports the Roadmap for Peace which espouses exactly the same requirements... and whose ultimate aim is the creation of a democratic and independent Palestinian state.

To highlight U.S. and international efforts to achieve peace in the Middle East, a brief historical review is in order.

- The Camp David Accords led directly to the 1979 Israel-Egypt Peace Treaty.

- The Madrid Conference was hosted by the government of Spain and co-sponsored by the USA and the USSR. It convened on October 30, 1991, and lasted for three days. It was an early attempt by the international community to start a peace process through negotiations involving Israel and the Palestinians.

- The Oslo Accords, agreed in Norway on August 20,

1993, and signed at a public ceremony in Washington, D.C. on September 13, 1993, was a milestone in the Israeli-Palestinian conflict. This was the first direct, face-to-face agreement between Israel and political representatives of the Palestinians. It was intended to be a framework for the future relations between Israel and the Palestinians, when all outstanding final status issues between the two sides would be addressed and resolved in one agreement. Permanent issues such as Jerusalem, Palestinian refugees, Israeli settlements, borders, and security were deliberately left to be decided at a later stage.

- The Interim Agreement on the West Bank and the Gaza Strip, also known as Oslo 2, was signed by Israel and the Palestine Liberation Organization (PLO) on September 28, 1995. It became the basis and the reference point for subsequent negotiations and agreements such as the Hebron Protocol of 1997 and the Wye River Memorandum of 1998, and it is a basis for the latter Road Map for Peace which calls for the creation of a democratic independent Palestinian state, part of the two-state solution for Middle East peace.

- The Wye River Memorandum, signed on October 23, 1998, was an agreement negotiated between Israel and the Palestinian Authority to implement the earlier Interim Agreement of September 1995.

- The Sharm El Sheikh Memorandum was signed on

September 4, 1999, by Prime Minister of Israel Ehud Barak and PLO Chairman Yasir Arafat. Its purpose was to implement the Interim Agreement (Oslo II) and all other agreements between the PLO and Israel since 1993. The two sides agreed to resume the Permanent Status negotiations to achieve the goal of reaching a Permanent Status Agreement. They reaffirmed that the negotiations on the Permanent Status will lead to the implementation of Security Council Resolutions 242 and 338. They agreed to make a determined effort to conclude a framework agreement and setting a timetable to achieve these goals. The timetable for final status talks to deal with Jerusalem, borders, refugees, settlements, and a framework agreement on permanent status (FAPS) was to be achieved by February 2000 with a permanent agreement signed by September 2000.

- The Middle East Peace Summit at Camp David of July 2000 took place between U.S. President Bill Clinton, Israeli Prime Minister Ehud Barak, and Palestinian Authority Chairman Yasir Arafat. It was an unsuccessful attempt to negotiate a "final status settlement" to the Israeli-Palestinian conflict.

- The Taba Summit between Israel and the Palestinian Authority was held in January 2001 at Taba in the Sinai Peninsula. These talks aimed at reaching the "final status" negotiations to end the Israeli-Palestinian conflict, and came closer to reaching a final settlement than any previous or subsequent peace talks. The talks were discontinued due to upcoming Israeli elections.

As can be seen by the record, U.S. and international efforts to reach a comprehensive settlement for peace in the Middle East and the establishment of an independent and democratic Palestinian state were proceeding nicely until early 2001. One might consider that we, as a global community, were in the end game, late in the fourth quarter or in the bottom of the ninth inning, to use sports analogies – but perhaps 'sudden death' would be more apt.

To have come so far and not taken the ball into the end zone, to have failed to cross the finish line when we were so close, indicates that there must be a very determined and powerful force preventing it. There must be an opposing power, a well-organized political entity whose objective is to prevent any final settlement of the crucial issues in the Palestinian/Israeli conflict. This antagonistic element is opposed to any agreement that would allow the establishment of an independent and democratic Palestinian state.

Ariel Sharon was elected prime minister of Israel in February 2001, and according to former President Jimmy Carter, Sharon was committed to the rejection of the Oslo peace agreement.

Historically speaking, Ariel Sharon, like other Israeli politicians from the right-wing Likud, made statements and policies that indicated his intention to kill the peace process. In 1977, Menachem Begin created the Likud party, which maintains the position that the land of Gaza and the West Bank belong to the State of Israel and will not be given up in a peace agreement.

In the early 1980s, during the presidency of Ronald Reagan, Israel announced the annexation of the Golan Heights and increased their efforts to build Jewish settlements throughout the West Bank and Gaza. Since 1980, with the Likud in control of the government, the confiscation of Arab land has accelerated greatly with the building of illegal Jewish settlements in the West Bank being one of the government's top priorities.

Ariel Sharon stated that the East Bank of the Jordan is "ours but not in our hands, just as East Jerusalem had been until the Six-Day War." During the Clinton years, Prime Minister Benjamin Netanyahu, a Likud hawk, promised never to exchange land for peace. Then Foreign Minister Ariel Sharon declared the Oslo Agreement to be "national suicide" saying, "Everybody has to move, run and grab as many hilltops as they can to enlarge the settlements because everything we take now will stay ours."

In *Jewish History, Jewish Religion,* Israeli author Israel Shahak explained the reasons behind the actions of his country's government:

> The main danger which Israel, as a 'Jewish state' poses to its own people, to other Jews, and to its neighbors is its ideologically motivated pursuit of territorial expansion and the inevitable series of wars resulting from this aim... In 1956, I eagerly swallowed all of Prime Minister Ben Gurion's political and military reasons for Israel initiating the Suez War, until he pronounced in the Knesset on the third day of that war, that the real reason for it is 'the restoration of the Kingdom of David and Solomon' to its Biblical [Old Testament] bor-

ders ... The Biblical borders of the land of Israel, "which rabbinical authorities interpret as ideally belonging to the Jewish state" include the following areas: in the south, all of Sinai and a part of northern Egypt up to the environs of Cairo; in the east, all of Jordan and a large chunk of Saudi Arabia, all of Kuwait and a part of Iraq south of the Euphrates; in the north, all of Lebanon and all of Syria together with a huge part of Turkey (up to Lake Van); and in the west, Cyprus ... In May of 1993, Ariel Sharon formally proposed in the Likud Convention that Israel should adopt the 'Biblical borders' concept as its official policy.

Well, it looks like we have identified the opposition to the establishment of an independent Palestinian state. As we can see, up until shortly before September 2001, U.S. and international efforts to achieve a final resolution to the Israeli-Palestinian conflict were very close to their goal. Shortly before September 11, 2001, an Israeli government was elected whose stated objectives were in sharp opposition to the aims of the peace efforts of the United States and the international community.

Immediately after the 9-11 attacks, Israeli spokesman Benjamin Netanyahu stated publicly, "It is a very good thing," because it would strengthen American support for Israel. As if to confirm Netanyahu's sentiments, using 9-11 as justification, Israel's Prime Minister Ariel Sharon escalated the Israeli-Palestinian conflict, pummeling Palestinian infrastructure, homes, and businesses in the West Bank and Gaza on the pretext of fighting terrorism.

Shortly thereafter, Sharon's Chief of Staff Dov Weisglass admitted that the purpose of his government's policy to expand settlements in the West Bank was to undermine peace plans, stymie the creation of a Palestinian state, and halt talks about the right of return for Palestinian refugees:

> The significance of our disengagement plan is the freezing of the peace process. It supplies the formaldehyde necessary so there is no political process with the Palestinians. When you freeze the process, you prevent the establishment of a Palestinian state... Effectively, this whole package called a Palestinian state has been removed indefinitely from our agenda. All of this was done with the United States' blessing.

What? Wait a minute! This was done with the blessing of the government of the United States? What about our "unwavering official policies"? What about Israeli settlements in the West Bank being "illegal" and "obstacles to peace"? What about our official support for the creation of an independent and democratic Palestinian State as part of a just and final resolution to the Israeli-Palestinian conflict? Do we have more than one policy?

On March 28, 2001, at the Arab League meeting in Beirut, twenty-two nations endorsed a resolution introduced by Saudi Crown Prince Abdullah. It offered Israel normal relations with all Arab states if Israel complied with UN Resolutions 194 and 242. The next day, a massive Israeli military force surrounded and destroyed Yasir Arafat's compound in Ramallah. Later, the United States voted for a UN Security Council resolution demanding Israeli withdrawal from Ramallah, which Israel ignored.

Arab diplomats accused Ariel Sharon of deliberately sabotaging the peace overture. Crown Prince Abdullah called Sharon's assault "a brutal, despicable, savage, inhumane, and cruel action."

A "Roadmap" for resolving the Israeli-Palestinian conflict was announced in April 2003 by UN Secretary General Kofi Annan on behalf of the U.S., the UN, the European Union, and Russia (i.e. the Quartet). Kofi Annan stated:

> Such a settlement, negotiated between the parties, will result in the emergence of an independent, democratic Palestinian state living side by side in peace and security with Israel and its neighbors. The settlement will end the occupation that began in 1967, based on the Madrid Conference terms of reference and the principle of land for peace, UN Security Council Resolutions 242, 338, and 1397, agreements previously reached by the parties, and the Arab initiative proposed by Saudi Crown Prince Abdullah and endorsed by the Arab Summit in Beirut.

The Palestinians accepted the Roadmap in its entirety. The Israeli government announced several caveats and prerequisites, some of which would preclude any final peace talks. Some of the Israeli provisos were: Israeli control over Palestine, including the entry and exit of all persons and cargo, plus its airspace and electromagnetic spectrum (radio, television, etc.). No discussion of Israeli settlements in Judea, Samaria [the West Bank] and Gaza or the status of the Palestinian Authority and its institutions in Jerusalem. No reference to the key provisions of UN Resolution 242, and the waiver of any right of return of refugees, among others.

The practical result of all this, according to former President Jimmy

Carter, is that the Roadmap for Peace has become moot, with only two results: Israel has been able to use it as a delaying tactic with an endless series of preconditions that can never be met while proceeding with plans to implement its unilateral goals; and the U.S. has been able to give the impression of positive engagement in the "peace process."

With Ariel Sharon and George W. Bush in office, the so-called "peace process" went nowhere.

In early 2005, Jimmy Carter again arrived in Israel. In *Palestine: Peace Not Apartheid,* he describes the "most disturbing intrusions of the great dividing wall being built by the Israelis."

Described as a 'security fence', Carter wrote about the Israeli wall of separation:

> "...its other purpose became clear as we observed its construction and examined maps of the barrier's ultimate path through Palestine. Including the Israeli-occupied Jordan River Valley, the wall would take in large areas of land for Israel and encircle the Palestinians who remained in their remnant of the West Bank. This would severely restrict Palestinian access to the outside world. 'Imprisonment Wall' is more descriptive than 'security fence.'

Sharon's purpose was to implement the unilateral disengagement policy and to complete building a wall to separate Palestinians from territory to be claimed by Israel, according to President Carter.

In Carter's book, he says the developments in the wake of 9-11 have taken us further from a final resolution and the creation of an independent and democratic Palestinian state. Carter wrote:

With increasing control of East Jerusalem, with relative security from the wall surrounding what is left of the West Bank, and with thousands of remaining settlers east of the wall protected by a strong occupying force, there is a temptation for some Israelis simply to avoid any further efforts to seek a peace agreement based on the Quartet's Roadmap or good-faith negotiations on any other basis...

In this diplomatic vacuum, Israeli leaders have embarked on a series of unilateral decisions, bypassing both Washington and the Palestinians...Utilizing their political and military dominance, they are imposing a system of partial withdrawal, encapsulation, and apartheid on the Muslim and Christian citizens of the occupied territories. The driving purpose for the forced separation of the two peoples is...the acquisition of land...

The future prospects for the West Bank are...dismal. Especially troublesome are the huge dividing wall in populated areas and an impassable fence in rural areas. The governments of Ariel Sharon and Ehud Olmert have built the fence and wall mainly within Palestinian territory, intruding deeply into the West Bank to encompass Israeli settlement blocs and large areas of other Palestinian land. It is projected to be at least three and a half times as long as Israel's internationally recognized border and already cuts directly through Palestinian villages, divides families from their gardens and farmland...

One example is that the wandering wall almost completely surrounds the Palestinian city of Qalqilya with its 45,000 inhabitants, with most of the citizens' land and about one-third of their water supply confiscated by the Israelis. Almost the same encirclement has occurred around 170,000 citizens of Bethlehem, the birthplace of Jesus.

First, a wide swath must be bulldozed through communities before the wall can be built. In addition to the concrete and electrified fencing materials used in the construction, the barrier includes two meter deep trenches, roads for patrol vehicles, electronic ground and fence sensors, thermal imaging and video cameras, sniper towers, and razor wire – almost entirely on Palestinian land. The area between the closed segregation barrier and the Israeli border has been designated a closed military region for an indefinite period of time. Israeli directives state that every Palestinian over the age of twelve living in the closed area has to obtain a 'permanent resident permit' from the civil administration to enable them to live in their own homes...

To summarize, whatever territory Israel decides to confiscate will be on its side of the wall, but Israelis will still control the Palestinians who will be on the other side of the barrier...

Since 1945, the International Court of Justice has functioned essentially as the judicial arm of the United Nations system, and in July 2004 the court determined that the Israeli government's construction of the segregation wall in the occupied West Bank was illegal...The court called on Israel to cease construction of the wall, to dismantle what has already been built in areas within the occupied Palestinian territory, and to compensate Palestinians who suffered losses as a result of the wall's construction. The Israeli Supreme Court has chosen not to accept the International Court's decision...

The wall ravages many places along its devious route that are important to Christians. In addition to enclosing Bethlehem in one of its most notable intrusions, an especially heartbreaking division is on the southern slope of the Mount of Olives, a favorite place for Jesus and his disciples, and very near Bethany, where they often visited Mary, Martha, and their brother, Lazarus. There is a church named for one of the sisters, Santa Marta Monastery, where Israel's thirty-foot concrete wall cuts through the property. The house of worship is now on the Jerusalem side, and its parishioners are separated from it because they cannot get permits to enter Jerusalem. Its priest, Father Claudio Ghilardi, says, 'For nine hundred years we have lived here under Turkish, British, Jordanian, and Israeli governments, and no one has ever stopped people coming to pray. It is scandalous. This is not a barrier. It is a border. Why don't they speak the truth?'

Father Claudio adds a comment that describes the path of the entire barrier: 'The wall is not separating Palestinians from Jews; rather, Palestinians from Palestinians.' Nearby are three convents that will also be cut off from people they serve. These 2,000 Palestinian Christians have lost their place of worship and their spiritual center.

In addition to cutting off about 200,000 Palestinians in Jerusalem from their relatives, property, schools, and businesses, the wall is designed to complete the enclosure of a severely truncated Palestine, a small portion of its original size, compartmentalized, divided into cantons, occupied by Israeli security forces, and isolated from the outside world. In addition, a network of exclusive highways is being built across even these fragments of the West Bank to connect the new Greater Israel in the west with the occupied Jordan River valley in the east, where 7,000 Jews are living in twenty-one heavily protected settlements among about 50,000 Palestinians who are still permitted to stay there. The area along the Jordan River, which is now planned as the eastern leg of the encirclement of the Palestinians, is one of Palestine's most lucrative and productive agricultural regions. Most of its inhabitants were forcibly evicted in 1967, and the Israelis have not allowed these original families to return. Israeli customs officers keep lists of their names and are careful to prohibit their crossing any international

checkpoint into occupied territory, where they might
lay claim to their homes and farmland.

President Carter continues to describe the rather hopeless prospects
for the Palestinians, the result of developments that were allowed to
occur in the Middle East after the attacks of 9-11: "It is obvious that
the Palestinians will be left with no territory in which to establish a
viable state... The Palestinians will have a future impossible for them
or any portion of the international community to accept."

So it sounds as if a two-state solution to the peace process has become null and void. Was this the real reason for 9-11? Was it carried
out to create a condition of war, based on lies, deception, and fraud to
distract and obfuscate attempts to reach a two-state settlement, which
seemed within reach just before September 2001? Was it designed to
allow Israel to continue its unilateral goals of further expansion, to create a Greater Israel that reaches from the Euphrates to the Nile, ethnically cleansing the land of its original inhabitants? Have we established
in the Green Zone in Baghdad a base to conduct future operations
to assist our Zionist ally with her future expansionist conquests? Do
we have more than one policy here? As observers of history and geopolitics, it certainly makes more sense now than the ridiculous, "They
attacked us because they hate our freedoms" rubbish.

Recently, on April 25, 2009, the Israeli newspaper *Ha'aretz* reported:

> New foreign minister Avigdor Lieberman said on
> Wednesday that Israel was changing its policies on
> the peace process and was not bound by commit-
> ments it made at a U.S. sponsored conference to pur-
> sue creation of a Palestinian state...

A source in Prime Minister Benjamin Netanyahu's party confirmed Wednesday that his new government intended to distance itself from U.S. sponsored understandings on working towards a Palestinian state.

"Israel's government said Sunday that it would not halt construction of a planned housing project in east Jerusalem," *USA TODAY* reported on July 20, 2009. "Prime Minister Benjamin Netanyahu told his cabinet there would be no limits on Jewish construction anywhere in 'unified Jerusalem'" and "declared Israeli sovereignty over the entire city 'indisputable.'"

Six weeks later, Reuters reported: "Israel approved on Monday the building of 455 settler homes in the occupied West Bank. A Defense Ministry list of the first such building permits since Prime Minister Benjamin Netanyahu took office in March showed the homes would be erected in areas Israel intends to keep."

As President Jimmy Carter wrote in *Palestine: Peace Not Apartheid*:

The overriding problem is that, for more than a quarter century, the actions of some Israeli leaders have been in direct conflict with the official policies of the United States, the international community, and their own negotiated agreements... Israel's continued control and colonization of Palestinian land have been the primary obstacles to a comprehensive peace agreement in the Holy Land. In order to perpetuate the occupation, Israeli forces have deprived their unwilling subjects of basic human rights. No objective person could personally observe existing conditions in the West Bank and dispute these statements.

Two other interrelated factors have contributed to the perpetuation of violence and regional upheaval: the condoning of illegal Israeli actions from a submissive White House and U.S. Congress during recent years, and the deference with which other international leaders permit this unofficial U. S. policy in the Middle East (emphasis added) to prevail.

In order to achieve its goals, Israel has decided to avoid any peace negotiations and to escape even the mild restraints of the United States by taking unilateral action, called 'convergence' or 'realignment,' to carve out for itself the choice portions of the West Bank, leaving Palestinians destitute within a small and fragmented remnant of their own land.

The only rational response to this continuing tragedy is to revitalize the peace process through negotiations between Israelis and Palestinians, but the United States has, in effect, abandoned this effort.

In 1796, George Washington gave his Farewell Address which contained many important parting words of advice for future generations of politicians and citizens alike, the disregard for which has helped bring us to this sad post 9-11 political world we find ourselves in. President Washington said:

Hence, likewise, they will avoid the necessity of those overgrown military establishments, which under any form of government, are inauspicious to liberty, and which are to be regarded as particularly hostile to republican liberty...

Nothing is more essential than that permanent, inveterate antipathies against particular nations, and passionate attachment for others should be excluded; and in place of them, just and amicable feelings towards all should be cultivated. The nation which indulges towards another a habitual hatred or a habitual fondness is in some degree a slave. It is a slave to its animosity or to its affection, either of which is sufficient to lead it astray from its duty and its interest…

So likewise, a passionate attachment of one nation for another produces a variety of evils. Sympathy for the favorite nation, facilitating the illusion of an imaginary common interest in cases where no real common interest exists, and infusing into one the enmities of the other, betrays the former into a participation in the quarrels and wars of the latter without adequate inducement or justification. It also leads to concessions to the favorite nation of privileges denied to others which is apt doubly to injure the nation making the concessions; by unnecessarily parting with what ought to be retained, and by exciting jealousy, ill-will, and a disposition to retaliate, in the parties from whom equal privileges are withheld. And it gives to ambitious, corrupted, or deluded citizens, (who devote themselves to the favorite nation), facility to betray or sacrifice the interests of their own country, without odium, sometimes even with popularity; gilding, with the appearance of a virtuous sense of obligation, a commendable deference for public opinion, or a laudable zeal for public good, the base or foolish compliance of ambition, corruption, or infatuation.

Against the insidious wiles of foreign influence (I conjure you to believe me fellow citizens) the jealousy of a free people ought to be constantly awake, since history and experience prove that foreign influence is one of the most baneful foes of republican government.

Excessive partiality for one nation and excessive dislike of another cause those whom they actuate to see danger only on one side, and serve to veil and even second the arts of influence on the other. Real Patriots who may resist the intrigues of the favorite are liable to become suspected and odious, while its tools and dupes usurp the applause and confidence of the people, to surrender their interest.

The great rule of conduct for us in regard to foreign nations is in extending our commercial relations, to have with them as little political connection as possible...

It is our true policy to steer clear of permanent alliances with any portion of the foreign world...

Harmony, liberal intercourse with all nations, are recommended by policy, humanity, and interest.

As you read Christopher Bollyn's *Solving 9-11: The Deception that Changed the World*, you will understand just exactly who and what foreign political interest actually attacked us on September 11, 2001. These foreign political interests with their traitors (George Washington referred to these types as tools and dupes) inside our U.S. political establishment attempted to deceive us in order to pursue their foreign-sponsored political will and expansionist policies in the Middle East.

As you read, the real perpetrators of the 9-11 attacks will become apparent, and they will be identified. The motive will become clear, and you will see this peg as a natural fit. You will understand that our country is filled with "ambitious, corrupted, and deluded citizens (in positions of political power, office holders, judges, the press, etc.) who devote themselves to a foreign nation, and have sacrificed the interests of their own country, with popularity, gilding, with the appearance of a virtuous sense of obligation. You may even find yourself supporting a new investigation into the attacks of 9-11.

So what else should one do when he or she finds that their government has attempted to deceive them, in order to pursue unofficial policies through the arts of lies, fraud, deception, and cover-up? For Christopher Bollyn and like-minded believers, the Scriptures are clear. "And have no fellowship with the unfruitful works of darkness, but rather expose them." (Ephesians 5:11, NKJV)

Glen Stanish is a professional pilot and the author of "Where is the Wreckage of UAL 93?" and *Uncle Sam's Christian Patriots*, a book about the attacks of 9-11.

The deathly precision of the attacks and the magnitude of planning would have required years of planning. Such a sophisticated operation would require the fixed frame of a state intelligence organization, something not found in a loose group like the one led by the student Mohammed Atta in Hamburg.

Eckehardt Werthebach,
former president of Germany's
Verfassungsschutz intelligence service,
to the author, December 2001

Chapter I

9-11 Through the Eyes
of an American Skeptic

As a journalist with an independent weekly newspaper based in Washington, D.C., I became caught up in the events of 9-11 from the minute it happened and was able to write freely about the terror attacks that were exploited to start the pre-planned War on Terror.

From my position as a skeptic of the unproven official version, I have examined the facts and evidence since the day it happened and have concluded that the U.S. government and controlled media have engaged in a conspiracy to deceive the world about what really happened on that terrible day.

The Dream

The early morning hours of 11 September 2001 found me with my family driving through New York City en route to Washington, D.C. after a weekend trip to Stowe, Vermont. We had visited the Trapp family lodge and gotten a late start from Stowe on Monday afternoon. By the time we reached New York City, our two small children were fast asleep in the back seat of the car.

Because the hotels were either full or outrageously expensive, I was left with no choice but to continue driving down the highway when I should have been sleeping. To keep me awake as I drove through New York City, my wife Helje described a vivid dream she had had a week earlier, the night before we had left our home near Chicago.

In her dream we were driving toward a city with a skyline of densely packed skyscrapers when a large airplane flew right at us and plunged into the road about 50 meters in front of our car. She turned and saw the plane emerge from the ground behind us and another plane coming at us from another angle. This was a strange dream in which she felt that our family had been under attack. Helje's dream turned out to be an eerie and uncanny premonition of what was to happen in the skies of New York City less than eight hours later.

It was about 3 a.m. in the morning of September 11 when we finally found an affordable hotel room just inside the state of Maryland on Interstate 95. The kids woke up and jumped on the beds and then we all fell asleep about a half-hour later.

I woke up about 8:30 a.m. and went down to the lobby for a cup of coffee. The television was on in the breakfast area reporting that a plane had struck the North Tower of the World Trade Center in Manhattan. I grabbed some pastries and coffee and hurried back to the room and turned the television to the news channel.

The children and I went to get more donuts and coffee and were on our way back to the room when the second plane hit the South Tower. Helje had seen it happen live on television. We were shocked by the events and realized that America was under attack. I immediately called my office in Washington, D.C. and told my boss that kamikaze airplanes had hit the World Trade Center. He thought I was joking. I said I wouldn't joke about such a thing and told him to turn on the radio. I called the office again after the Pentagon was hit and said we would not be coming to Washington but were heading home to Chicago. Having no idea what would happen next, I thought it would be best to take the country roads and stay away from big cities.

We drove through rural Lancaster County past Amish farmers harvesting a very tall corn crop. I stopped and walked into the fields to ask some of the German-speaking farmers if they knew what had happened in New York City. They said they had not heard anything about it and carried on working with their horse-drawn harvester.

Our route from Pennsylvania to Chicago took us near the site in Shanksville where Flight 93 supposedly crashed, but I had no desire to go to the scene of the disaster. We stopped for lunch in a small town. The diner was full of people but nobody was talking. The people sat quietly, as if mesmerized, listening to the news on the radio.

Indications of Israeli Involvement

We listened to the radio as we drove across Pennsylvania. It was a beautiful sunny day with a bright blue sky. About noon I heard a news report that five "Middle Eastern" men had been seen in New Jersey videotaping and celebrating the destruction of the World Trade Center. Most people automatically associate "Middle Eastern" with "Arab". This early news report immediately planted in the public mind the idea that Muslims were behind the terror attacks. This line of thinking quickly became the accepted explanation and although it remains unproven, became the official version of 9-11.

The first indication that the attack on the World Trade Center was an elaborate "false flag" operation came with the arrest of the five men on the New Jersey side of the Hudson River. These men, described as "Middle Eastern" in the first media reports, were later identified as Israelis. A false-flag operation is a crime which is designed and carried out so that another party or nation is blamed.

The five jubilant Middle Eastern men, who had filmed themselves smiling and celebrating with the burning World Trade Center in the background, were identified as Sivan and Paul Kurzberg, Oded Ellner, Omer Marmari, and Yaron Schmuel. Two of them were actually known to U.S. law enforcement as agents of Israeli intelligence, a fact that was ignored by the media.

The Israelis had been observed taking video or photos of themselves with the World Trade Center burning in the background. Sivan Kurzberg told the police that the men had been driving in their van in the immediate vicinity of the towers that morning. He was photographed flicking a lighter with the burning towers behind him.

A woman who had observed the jubilant Israelis said she was struck by the expressions on the men's faces. "They were like happy, you know," she said. "They didn't look shocked to me. I thought it was very strange."

When they were arrested, Sivan, the driver of the van, told the police, "We are Israeli. We are not your problem. Your problems are our problems. The Palestinians are the problem."

The story of the five men celebrating the destruction of the Twin Towers was dropped from the national news when it became known that they were not Arabs or Muslims from the Middle East, but Israelis.

The noteworthy fact that these men, who clearly had prior knowledge of the attacks, were in fact Israelis, and that they had been arrested at gunpoint with box cutter knives, multiple passports, and thousands of dollars in cash driving a van that tested positive for explosives was only reported by Paolo Lima in a local New Jersey newspaper, the *Bergen Record*, the following day.

This important information, however, was completely ignored by the *New York Times* and the other national mass media outlets based across the river in New York City. I discussed the details with Paolo Lima on the phone and this important and suppressed story became the subject of my first article about 9-11. I realized then, during the first week after 9-11, that the mainstream news media was ignoring and covering up important information and evidence about the terrorist attacks.

There would be, for example, no reporting in the mainstream media of the evidence of Israeli involvement or prior knowledge of the attacks. This was just the beginning of the censorship the media was to impose on the events of 9-11.

The possibility that these men could be Israeli intelligence agents involved in a spectacular "false flag" terror attack was discussed in my article that went to print in *American Free Press* on September 20, 2001.

Months later, *Forward*, a well-known New York-based Jewish newspaper, confirmed that Urban Moving Systems, the Weehawken, New Jersey-based "moving" company that the men worked for, was actually an Israeli intelligence front operation and that at least two of the men, evidently the Kurzberg brothers, were known agents of Mossad, Israeli military intelligence.

Dominic Suter, the owner of the company and a suspect in the terror attacks, was allowed to flee to Israel after the Federal Bureau of Investigation had initially interviewed him, but before they could interrogate him a second time. He has not been extradited to the United States.

After being held for 10 weeks, the five Israelis were sent back to Israel on visa violations. Ellner, Marmari, and Schmuel appeared on an Israeli television show, without the Kurzberg brothers, in November 2001. The three Israelis confessed that their mission had been to document the 9-11 attacks. "The fact of the matter is that we come from a country that experiences terror daily," Oded Ellner said. "Our purpose was to document the event."

The Israelis prior knowledge of the attacks reveals their evident complicity in the murder of some 3,000 people. One would think that such a revealing public admission by a suspect, claiming prior knowledge of the terror attack and saying that his purpose "was to document the event" would be extremely newsworthy information in the United States.

Sadly, this was not the case. Rather than discuss the evidence, the mainstream media promoted an unproven version of events in which the blame was assigned to nineteen Arabs with ties to Osama Bin Laden and Al Qaida.

There were other conspicuous indications of Israeli involvement in 9-11 from the beginning. On the day of the bombings, Benjamin Netanyahu, the Israeli politician from the right-wing Likud Party, openly stated that he viewed 9-11 as a *positive* development in an interview with James Bennet of the *New York Times*:

Asked tonight what the attack meant for relations between the United States and Israel, Benjamin Netanyahu, the former prime minister, replied, "It's very good." Then he edited himself: "Well, it's not good, but it will generate immediate sympathy."

Netanyahu predicted that the attack would "strengthen the bond between our two peoples, because we've experienced terror of so many decades, but the United States has now experienced a massive hemorrhaging of terror." The *New York Times* published Netanyahu's comments in an article titled "Spilled Blood is Seen as Bond That Draws Two Nations Closer," on 12 September 2001.

Journalists who challenge the official version with evidence and facts are marginalized as "conspiracy nuts." I have been slandered by the media simply because I have investigated the evidence of Israeli involvement in the terror attacks.

The personal attacks against me led to an assault by three heavily-armed unidentified men who assaulted me at my home in August 2006. The names of these men, who turned out to be undercover police, were kept secret for a month. Their assault left me with a fractured right elbow and shocked with 50,000 volts from a police device known as a TASER. This outrageous and illegal assault occurred at my home in front of my wife and eight-year-old daughter.

I was taken to jail and subsequently charged with resisting arrest and aggravated assault, both misdemeanor charges. In the Chicago system of justice, one is forced to plead guilty and accept the sentence meted out by the judge. I refused to plead guilty, however, and spent nearly one year trying to defend myself against the baseless charges and malicious prosecution.

In early June 2007, I was found guilty of both misdemeanors after a seriously flawed four-day trial in which the police were allowed to destroy the video evidence and then openly lied on the stand. My expert witness and evidence were not allowed to be presented by the

Cook County judge, Hyman Riebman, a Zionist Jew. Having seen that there was no way to obtain justice in the corrupt court system, I was compelled to leave Chicago with my family before the date of sentencing. It would have been irresponsible for me to allow this criminal system to harm me and my family more than it already had.

The Odigo Warnings

In the first days and weeks after 9-11, I paid very close attention to the large number of Israeli terror suspects arrested, which was more than two hundred by November 2001. I also investigated the published reports that an Israeli text messaging service had been used to warn Israelis of the attacks in New York - hours before they occurred. Many Israelis were evidently forewarned of the attacks through an Israeli instant messaging service called Odigo. This story, which presents the clearest evidence of Israeli prior knowledge of the attacks, was reported only very briefly in the U.S. media – and then forgotten.

According to the published reports, Israel-based employees of Odigo reported having received warnings of an imminent attack at the World Trade Center hours before the first plane hit the north tower. Odigo, an Israeli-owned company, had its U.S. headquarters two blocks from the World Trade Center, but the forewarned Odigo employees did not pass the terror warning on to the authorities in New York, an act that would have saved thousands of lives.

Two weeks after 9-11, Alex Diamandis, Odigo's vice president, said, "The messages said something big was going to happen in a certain amount of time, and it did – almost to the minute." "It was possible that the attack warning was broadcast to other Odigo members, but the company has not received reports of other recipients of the message," Diamandis said. According to a report in the *Jerusalem Post*, Israel's foreign ministry had collected the names of four thousand Israelis believed to have been in the areas of World Trade Center and the Pentagon at the time of the attack, yet only one was reported to have died in the Twin Towers. Based on the number provided by the Israeli government of the number of Israelis thought to have been at the World Trade Center at the time of the attacks, it seems evident that most of them got the warning.

Odigo, which offers real-time messaging, has a feature called "People Finder" which allows a user to send an instant message to a large group based on a common characteristic, such as Israeli nationality. "People Finder" allows Odigo users to search for online "buddies," with filters like Israeli nationality, while maintaining user privacy at all times. The message was probably sent in Hebrew. The Internet address of the sender of the warning was allegedly given to the FBI. Two months later it was reported that the FBI was still investigating the matter. Since then there have been no further media reports about the Odigo warning of 9-11.

These two news stories about the fake Israeli "movers" and the Odigo messages, which clearly indicated that some Israelis had very specific prior knowledge of the attacks, were published in American and Israeli newspapers shortly after 9-11. Had the recipients of these Odigo instant messages contacted the New York police department, thousands of lives could have been saved. The question that has not been asked is why didn't they?

Cui Bono?

There were several early indications that Israelis were involved in 9-11 and that it was a spectacular "false flag" terror attack designed to serve as a *casus belli* that could be used to drag the United States into the "War on Terror." Apart from the previously mentioned evidence of Israeli prior knowledge, there were also the incredibly insensitive comments of Netanyahu about 9-11 being "very good" in his view.

Netanyahu, it should be noted, is the author of several books which call for the western nations to engage in a global "War on Terror." Since 1986, Netanyahu has urged the United States and western democracies to take up arms against the enemies of Israel in the name of "fighting terrorism," which is the title of one of his books. The "terrorists" that Netanyahu wants the West to wage war on, however, all happen to be the people and states opposed to Israel's illegal occupation of Palestinian land.

I approached the 9-11 investigation with a twenty-five year history of living in and following the events of the Middle East. After many years of traveling in Europe and the Middle East, I obtained a degree in History from the University of California at Santa Cruz in 1992. My academic emphasis was on Palestine and Israel. After the first U.S. war against Iraq, which I was actively opposed to, I spent my final year of university researching the Soviet occupation of the newly liberated Baltic republics and completing my courses at the University of Bergen in Norway.

Fate brought me into the proximity of another mass disaster on the morning of September 28, 1994, when I arrived by ship in Sweden and learned that the Baltic ferry named *Estonia* had sunk during the night with 852 victims lost at sea. My wife's first husband, a famous Estonian singer named Urmas Alender, was among the missing. While it was abundantly clear that something much more explosive than a "monster wave" had sunk the ferry, the Swedish government and media pretended that natural forces had caused the catastrophe. In the process of investigating what happened in the ferry disaster, I came to realize that a modern "democratic" state, like Sweden, could actually be complicit in the cover-up of the mass murder of hundreds of its own citizens.

In 2000, when I began working as a journalist for the Washington-based *Spotlight*, I turned my attention to the mysterious 1996 crash of TWA Flight 800 off the coast of New York. I attended the National Transportation Safety Board's (NTSB) presentation of their findings of what had caused the "crash" of Flight 800 and was appalled at the obvious cover-up. I noticed how the three Jewish members of the board dominated the presentation. The two-day event ended with the outrageous dismissal of the testimonies of more than one hundred eyewitnesses, who had testified to having seen a streaking object hitting the aircraft in flight. This eyewitness evidence was categorically dismissed because, according to the youngest member of the board, based solely on the time of day, all of the one hundred witnesses must have been drunk and hallucinating. After the presentation of the NTSB findings there was no press conference or session allowing for any questions from the media or public. This was clearly another cover-up.

I had also studied the Israeli attack on the *USS Liberty* and had seen how the U.S. government and military had covered up the truth of the Israeli military attack on the unarmed Navy vessel off the coast of Egypt in 1967. With this background I approached the events of 9-11. Well aware of the history of false-flag terror, the overwhelming Zionist influence in government and media, and corrupt official investigations of recent mass disasters, I was skeptical from the start.

Evidence of Explosions Ignored

The administration of George W. Bush rushed the nation and its allies into war in Afghanistan within one month of the 9-11 attacks using the unsolved crime as the *casus belli* to justify a war of aggression that had been planned long before. The war against the government of Afghanistan, called Operation Enduring Freedom by the government and military, began on October 7, 2001.

The week before the war began I wrote an article about the immense oil and gas reserves of the Caspian Basin and the new "Great Game" to gain control of these valuable energy resources. I also wrote several articles about the long-standing business and personal ties between George W. Bush and the Bin Laden family. One month after 9-11, I wrote about how the mass media was ignoring the large number of eyewitness accounts describing explosions at the World Trade Center before the collapse of the Twin Towers and Building 7.

"Despite reports from numerous eyewitnesses and experts, including news reporters on the scene, who heard or saw explosions immediately before the collapse of the World Trade Center, there has been a virtual silence in the mainstream media," I wrote in the article titled "Some Survivors Say 'Bombs Exploded Inside WTC.'"

"After the airplanes hit the World Trade Center there were some explosive devices inside the buildings that caused the towers to collapse," Van Romero, an explosives expert and former director of the Energetic Materials Research and Testing Center at New Mexico

Tech, told the *Albuquerque Journal* minutes after the collapses. The collapse of the structures resembled controlled implosions used to demolish old structures and was "too methodical to be a chance result of airplanes colliding with the structures," Romero said. Coming from a man who is an expert in the effects of explosives on structures, Romero's comments carried a lot of weight, in my opinion.

"It would be difficult for something from the plane to trigger an event like that," Romero said. If explosions did cause the towers to collapse, "It could have been a relatively small amount of explosives placed in strategic points."

"One of the things terrorist events are noted for is a diversionary attack and secondary device," he said. Then suddenly, ten days after the attack, without any explanation, Romero did a complete about-face in his analysis of the collapse. "Certainly the fire is what caused the building to fail," he told the *Albuquerque Journal* on September 21, 2001.

A friend of mine from Brooklyn told me that he had been standing among a crowd of people on Church Street, about two blocks from the South Tower (WTC 2), when he saw "a number of brief light sources being emitted from inside the building between floors 10 and 15." He saw about six of these brief flashes, accompanied by "a crackling sound" immediately before the tower collapsed.

Even a veteran 51-year-old fire fighter, Louie Cacchioli, told *People* magazine that he had witnessed explosions in the South Tower: "I was taking firefighters up in the elevator to the 24th floor to get in position to evacuate workers. On the last trip up a bomb went off. We think there were bombs set in the building."

What is most peculiar about the eyewitness reports of explosions was that they were completely ignored by the mainstream news media, even when the reports came from their own reporters on the scene. Stephen Evans of the BBC, for example, was in the South Tower where he witnessed "a series of explosions" and felt a "big explosion, from much, much lower." Yet the BBC, like the rest of the mainstream media failed to investigate or even discuss the evidence of explosions in the towers.

How did the editors of the mass media networks in the United States and Britain make the decision not to discuss the evidence of explosions even when the information came from their own reporters on the scene? Eyewitness reports and images of explosions were broadcast only once and then swept under the carpet. It soon became quite clear that the mass media was censoring any discussion of the evidence of explosions in the World Trade Center.

Within a few weeks I realized that the media and government were working together to deceive the public about what had really happened on 9-11 and that there was a massive conspiracy afoot to promote a false version of events in order to gain public support for a previously planned war policy in the Middle East. The mass media was clearly engaged in a comprehensive propaganda campaign to instill fear in the public. I decided that Europe would probably be a safer and saner place to be, so at the end of November, after the Thanksgiving holiday, we flew to Germany.

The Destruction of Evidence

In Germany, I had the opportunity to interview Andreas von Bülow in Bonn. Von Bülow is the author of two books about 9/11 and a former member of the *Bundestag* (the German parliament). While in the government, he served on the parliamentary commission which oversees the three branches of the German secret service. Von Bülow told me that he thought Israel's intelligence service, the Mossad, was behind the 9-11 attacks. These attacks, he said, were carried out to turn public opinion against the Arabs and boost military and security spending.

"You don't get the higher echelons," von Bülow said, referring to the "architectural structure" which masterminds such terror attacks. At this level, he said, the organization doing the planning, such as Mossad, is primarily interested in affecting public opinion. The terrorists who actually commit the crimes are what von Bülow calls "the working level," such as the nineteen Arabs who allegedly hijacked the planes on September 11. "The working level is part of the deception," he said.

"Ninety-five percent of the work of the intelligence agencies around the world is deception and disinformation," he said, which is widely propagated in the mainstream media creating an accepted version of events. "Journalists don't even raise the *simplest* questions," he said. "Those who differ are labeled as crazy."

Eckehardt Werthebach, the former president of the *Verfassungsschutz* (a branch of German intelligence), told me that "the deathly precision" and "the magnitude of planning" behind the attacks would have needed *"years of planning"*. Such a sophisticated operation, Werthebach said, required the "fixed frame" of a state intelligence organization, something not found in a "loose group" of terrorists. Both Werthebach and von Bülow said the lack of a complete "blue ribbon" investigation, with congressional hearings, into the events of September 11 was incomprehensible. These men made more sense to me than anyone in the U.S. government or media.

As incomprehensible as it might seem, the Bush administration delayed and avoided an official investigation for as long as possible – at least until all of the evidence was destroyed. The steel from the World Trade Center was quickly shipped to Asia where it was melted down. The evidence from the crime scene was being destroyed as quickly as possible. This was clearly criminal, yet the highest authorities in the U.S. government and the Department of Justice were allowing it to happen.

Molten Metal

9-11 is an unsolved crime and I have done what I can to solve it using the available evidence. In the summer of 2002, for example, I wrote an article about the seismic data that showed unexplained spikes occurring at the beginning of each collapse.

In my research into the removal of the rubble, I learned from one of the contractors and a demolition expert that molten metal had been discovered at the bottom of the rubble pile in the lower basement levels. This molten metal was described to me as "molten steel" by Peter Tully, president of Tully Construction of Flushing, New York, and Mark Loizeaux, president of Controlled Demolition, Inc. (CDI) of Phoenix, Maryland.

The molten steel was found "three, four, and five weeks later, when the rubble was being removed," Loizeaux said. He said molten steel was also found at WTC 7, the 47-story building owned by Larry Silverstein, which collapsed mysteriously in the late afternoon. Loizeaux said, "If I were to bring the towers down, I would put explosives in the basement to get the weight of the building to help collapse the structure."

The molten metal found beneath the rubble was clearly important evidence that could explain how the towers were brought down. Because each tower was held up by 47 huge core columns, there had to be an explanation for what caused these columns to fall. The official explanation that fires had caused the floor trusses to give way failed to explain what happened to the core columns. To explain the extremely quick collapse of the core columns, the seismic spikes and molten metal seemed to be very important clues.

Steven E. Jones, a professor of physics at Brigham Young University (BYU) in Utah, contacted me in the summer of 2005 and asked me what I had learned about the discovery of molten metal at the World Trade Center. I told Jones exactly what Peter Tully and Mark Loizeaux had said about the discovery of molten iron in the basements of the Twin Towers and Building 7. After studying the reports and photographs of molten metal, Jones had been able to obtain some fragments of the metal. He concluded that the fragments were primarily iron and possible evidence that Thermite had been used to demolish the buildings.

Encouraged by his research, I visited Professor Jones on the campus of Brigham Young University in the spring of 2006. From Provo, Utah, I then traveled by train to the University of California at Davis where I met with Professor Thomas A. Cahill, an expert on airborne particles. Dr. Cahill had conducted a study of the particles contained in the thin bluish smoke that rose from the rubble for nearly four months after 9-11. Cahill's air sampling began on October 2 and continued until late December 2001, when the last fires were finally extinguished.

Asked why it took so long to begin a scientific evaluation of the air contamination that accompanied the destruction of the World Trade Center, Dr. Cahill said he had assumed that there were scores of agencies and scientists monitoring the air quality in New York City after 9-11. "I assumed it was happening. I could not believe it was not," Cahill said. "The EPA [Environmental Protection Agency] did nothing."

Cahill's work revealed the presence of extremely small metallic aerosols in unprecedented amounts in the plumes coming from the burning WTC rubble. Most of the particles in these plumes were in the categories of ultra-fine and nano-particles: from 0.26 to 0.09 microns. The extraordinarily high level of ultra-fine aerosols was one of the most unusual aspects of the data, Cahill said. "Ultra-fine particles require extremely high temperatures," he said, "namely the boiling point of the metal."

Since the scientific data supports the theory that some form of Thermite was used to destroy the towers, the question is how it got onto the 81st floor of the south tower, where large amounts of molten metal were seen falling before the collapse?

The official final report of the fires does not explain what was on the 81st floor, which seems odd because this is the floor, leased by Fuji Bank, into which the airplane crashed. A former employee of the bank came forward and told me that the bank had reinforced the floor in 1999 to support a very heavy load of computer back-up batteries. "The whole floor was batteries," he said, "huge battery-looking things." They were "all black" and "solid, very heavy" things, which had been brought in during the night. They had been put in place during the summer prior to 9-11, he said. But were they really batteries? "It's weird," he said. "They were never turned on."

So, what really was on the 81st floor of the South Tower? What was in these heavy "battery-looking things?" Were they batteries, or were they Thermite? And is it more than a coincidence that both planes flew directly into secure computer rooms in both towers and that both spectacular explosions showed evidence of Thermite-produced white smoke?

The Cover-up Continues

Despite the legal difficulties, slander, criticism, and other setbacks, I have continued to examine the evidence from 9-11 and ask the questions that demand to be answered. The lost lives of the thousands of victims of the terror attacks and the illegal wars that have been waged in the name of 9-11 deserve to be honored with the truth, not a pack of lies pushed by the controlled media onto a gullible public.

It would be naïve and foolish for us to expect the truth from a government that has been shown to have repeatedly lied to the media and international community in order to accomplish its dubious goals. The truth of 9-11 will certainly not be given to us on a silver platter. It is something we will have to fight for.

Someday, perhaps, if it's decided that the stories can be told, you'll see that the state [Israel] has been involved in acts which are a thousand times more dirty than anything going on in Colombia. But these things were decided by the government, in cabinet meetings. As long as the government decides to do something, something that the national interest demanded, then it is legitimate. But if an individual wants to do the same thing, it isn't. That's just the way it is. It's very simple.

Lieut. Gen. Rafael Eitan,
Israeli Chief of Staff, 1978-83,
"The Colombia Connection,"
Jerusalem Post, September 1, 1989

Chapter II

The Planes of 9-11

Unlike those researchers and writers who say they have "moved beyond 9-11," I have persevered in my efforts to solve this heinous crime. How can one abandon the pursuit of the truth about 9-11 before the crime has been solved? During the decade after the terrorist attacks in which some 3,000 innocent people died, the federal judge who presided over the 9-11 tort litigation waged a judicial war of attrition against the families of the victims to prevent their cases from ever going to trial. In the end, every one of the 9-11 families was forced into an out-of-court settlement. The 96 families that refused the government compensation money and held out for years to have a trial to find the truth never got their day in court.

How can Americans tolerate such injustice? How can we forget the thousands of people who died on 9-11? How can we ignore the death and destruction that has, as a result, been wrongfully inflicted on the innocent people of Iraq, Afghanistan, Lebanon, and Palestine? Who can accept corrupt and irresponsible administrations dragging our military from one illegal war to another in the utterly fraudulent "War on Terror," which the Bush administration promised will last for generations?

If we, as Americans, don't demand the truth about 9-11, who and what do we really stand for? The policies of the Bush and Obama administrations were based on an unproven interpretation of the events of 9-11. What does it mean to be a citizen of "the land of the free and the home of the brave" if we allow our minds and our nation to be so easily hijacked by government lies and propaganda? After being attacked by undercover police at my home in August 2006 and maliciously prosecuted in a seriously flawed trial, I increased my efforts to solve 9-11. As the cover-up became more obvious and the guilty parties revealed themselves it made sense to intensify the pressure, not give up.

The Fraudulent War on Terror

I cannot accept mass murder, occupation, and genocidal wars of aggression. Nor can I accept the corruption of our values and destruction of our basic American rights to facilitate the massive fraud known as the "War on Terror." With the passage of time, it has become quite clear that 9-11 was carried out to kick-start the global "War on Terror" with its pre-planned wars of aggression.

In December 2001, veteran German intelligence professionals told me that 9-11 had been executed by a state-sponsored criminal network and had required years of planning. Eckehardt Werthebach, the former president of Germany's domestic intelligence service, Verfassungsschutz, told me in 2001 that "the deathly precision" and "the magnitude of planning" of the 9-11 attacks would have required "years of planning." Such a sophisticated operation, Werthebach said, would require the "fixed frame" of a state intelligence organization, something not found in a "loose group" like the one allegedly led by Mohammed Atta while he studied in Hamburg.

If Werthebach's analysis is correct, and I have every reason to believe it is, the official version is nothing but a pack of lies. This would mean that the members of the criminal network are still occupying the highest positions of power in the United States, Israel, and other nations. The members of this network are dedicated to preventing the evidence from being released because it would expose the real perpetrators. This is the only logical reason why the 9-11 evidence has been suppressed, the investigation controlled, and the litigation and discovery processes obstructed.

At this point, it should be clear that 9-11 will never be solved by the federal government, politically appointed investigators, law enforcement agencies, or the corrupt courts. These controlled agencies, like the Zionist-controlled media, are only interested in controlling the information and preventing the real truth from being revealed. This crime will only be solved by concerned and dedicated independent researchers.

The Zionist Strategy

9-11 was a very sophisticated operation, as Werthebach said, which required the "fixed frame" of a state intelligence organization. It was carefully planned years in advance and carried out for one strategic purpose: to kick-start the Zionist-planned "War on Terror."

The rabid Zionist Neo-Cons who dominated the Bush administration pushed the "War on Terror" with its criminal wars of aggression, occupation, and Balkanization in the Middle East as the strategic response to 9-11. Likewise, the Zionist media moguls, who dominate the U.S. mass media, promoted the "War on Terror" as the suitable and proper response to the terror atrocity, a crime of mass murder which they refused to investigate.

An Israeli official named Oded Yinon revealed the Zionist strategy to Balkanize the entire Middle East into ethnic mini-states in the early 1980s. The plan for a global "War on Terror" to accomplish this goal has been articulated since the mid-1980s by Benjamin Netanyahu, the Israeli prime minister of the extreme right-wing Likud party. The Israeli military's plans to realize these strategic goals were evidently in the works for at least twenty years before 9-11.

The Hoax of 9-11

9-11 is, in fact, a gigantic hoax. Only by exposing the terrorist masterminds behind 9-11 will we reveal the criminals behind the fraudulent "War on Terror" and the epidemic of "false flag" terrorism that plagues the world. False flag terrorism is a crime designed and committed with the intention that the blame will fall on a targeted faction, state, or organization. The media outlets, which the criminals control, facilitate the blame game by promoting the false version and stifling any independent investigation or truthful analysis of the crime.

After all, 9-11 remains an unsolved crime. It is, however, rather obvious who is responsible for blocking discovery and obstructing justice for the victims and their relatives. At every critical point where the events and circumstances of 9-11 should have been investigated and discussed, there has been a Zionist, a dedicated devotee of the State of Israel, occupying a key position and acting as the controller and censor of evidence - the gatekeeper of information.

I have seen this pattern in earlier cover-ups. The same pattern was used with the sinking of *Estonia* in the Baltic Sea (1994) and the U.S. government's (NTSB) investigation of the downing of TWA Flight 800, two of the most egregious examples of government cover-ups in modern times. In each case, the three critical phases of the cover-up: investigation and access to evidence, media interpretation of the event, and related litigation, were all tightly controlled to prevent any meaningful discovery of what had really caused the disaster.

The people who are preventing the discovery of the facts in such cases are actually complicit in covering-up crimes of mass murder. Logically, there can be no reason for dedicated Zionists to obstruct the investigation of 9-11 other than to conceal the evidence of Israeli and Zionist involvement in the crimes.

The FBI, for example, under the command of the Israeli dual-national Michael Chertoff, was responsible for the confiscation and destruction of the crucial evidence from 9-11. Chertoff, as Assistant Attorney General of the Criminal Division of the Department of Justice, oversaw the non-investigation of 9-11 which resulted in the massive destruction of the steel - crucial evidence - from the World Trade Center. Chertoff went on to head the Department of Homeland Security, where he continued to control access to the evidence through the Sensitive Security Information (SSI) program.

The confiscated evidence includes video tapes of the Pentagon attack and physical pieces from the different aircraft involved. This evidence is critical to prove what happened and identify the aircraft involved in the attacks - but the FBI has refused to release this evidence. Neither President George W. Bush nor the U.S. Congress demanded that they do so. Under President Barack Obama the 9-11 cover-up was perpetuated and the war effort in Afghanistan increased. The destruction of the crucial evidence from 9-11 and the lack of a real investigation reveal the culture of corruption that prevails in Washington.

The appointed federal judges Alvin K. Hellerstein and Michael B. Mukasey and the former assistant attorney general Michael Chertoff did not confiscate and destroy the critical evidence and block discovery in order to protect fanatical Arab Muslims or conspiratorial Jesuits. These men are all dedicated Zionists and their efforts were exerted to protect Israel, the foreign state to which they are wholeheartedly devoted.

U.S. District Judge Alvin K. Hellerstein managed the 9-11 tort litigation in which not one single wrongful death case went to trial. Judge Hellerstein has close family ties to Israel - and the Israeli airport security company, ICTS, a key defendant in the tort litigation.

The Zionist role in 9-11 cover-up is obvious. The players who are involved in obstructing justice are known. Patriotic Americans must not abandon the pursuit of the truth. For those who died on 9-11, for our nation and our posterity, we are obliged to find and expose those who are responsible for the crimes and cover-up of 9-11.

The Evidence of Israeli Involvement

I have pursued the leads of Israeli involvement simply because the evidence indicates that the Israeli military and intelligence had prior knowledge and involvement in 9-11. The five jubilant Israeli Mossad agents who were caught celebrating and filming themselves in front of the destruction of the World Trade Center, and their subsequent public statements, clearly indicate that the Mossad had prior knowledge of 9-11.

The text message warnings of the attacks sent over the Israeli-owned Odigo instant messaging system several hours prior to the attacks are further evidence of Israeli prior knowledge. Furthermore, the Israelis have a long history of committing "false flag" terror attacks, particularly against American targets. The Israeli attack on the USS Liberty in 1967 and the Israeli terrorist bombings of U.S. and British civilian targets in Egypt during the 1954 Lavon Affair are the first that come to mind.

If the evidence indicated that Saudis, Pakistanis, or even Jesuits were behind the attacks, I would investigate them. The evidence, however, points to Israelis being involved - so I look there. There has been no independent investigation of 9-11 done by the controlled media other than Carl Cameron's now deeply-buried four-part series on FOX News in December 2001. Think about this for a minute. The mass media in the land of the "free press" has not done any independent investigation about the crime of the century.

The evidence of Israeli involvement in 9-11 is so obvious that senior editors in the controlled media don't even let their journalists approach the subject. The journalists of the "free press" in the United States are confined to the same "Auschwitz of the mind" as the American public they write for. This is a self-imposed limit on what they allow themselves to think or express, in particular about Israel because of the Jewish suffering of World War II. Journalists know very well that to touch the subject of Israeli involvement in 9-11 would be like touching a live wire. Likewise, when it comes to tracking the Israeli criminal network that has operated in the United States for decades, the U.S. media is a dog that won't bark - or hunt.

The extent of Zionist control over the U.S. mass media, including the Internet, is astounding. The mass media has effectively prevented most Americans from understanding who is really behind the false-flag terror attacks of 9-11, and, by extension, the illegal and genocidal wars in Afghanistan, Palestine, Lebanon, and Iraq. The controlled media has also left Americans with an extremely distorted view of the Middle East, Zionism, and the history of the Zionist state, Israel.

Israel – A Terrorist State

Israel is a nation which was founded by terrorists, ruthless men with histories of committing genocidal crimes and false-flag terror attacks. Israel was created in 1948 in Palestine on land that was "ethnically cleansed" of its indigenous Christian and Muslim inhabitants.

Ariel Sharon, the former prime minister who has been in a coma since January 4, 2006, is a prime example of an Israeli terrorist. Sharon came to power in early 2001, about the same time as George W. Bush, some eight months before 9-11. Sharon is a well-known terrorist and génocidaire, i.e. a person who has been involved in genocide.

Sharon has supervised numerous terrorist atrocities, such as the 1982 massacre in Sabra and Shatila refugee camps, in which thousands of innocent people were massacred. Sharon is a Zionist extremist who believes that every Jew should live in Israeli-occupied Palestine. Realistically, what else besides terrorism and bloodshed should one expect from such fanatical and genocidal terrorists?

The sons and daughters of the original Zionist terrorists have occupied the highest positions of power in the Israeli government. Tzipora Malka "Tzipi" Livni, for example, the foreign minister (2006-09), is the daughter of the former terror chief of the Irgun. Born in Tel Aviv in July 1958, "Tzipi" is the daughter of Eitan Livni (born Yerucham Bzozowitch in Grodno, 1919), a Polish-born Irgun terrorist associated with the bombing of the King David Hotel in Jerusalem.

Steven Erlanger of the *New York Times* (5 February 2006) wrote an article about Livni entitled "Israel's Top Envoy":

Tzipi Livni, 47, is the first woman to serve as Israel's

foreign minister since Golda Meir. Some think she
may be the first since Ms. Meir to be prime minister.

She is also a deeply Israeli figure, the daughter of Zionist guerrillas - terrorists in some eyes - who met in
the Irgun, the underground organization that fought
the British and the Arabs, and that blew up the British headquarters in the King David Hotel in 1946,
killing 91 people.

Her father, Eitan Livni, was the head of operations for the Irgun terrorists, and on his gravestone is the map of Greater Israel, extending over
both sides of the Jordan River. Erlanger suggests that blowing up a
hotel and killing 91 people is only seen as a terrorist act "in some eyes."

Israeli False-Flag Terrorism

The fact that the Israeli political leadership and military command
decided to launch a vicious attack on a defenseless U.S. reconnaissance ship, the USS Liberty, off the coast of Gaza in June 1967 and
kill every man on board illustrates that the Israelis are fully capable
of committing such atrocities in their attempts to blame their enemies and achieve their strategic goals. Dedicated Zionists will defend
these acts of Israeli false flag terrorism as the "pragmatic" thing to do
— and attack those who disagree as being anti-Semitic.

The Zionist-controlled media adamantly refused to conduct its
own investigation of 9-11, the seminal event of the "War on Terror".
Controlled news outlets like the New York Times promoted the pre-
planned wars of aggression against Afghanistan and Iraq with propaganda pieces and false reports about weapons of mass destruction,

such as those provided by Judith Miller. Miller is the daughter of William Miller, a Jewish immigrant from Pinsk, Russia, who started out as a New Jersey nightclub owner and made it big as entertainment director of the Sahara, Dunes, Flamingo, and International hotels in Las Vegas.

False flag terror acts are an Israeli specialty, as Dr. Kaasem Khaleel points out in his book *Wrongly Blamed* (2007). "Public terror was invented by the Israelis," Khaleel wrote citing Christopher Sykes' book *Crossroads to Israel*:

> To achieve their political goals, Zionists are dependent on terror. These terror acts are used as a distraction. Even though the Israelis are the sources, they effectively blame others. The fabricated terror they commit is an assault on people's intelligence. Thus people are being purposely misled regarding the real source of these crimes.

The Zionist-controlled media has purposely misled the public about 9-11 for the same reason as the Zionist judges, investigators, and commissioners: to protect the evidence of Israeli involvement from being exposed. The controlled U.S. media works with the Zionist criminal network and allows it to flourish by failing to investigate and identify the companies and individuals involved.

The Planes of 9-11

9-11 was an act of false flag terror in which four allegedly "hijacked" airplanes were used as weapons of mass destruction. There are, however, many unanswered questions about the airplanes involved. There are many observations about these planes which suggest they were not the civilian airliners they are said to have been. The plane that struck the South Tower, for example, had unusual shapes, bulges, and holes, which have led many analysts to believe it was a Boeing 767-300 refueling tanker that had been disguised as a 767-200 United Airlines passenger jet.

Durable parts from the two jets that struck the twin towers, such as landing gear and engines, landed on buildings and streets of Manhattan. On these engines and landing gear are many numbered time-tracked parts which could prove precisely which aircraft they had been put on and when they had been serviced, but the FBI has refused to present this evidence to make its case. Why wouldn't the FBI present this evidence if it had it?

The only possible explanation for the FBI's failure to present this evidence is that it does not match the planes they claim hit the buildings or "crashed" in Pennsylvania. If the planes that were involved in the attacks on the World Trade Center were, in fact, not United Airlines Flight 175 and American Airlines Flight 11, but remotely-controlled tankers painted to look like civilian aircraft, who could have produced such disguised planes and inserted them into the NORAD anti-terrorism exercise that was taking place in the airspace of the East Coast on the morning of 9-11?

Israel Aircraft Industries (IAI)

Given the evidence of Israeli prior knowledge, some obvious questions arise: Did the Israelis have the capability to carry off such a complex operation? If they did, is there a link between their capability and the events of 9-11? The answer to both questions is yes.

The Israeli military and its intelligence agencies have long had the capability to convert and disguise large-body aircraft in the United States, and their companies that do this kind of work are connected to International Consultants on Targeted Security (ICTS NV). ICTS is the Israeli airport security company, based in the Netherlands, that is a prime suspect in the "false flag" terrorism of 9-11. ICTS was a key defendant in the 9-11 tort litigation until Judge Alvin K. Hellerstein dismissed the Mossad-linked company from the case in May 2011.

The Israeli military has spawned several aircraft leasing and maintenance companies in the United States since the late 1960s. There is, in fact, a network of Israeli-controlled aviation companies operating in the United States which were all started by Israel Aircraft Industries (IAI), now known as Israel Aerospace Industries. IAI is a wholly-owned subsidiary of the Israeli Defense Ministry, which produces and maintains planes and missiles.

One of the Israeli military's aviation companies spawned in the United States was an aircraft leasing company named ATASCO, which began operating in the United States in the early 1970s. I began investigating ATASCO in August 2006. As a matter of fact, I had spoken with Shalom Yoran, the Israeli chairman of this now defunct Israeli company, about six hours before a squad of three undercover police arrived at my house and, without cause or provocation, tackled me on my front lawn. While I was pinned down beneath two men, one kneeling on the temple of my head, they applied a TASER directly to my back and gave me a shock of 50,000 volts. The police assault at my home on August 15, 2006, left me with a fractured elbow.

I had come across Shalom Yoran's name while researching Amit and Naftali Yoran, the suspicious young Israelis who oversaw cyber-security for the U.S. government and military computers prior to and after 9-11.

Shalom Yoran has an extremely suspicious and unusual profile for an Israeli immigrant to the United States. He was in the original Israeli air force of 1948 and is a founder and former head of Israel Aircraft Industries. Yoran was instrumental in building the IAI into an internationally recognized company and the largest industry in Israel.

Before Yoran emigrated to the United States, which is very unusual for Israelis of his age and with his high-level military background, he had spent the previous ten years as senior vice president of IAI and as president of IAI's parent company, Bedek. Israelis like Yoran don't usually come to America as immigrants - they are sent there on a mission.

Israel Aircraft Industries was established in 1953 as Bedek Aviation Company, five years after the establishment of the State of Israel. Today, Bedek is the senior group of Israel Aerospace Industries and specializes in aircraft operation, conversion, maintenance, and overhaul. In 1975, when Yoran "left" Bedek and IAI at the unusually young retirement age of fifty, the corporation had 22,000 employees, of which 4,000 worked in the Bedek Division. In reality, Yoran didn't leave Bedek and IAI at all; he was sent by the Israeli military to the United States to manage one of their most important operations - ATASCO.

In his on-line biographies, Yoran says he was appointed to this position: "When he retired at the age of fifty [ca. 1975], he was appointed the President of Atasco, an American Flight company for cargo shipment and maintenance."

His 2003 biography on the website of Tel Aviv University (TAU) has a similar tale: "At the age of fifty, Shalom Yoran retired from the Israel Aircraft Industries. In 1978 he moved to the U.S. where he became chairman of ATASCO USA - a private aircraft trading and service company. ATASCO bought and leased airplanes to major airlines around the world. The company also had an aircraft maintenance and modification plant in Smyrna, Tennessee.

"Shalom Yoran continues to be chairman of ATASCO USA," the 2003 TAU entry noted. How could an Israeli be appointed to be president or chairman of an "American" company, unless that company were actually an Israeli company disguised as an American company? And why would an Israeli company doing business in the United States want to disguise the fact that it is Israeli-owned in the first place?

The ATASCO-Bedek Connection

ATASCO USA was, of course, created and owned by the Israeli military and connected to the Mossad, but this information is not easily found. There has only been one article that I have found that mentions what ATASCO has been doing for the past 36 years in the United States, since it was first created by the Israeli Defense Ministry in 1971. That article, entitled "Ugandan Plane Deal Believed Key to Israeli Spy Operation," was published in the *Washington Post* of September 11, 1978.

This investigative article, which involved an international team of journalists that included an Israeli, focused on the "mysterious Israeli tycoon and the Mossad, Israeli's intelligence service," and how they had provided the Ugandan dictator Idi Amin with two Boeing 707 jetliners as part of an Israeli effort to spy on Libya. The "big winner" and tycoon in this Mossad spying operation was Shaul Nehemia Eisenberg (1921-1997), "the reclusive Israeli entrepreneur at its center."

Eisenberg was, as the *Washington Post* reported in 1978, the central figure in the Mossad spying operation on Libya:

> The chief Eisenberg firm in these deals was Aircraft Trading and Services Inc., or Atasco. Headquartered in Asia House, Eisenberg's luxury building in Tel Aviv, Atasco also has branches in the "Eisenberg Building" in New York and in London.
>
> Atasco was put together in 1971 by executives of Israeli Aircraft Industries, a wholly owned subsidiary of the Israeli Defense Ministry that makes planes and missiles.
>
> Eisenberg got into Atasco as an equal partner with Israeli Aircraft for $500,000 in cash. After the 1973 Middle East War, Israeli Aircraft, staggered by scandals, sold its share in Atasco to Eisenberg, leaving him its sole owner.
>
> The rest of Atasco's original capital, $5 million, came from the U.S. Export-Import Bank, which is supposed to make loans to promote American exports.
>
> The Ex-Im Bank certainly found the right man in Eisenberg. He quickly turned into an eager customer for Pan American Airways' used Boeing 707s.
>
> Atasco bought 12 or 15 of the advance series "C" 707s that Pan Am was selling and purchased six out of ten earlier series "C" 707s being sold by the airline.
>
> At its Israeli hangars, currently jammed with 707s

bearing obscure markings, Atasco remodels the interiors to suit customers, and paints on their proud colors - Iran Air, Tarom of Romania, Uganda Airlines.

In May 1976, Atasco sold the 707 that was once Pan Am's "Clipper Jupiter" to a firm in Zurich, which dealt it on to Amin.

Intelligence sources say that the head of this Zurich firm is a 15-year veteran of Mossad, the Israeli intelligence agency, and the firm is an agency "laundry." It exists, these sources say, to pass on Mossad funds for deals in which the Israeli secret service is interested.

The *Washington Post*, one of the most important newspapers in the United States, is a leading national newspaper of record. Oddly, however, the extremely important information contained in this article about ATASCO was never repeated in any of the subsequent articles in which this mysterious company was mentioned, for example, when Gerald L. Gitner, an aviation executive with Pan Am, TWA, and a host of smaller airlines, was appointed Chief Executive Officer (CEO) of ATASCO USA, Inc.

In 1986, when Gitner became CEO of the Israeli-owned company with a documented history of murky business, the company was described as a New York aircraft leasing and brokerage company. ATASCO's previously published history of involvement in Mossad operations was never mentioned. Gitner, who was CEO of Mossad's "privately held" aircraft leasing and maintenance company until 1990, was involved in the dismemberment and selling off of the assets of the once prosperous Pan Am and TWA airlines.

In October 1986, when Gitner was appointed CEO of the Mossad-run ATASCO U.S.A. Inc., he was or had been a senior executive with PanAm Corporation and TWA. He was the president of Texas Air Corporation, the holding company for Continental Airlines and New York Air, when he was appointed president and CEO of ATASCO U.S.A., "a private aviation concern involved in commercial aircraft leasing and heavy aircraft maintenance."

Gitner was also co-founder and president of People Express Airlines. The *Houston Chronicle* of October 3, 1986, however, only identified ATASCO as "an aircraft leasing and brokerage company."

Shaul Eisenberg – "World Entrepreneur"

In November 1982, when Eisenberg became involved in the Tregaron deal and tried to take over a large piece of prime real estate in Washington, D.C., the *Washington Post* wrote about Mossad's "world entrepreneur" and their point man in China - and Panama:

> Eisenberg was profiled in a 1981 Business Week article as a businessman of enormous wealth, diversity of business interests, and a proclivity for secretiveness in his dealings. He owns a worldwide network of corporations. His largest company, United Development Inc., was set up in Panama in 1960.
>
> Eisenberg essentially acts as a middleman, according to reports on his dealings, assembling consortiums of manufacturers, builders and banks to construct industrial facilities of all types.

Since Eisenberg was the "sole owner" of ATASCO since 1973, the

Mossad's "aircraft trading and services" company naturally began its murky business on the American continent in Panama. In 1978 the *Washington Post* reported that there were "frequent but unsubstantiated reports that Eisenberg operates mostly from Central America." Eisenberg was also the "Panamanian honorary general consul in Tel Aviv," the *Post* reported.

The first mention of ATASCO other than the 1978 article in the *Washington Post* was in the *New York Times* on October 29, 1981, when it reported that Emery Air Freight had purchased a Boeing 727-100 from Atasco-Panama.

IDF – Israeli Drug Forces?

Israel Aircraft Industries also has a branch, IAI Sucursal Colombia, in Bogota, Colombia. Colombia is a nation better known for the production and distribution of cocaine than aircraft. Why would IAI establish aircraft leasing and maintenance facilities in Colombia and Panama?

Is airlifting drugs a central part of the IAI operations in Latin America? Does the Mossad use IAI facilities in Colombia to run its own drug smuggling routes to fund its operations? Does Mossad drug smuggling involve American politicians (and intelligence agencies) which it controls through criminal complicity?

There are a number of indications that the Mossad is deeply involved in the Colombian drug trade. A horde of Mossad operatives, disguised as Israeli art students, were targeting the offices and personnel of the U.S. Drug Enforcement Agency (DEA) for two years prior to 9-11. Why would the Mossad be seeking to penetrate the DEA if it were not involved in drug smuggling?

It is well known that Israeli criminal gangs are heavily involved in illicit drug smuggling. The Israeli newspaper *Haaretz*, for example, reported in 2003 that Israel is at the center of the international trade in the drug Ecstasy, according to a document published by the U.S. State Department. "In recent years, organized crime in Israel, some with links to criminal organizations in Russia, have come to control the distribution of the drug in Europe, according to a Bureau for International Narcotics and Law Enforcement Affairs document," *Haaretz* reported. "During 2000, 80 percent of the Ecstasy seized in North America originated in the Netherlands, which is the largest production center, along with Belgium and Poland. The State Department is certain that Israeli organizations are linked to the laboratories in the Netherlands and are responsible for the worldwide distribution.

"Israeli drug distribution organizations are currently the main source for distribution of the drug to groups inside the U.S., to smuggling through express mail services, through couriers on commercial flights and, recently, through air cargo," the report stated. It should be noted that the Israeli airport security firm ICTS handles airport security at Schiphol, the international airport of Amsterdam. Why is the Mossad-linked airport security company based in Holland?

The rumors about the Bush and Clinton families being involved in large scale drug smuggling operations are legendary. From George H.W. Bush's days in the Texas oil business and as head of the CIA to his position as a director of the Prozac giant Eli Lilly and Company, the drug trade is a central part of the Bush family business.

The allegations about Governor Bill Clinton's involvement in the drug smuggling operation in Mena, Arkansas are equally legendary. Aircraft were used to smuggle drugs and weapons through the airport in

SOLVING 9-11

Mena in the 1980s while Clinton protected the entire operation. "Given the scope and implications of the Mena story, it may be easy to understand the media's initial skepticism and reluctance," Sally Denton and Roger Morris wrote in their July 1995 article "The Crimes of Mena":

> Mena, from 1981 to 1985, was indeed one of the centers for international smuggling traffic. According to official I.R.S. and D.E.A. calculations, sworn court testimony, and other corroborative records, the traffic amounted to thousands of kilos of cocaine and heroin and literally hundreds of millions of dollars in drug profits. According to a 1986 letter from the Louisiana attorney general to then U.S. attorney general Edwin Meese, [Adler Berriman Seal, or "Barry"] Seal "smuggled between $3 billion and $5 billion of drugs into the U.S."

Adler Berriman Seal had been a pilot with TWA from 1966 to 1974, according to his on-line biography. Gitner, who began his career at TWA in 1968 was a vice president when he also left TWA in 1974 to join the much smaller Texas International Airlines.

The numerous reports and allegations of involvement in drug smuggling are what the Bush and Clinton families have in common. These are the families which have dominated the executive branch of the United States government since 1981. There was either a Bush or Clinton in the White House from January 1981 until January 2009. Is the illegal drug business the central criminal activity that the Bush and Clinton families have participated in with the Israeli Mossad?

If the reports, allegations, and rumors are true, the illegal drug trade

40

THE PLANES OF 9-11

is where the interests of the Bush family, the Clintons, the CIA, and the Mossad all come together. This would explain the choice to invade and occupy Afghanistan, where opium production is now at record levels after having been nearly eradicated under the Taliban regime. This would also explain the unusual pressure to medicate the 9-11 relatives with mind-altering drugs like Prozac. It appears that drug smuggling could very well be the illegal enterprise at the center of the criminal network behind 9-11. This is a subject that deserves further investigation.

"Clipper Jupiter" and Zimex Aviation

In the 1978 article about Eisenberg and the Mossad the *Washington Post* reported that ATASCO had sold the Boeing 707, which had been Pan Am's "Clipper Jupiter," to a firm in Zurich, which had immediately transferred ownership to Idi Amin in Uganda:

> Intelligence sources say that the head of this Zurich firm is a 15-year veteran of Mossad, the Israeli intelligence agency, and the firm is an agency 'laundry.' It exists, these sources say, to pass on Mossad funds for deals in which the Israeli secret service is interested.
>
> Pan Am's "Clipper Jupiter," with tail registration number N766PA, was sold to a Zurich-based company called Zimex Aviation on May 12, 1976. The same day, Zimex Aviation transferred the plane with a new tail number, 5X-UAL, to Uganda Airlines.

The "15-year veteran of Mossad" would be Hans Ziegler, who headed Zimex as reported in *The Oregonian* on August 22, 1988:

Charles Hanner, then a Page [Airways] vice president, testified by deposition that he had been introduced to Amin by Hans Ziegler, a veteran agent of Mossad, the Israeli military intelligence service. Ziegler's Swiss company, Zimex Aviation, had sold a number of aircraft to Middle Eastern potentates and to Amin's friend Moammar Khadafy, the Libyan dictator.

ATASCO Ties to 9-11

Gitner reportedly stayed with ATASCO from October 1986 through December 1989. In 1989, Gitner was appointed to head Presidential Airways of Herndon, Virginia. Gitner later served on the board of directors of another Mossad-run company, ICTS, one of the key defendants in the 9-11 tort litigation. Along with a handful of senior Israeli Mossad veterans, Gitner was a director of ICTS from at least 1997 through 2005. ICTS was responsible for airline security and passenger screening at Boston's Logan Airport on 9-11.

International Consultants on Targeted Security (ICTS NV) is the Mossad-linked company that owns Huntleigh USA, the airline security company that oversaw the passenger screening operations at Boston's Logan Airport on September 11, 2001. How would Gitner be a director or CEO of a Mossad-run company like ATASCO or ICTS if he were not working for the Mossad? Has Gerald Gitner from Boston been working with the Israelis since he began at TWA in the late 1960s? Is this the reason he left TWA and began working for Texas International?

Bedek's Specialty - Boeing 767 Conversions

IAI is "a world leader in aircraft conversion and modernization programs, unmanned air vehicles (UAVs), communication programs and defense electronics," according to the company's website. Shalom Yoran's company, Bedek Aviation Group, reportedly converted its first Boeing 767 from a passenger to cargo jet in early 2000. The converted passenger jet was the first of eleven 767s to be converted for Airborne-Express, according to the *Jerusalem Post* of April 4, 2000. "Bedek is one of the world's leaders in plane conversions," the Israeli newspaper reported.

In early 2001, Bedek delivered a refurbished Boeing 707 refueling tanker for the Israeli air force, according to the *Jerusalem Post* of February 22, 2001. "The number of [Israeli] refueling tankers is classified," the *Post* reported. "The first 707 air refueling tanker converted for the Air Force was delivered twenty years ago." This Israeli report indicates that Bedek has been converting Boeing aircraft into tankers since the early 1980s.

"The main benefit of this present aircraft is in its versatility, its quick conversion from a refueling tanker to a cargo jet. In this way, the aircraft can be used as a cargo plane in times of peace and a refueling tanker in an emergency," an IAI statement said.

IAI in Miami – Commodore Aviation

"Boeing has been working with Israel Aircraft Industries Ltd. for 30 years," the *Seattle Post-Intelligencer* reported in October 1998.

Miami International Airport has long been the site of one of Bedek's maintenance stations, along with Paris, Moscow, Baku, and Baikal, according to the *Jerusalem Post* of January 13, 1995. The Bedek operation in Miami was known as Commodore Aviation. IAI and Bedek had "offices in Arlington, Va.; New York City; Princeton, N.J., for its Galaxy Aerospace subsidiary; and in Miami for its Commodore Aviation unit," according to the *Seattle Post-Intelligencer* article from 1998.

Florida Governor Jeb Bush made a four-day trade mission visit to Israel in November 1999 during which he appealed to the state-owned Israel Aircraft Industries to expand their business operations in Florida. IAI's Miami-based Commodore Aviation was already the largest Israeli business presence in Florida in 1999 with about 500 employees, the *Stuart News* (Florida) reported.

In 2003, Commodore Aviation, "part of IAI's Bedek Aviation Group," pulled out of Miami, reportedly owing nearly a million dollars to the Miami airport, and moved to Rome, New York, where it renamed its operation the "Empire Air Center."

"Commodore has been searching for a new location since June 2002 and owes $800,000 in back rent to Miami International Airport, where it's currently based," South Florida CEO reported in May 2003, when it announced Commodore Aviation's move to New York and its name change.

Like ATASCO, Commodore has been generously funded by the U.S. taxpayer. Commodore Aviation actually made money by its move to the former Griffiss Air Force Base, where it operates in a massive hangar in which B-52 bombers and tankers were once serviced. The move profited Commodore, which received some $25 million in grants and tax incentives from federal and New York government sources, the *Jerusalem Post* reported on November 21, 2003. "The whole relocation didn't cost IAI one dollar," said Gerry Stoch, New York state's economic attaché in Israel.

I sat with former Mossad chief Isser Harel for a conversation about Arab terrorism. As he handed me a cup of hot tea and a plate of cookies, I asked him, "Do you think terrorism will come to America, and if so, where and why?"

Harel looked at his American visitor and replied, "I fear it will come to you in America. America has the power, but not the will, to fight terrorism. The terrorists have the will, but not the power, to fight America — but all that could change with time. Arab oil money buys more than tents."

As to the where, Harel continued, "New York City is the symbol of freedom and capitalism. It's likely they will strike the Empire State Building, your tallest building [he mistakenly thought] and a symbol of your power."

... Twenty-one years later, the first part of Harel's prediction came true; except, of course, that the Twin Towers of the World Trade Center were much taller than the Empire State Building.

Michael D. Evans on what Israeli intelligence chief Isser Harel told him in September 1980, "America the Target," *Jerusalem Post*, September 30, 2001

Chapter III

America the Target: 9-11 and Israel's History of False Flag Terrorism

The Israeli military has a history of owning and operating private aircraft leasing and maintenance companies in the United States. These privately-held aviation companies, created by the Israeli military and linked to its state-owned aviation industry, had the capability and advanced avionics required to convert Boeing aircraft into remote-controlled drones like those that evidently struck the World Trade Center (WTC) on 9-11.

Given the Israeli military's capability to carry out the attacks, the evidence of Israeli prior knowledge raises a fundamental question that must be asked: Would the Israeli military conduct such an outrageous act of terror?

Millions of Americans have blindly accepted, without any proof, the government and controlled media's fictitious tale that nineteen Arabs, who lacked basic piloting skills, were responsible for the coordinated precision aerial attacks and subsequent carnage and destruction of 9-11. On the other hand, the same government and media have shown absolutely no interest in probing the evidence or looking into the many unanswered questions surrounding the attacks. There can only be one logical explanation for such persistent avoidance of the evidence by the people who should be leading the investigation. They have avoided the evidence because it contradicts the fiction they have presented to the public.

The number of people who realize that the government and media have lied about 9-11 is significant and continues to grow all the time. The pack of lies surrounding the attacks has been thoroughly exposed and can no longer be supported. Unable to defend their fiction in the face of facts and evidence presented by honest scientists and writers, the defenders of the 9-11 lie use disinformation, defamation, and slander to try and prevent the truth from spreading like wildfire.

Israeli Prior Knowledge

While the evidence indicates that the Israelis had prior knowledge of 9-11, commonly-held misconceptions about Israel and a general lack of understanding of Zionism's brutal history of terrorism prevent most people from comprehending the Israeli connection. The ignorance of Zionist history, cultivated by the controlled media, prevents people from understanding reality in the Middle East. It is essential to have a grasp of the history of previous Israeli attacks on the United States to understand 9-11. This chapter examines a few little-known, but key events in the history of Israeli false-flag terror attacks and the people behind them. The names and events discussed in this chapter are at the center of Zionist terrorism, false-flag and otherwise.

"False-flag" terrorism means an act of terror planned and perpetrated by one party for the purpose of having the blame assigned to its enemy for political or strategic purposes. False-flag attacks are designed to foment hostility or instigate war between groups or nations. 9-11, like many of the terror attacks that have occurred in occupied-Iraq, was a textbook false-flag operation.

Very rarely has the United States, oceans away from the conflicts of Europe and Asia, actually been attacked by foreign militaries. The British invasion during the War of 1812 and the Japanese bombing of Pearl Harbor in 1941 are the only foreign attacks, prior to 9-11, that come to mind. Although 9-11 is disguised and interpreted by the government and media as an act of terrorism carried out by Islamic fanatics, the evidence indicates that it was a carefully planned false-flag attack carried out by the Israeli military after years of planning and preparation.

Evidence of Israeli Involvement

This is not a hypothesis that can be easily dismissed as based on speculation or prejudice. There is solid evidence that Israeli intelligence agencies had prior knowledge of 9-11, which is indicative of involvement in the attacks. Public statements made by key terror suspects, the five jubilant "movers" arrested in New Jersey, for example, who were actually Israeli intelligence agents, indicate that they possessed prior knowledge of the attacks.

In November 2001, after two months in U.S. custody, three of the five agents appeared on Israeli television and admitted, in plain Hebrew, that their purpose had been to document the event. The Israeli interviewer did not ask who had sent them, but it is quite clear they were working for Israeli intelligence.

The five fake movers from Urban Moving Systems of Weehawken, New Jersey, were actually operatives of the Israeli secret service. The five Israeli agents, described in early news reports as "Middle Eastern," had been sought by the FBI and New Jersey authorities after they had been seen celebrating and photographing the destruction of the World Trade Center. The Israelis made a video of themselves with the burning towers behind them as they flicked their cigarette lighters, laughed, and celebrated as hundreds of innocent people were being roasted alive. Reportedly, they had worn Palestinian or Arab garb, which was later found in their van.

The Israeli agents, who were caught with multiple passports, box cutters, and thousands of dollars stuffed into their socks, were driving a van that tested positive for explosives when they were arrested. Two of the five were actually on a list of foreign intelligence agents known to U.S. law enforcement authorities at the time.

ABC News did a follow up on the Israeli agents in June 2002:

> The arresting officers said they saw a lot that aroused their suspicion about the men. One of the passengers had $4,700 in cash hidden in his sock. Another was carrying two foreign passports. A box cutter was found in the van. But perhaps the biggest surprise for the officers came when the five men identified themselves as Israeli citizens.
>
> 'We Are Not Your Problem'
>
> According to the police report, one of the passengers told the officers they had been on the West Side Highway in Manhattan "during the incident" — referring to the World Trade Center attack. The driver of the van, Sivan Kurzberg, told the officers, "We are Israeli. We are not your problem. Your problems are

our problems. The Palestinians are the problem." The other passengers were his brother Paul Kurzberg, Yaron Shmuel, Oded Ellner, and Omer Marmari.

The five "movers" were evidently part of a much larger Israeli operation in New York City. The Urban Moving Systems company was later exposed as a Mossad "front" company, a fake agency set up to facilitate the terror operation. An American who worked with the company said he was shocked to see that the Israeli employees had openly rejoiced over the attacks.

In November 2001, the five Israeli terror suspects were returned to Israel on "visa violations" although they had repeatedly refused to take, and then failed, lie detector tests concerning their involvement in 9-11.

Instant messages warning of the attack at the WTC and predicting the bombing to the precise minute were sent via the Mossad-owned Odigo messaging system hours before the first plane hit the North Tower. These warnings are further evidence that Israeli intelligence had very specific and accurate knowledge of the terror attacks – long before they occurred.

In a complex and elaborately planned crime of mass murder and terrorism like 9-11, possession of specific prior knowledge like that held by the fake Israeli movers and the senders of the Odigo messages is evidence of complicity in the crime.

Had the recipients of the Odigo warnings contacted the authorities in New York City, thousands of lives would have been saved. If these people were not complicit in the crime, why didn't they contact the authorities? Taking the evidence of Israeli prior knowledge into consideration with the Israeli military's capability to launch such a sophisticated false-flag terror attack, the obvious question has to be asked: Would Israeli military agencies commit such an atrocious act of terrorism in the United States in order to achieve a strategic goal?

The question whether Israeli strategic planners would conduct a false-flag terror attack against the United States, their most powerful ally, in order to fix the blame on the Arabs, their enemies, raises –several specific questions:

1. Has the Israeli military conducted false-flag terror attacks against the United States in the past?

2. If so, are there links between the people or agencies involved in the previous terror attacks and 9-11?

3. Is there a strategic goal for which Zionist planners would commit such a terrorist atrocity?

4. If so, has that strategic goal been realized as a result of 9-11?

The answer to all four questions is yes. The Israeli military has a documented history of conducting false-flag terror attacks against the United States. It also has a history of withholding information from the United States about threats it had knowledge of.

Specific Zionist extremists are, furthermore, the prime suspects with the strongest motives for carrying out 9-11. The Zionist motive was to kick-start their long-planned U.S.-led "War on Terror" with a spectacular terror attack inside the United States. Like any other crime, solving 9-11 requires that we diligently investigate those suspects with strong motives and prior histories of committing similar crimes. There are Israeli suspects who fit this description. On the other hand, there is no reasonable Arab motive to attack the World Trade Center or the Pentagon. Why would Arabs or Moslems commit such a counter-productive act? Why would any Arab organization commit a senseless crime knowing that it would invite a U.S. military invasion of their nation or another Islamic nation? The Arab/ Islamic terror scenario for 9-11 makes very little sense.

Israel's History of Terror

We must use terror, assassination, intimidation, land confiscation, and the cutting of all social services to rid the Galilee of its Arab population.

David Ben Gurion, first prime minister of Israel, to the General Staff, May 1948

Zionists and Israelis have long employed terrorism as a tool and a tactic. Senior officials of the Israeli government, the Mossad, and Aman (Israeli military intelligence) have long histories of using terror as a tool. Zionists from Poland and Russia used terrorism to drive the native Palestinians from their land, homes, and villages during the war of 1947-48. Some 400 Palestinian villages and towns were obliterated and their populations massacred or sent into exile as refugees. Many of the Palestinian houses and villages were taken over by Jewish immigrants; others were razed to the ground.

The Zionists also began using terrorism as a tactic against the West in the 1940s, carrying out false-flag terror attacks against the United States and Britain as far back as the bombing of Jerusalem's King David Hotel on July 22, 1946. The bombing of the luxury hotel was ordered by Menachem Begin, the head of the Irgun, a Zionist terrorist organization during the 1930s and 1940s. Begin, a known terrorist, later became prime minister of Israel, a position he held during the 1982 invasion of Lebanon, which was led by Ariel Sharon, his defense minister. Begin, an avowed racist, had a Jewish supremacist view of the world, which he used to justify his crimes of terrorism and genocide. "[The Palestinians] are beasts walking on two legs," Begin said in a speech to the Knesset, as quoted by the Israeli writer Amnon Kapeliouk in his article "Begin and the Beasts" published in the *New Statesman* of 25 June 1982.

Zionist terrorists from the Irgun and Haganah militia, disguised as Arabs, set off seven large demolition bombs in the basement of the King David Hotel, which was the base for the British Secretariat and the military command in British-occupied Palestine. Ninety-one people were killed, most of them staff of the secretariat. The attack on the hotel was the deadliest attack against the British in the history of the Mandate. To this day, the Zionist bombing of the King David Hotel is the terrorist act which has caused the greatest number of casualties in the history of the Israeli-Arab conflict. Zionists are proud of the bombing as one of their key acts of terror that compelled the British to abandon Palestine.

David Ben Gurion, the head of the Haganah militia, advocated the use of terror and supported the bombing. Although publicly the Haganah condemned the bombing, many researchers insist that the Haganah had authorized it. "Everything was coordinated with the Haganah," Menachem Begin declared in a film from the Israel Broadcasting Authority's "Scroll of Fire" series.

Netanyahu's Support for Terrorists

Members of the Irgun, which carried out scores of terror bombings in the 1930s and 40s, and its political successors in the Likud party, hold the worldview that "political violence and terrorism" are "legitimate tools in the Jewish national struggle for the Land of Israel," according to Arie Perliger and Leonard Weinberg, authors of *Jewish Self Defense and Terrorist Groups Prior to the Establishment of the State of Israel: Roots and Traditions*.

Benjamin Netanyahu, the prime minister and leader of the Likud, attended a two-day anniversary celebration of the King David Hotel bombing in July 2006 with former terrorists of the Irgun and Haganah. The event was organized by the Menachem Begin Heritage House, the University of Haifa, and the Association of IZL [Irgun] Fighters. The seminar was held "to mark the 60th anniversary of the bombing of the King David Hotel, Jerusalem, by members of the United Resistance Movement (Haganah and Irgun)," the *Jerusalem Post* noted in its pre-event notices. The Israeli newspaper specifically noted that members of the Haganah and Irgun had been involved in the terrorist bombing.

One of the terrorists even led a tour of the hotel he had bombed. The fact that the right-wing politician and terror specialist, "Bibi" Netanyahu, had participated in a two-day event celebrating the bombing of the King David Hotel was reported in the *Jerusalem Post*, and in leading newspapers in Britain, France, and India – but not a single word about the event was printed in the controlled press of the United States, the nation supposedly fighting the "War on Terror."

Netanyahu's conspicuous role as the main speaker at an event celebrating an act of terrorism was not reported in any U.S. newspaper until Patrick Buchanan mentioned it in his article entitled "Moral Culpability for Qana," on August 2, 2006. Buchanan's comments, however, only appeared in independent regional newspapers in Pittsburgh, Wyoming, and Ohio:

> Rubbing our noses in our own cravenness, "Bibi" Netanyahu took time out a week ago to commemorate the 60th anniversary of the terror attack on the King David Hotel by Menachem Begin's Irgun, an attack that killed 92 people, among them British nurses. This was not a terrorist act, Bibi explained, because Irgun telephoned a 15-minute warning to the hotel before the bombs went off.

> Right. And those children in Qana should not have ignored Israeli leaflets warning them to clear out of southern Lebanon.

> Our Israeli friends appear to be playing us for fools.

In 1946, *The Times* (U.K.) described the Irgun as "terrorists in disguise." Sarah Agassi, it reported, was one of the "terrorists in disguise" involved in the bombing of the King David Hotel. She and a fellow agent had "cased" the hotel, while her brother and other terrorists had disguised themselves as Arabs delivering milk as they placed seven milk cans, each containing 50 kg. (110 lbs.) of explosives, in its basement.

The Zionists had important strategic reasons for the bombing, according to the *Jerusalem Post* of July 27, 2006:

> The bombing was a direct response to the events of the British Operation Agatha and the Black Sabbath of June 29, 1946, during which 17,000 British soldiers confiscated weapons and intelligence documents and arrested thousands of leaders of the Yishuv and Hagana activists.
>
> The documents, brought to the King David headquarters, revealed most of the Yishuv's operational plans and incriminated the Jewish Agency in the leadership of the United Resistance, as well as the IZL and the Lehi, against the British.
>
> The evidence would be used to try the Jewish activists and, quite possibly, to hang them.
>
> Twenty-five fighters took part in the carefully-planned and precisely executed bombing. Six of them, dressed as Arab laborers, placed the seven milk cans filled with 350 kg. of explosives, fitted with timers set to go off in 40 minutes, around the central support beam of the hotel's southern wing. Others spread explosives along the roads leading to the hotel to prevent reinforcements and emergency medical crews from arriving at the scene.

Netanyahu's Terrorist Roots

Netanyahu is the son of Ben Zion Netanyahu (born Mileikowsky in Warsaw, Poland). Ben Zion was the former senior aide of Vladimir "Ze'ev" Jabotinsky, the militant extremist founder of Revisionist Zionism and the Irgun. His son, Benjamin "Bibi" Netanyahu is also a leading advocate of the teachings of Jabotinsky. On July 8, 2007, Netanyahu was the keynote speaker at an event at the Jabotinsky Institute to mark the 67th anniversary of the death of the founder of the Irgun.

The Irgun, a Zionist terrorist organization dedicated to creating Greater Israel, is the political parent of Israel's extreme right-wing Likud party, which Benjamin Netanyahu currently heads. The Irgun was the "armed expression" of Revisionist Zionism, which was expressed by Jabotinsky as follows, according to Howard M. Sachar, author of *A History of Israel from the Rise of Zionism to Our Time*:

1. Every Jew has the right to enter Palestine;

2. Only active retaliation [i.e. terrorism] would deter the Arabs and the British;

3. Only Jewish armed force would ensure the Jewish state.

Terrorism Specialist

Netanyahu is also a terrorism specialist who has made a career out of promoting the Zionist agenda of a global "War on Terror" since the 1980s. When Netanyahu was asked, on the same day, about the terrorism of 9-11, he said, "It's very good." Who else, but a hardened terrorist complicit in the crime, would use the word "good" to describe 9-11? As James Bennet of the *New York Times* reported on September 12, 2001:

Asked tonight what the attack meant for relations between the United States and Israel, Benjamin Netanyahu, the former prime minister, replied, "It's very good." Then he edited himself: "Well, not very good, but it will generate immediate sympathy."

In 2006, the *Jerusalem Post* and other newspapers reported on Netanyahu's outspoken support for the terrorists who had bombed the King David Hotel in 1946. The Irgun's chief of operations at the time of the bombing was Eitan Livni, father of the Israeli Foreign Minister "Tzipi" Livni (2006-09). The high-level political connections in Israel with the Irgun terrorists of the 1940s are an indication of the influence they have on the Israeli political establishment, *The Hindu* [India] noted in an article entitled "Celebrating Terror, Israeli-style" on July 24, 2006:

> "We do not think that it is right for an act of terrorism, which led to the loss of many lives, to be commemorated," Britain's Ambassador to Israel, Simon McDonald, and its consul-general in Jerusalem, John Jenkins, protested weakly in a letter to the local Israeli administration in Jerusalem.

Previous Israeli Attacks on U.S. Targets

Eight years after the bombing of the King David Hotel, Israel carried out a series of false-flag terror bombings against U.S. and British libraries, theatres, and other government institutions in Egypt in a terror campaign designed to be blamed on Egyptian groups. This Israeli terror campaign of July 1954 is often referred to as the "Lavon Affair" after Pinhas Lavon, the Israeli defense minister at the time.

In June 1967, thirteen years after the Lavon Affair, the Israeli air force and navy deliberately strafed, bombed, napalmed, and torpedoed an unarmed U.S. vessel, the *USS Liberty*, and tried to kill all of the nearly three hundred crew members, simply to achieve a strategic goal. Recently released documents from the National Security Agency (NSA) confirm that the United States government at the time had evidence that the Israelis had deliberately attacked the *USS Liberty* knowing it was a U.S. vessel. Oliver Kirby, the NSA's deputy director for operations at the time of the Israeli attack on the *USS Liberty*, confirmed the existence of the transcripts to John Crewdson of the *Chicago Tribune* in 2007, saying he had personally read them:

Asked whether he had personally read such transcripts, Kirby replied, "I sure did. I certainly did."

> "They said, 'We've got him in the zero,'" Kirby recalled, "whatever that meant — I guess the sights or something. And then one of them said, 'Can you see the flag?'
>
> They said 'Yes, it's U.S, it's U.S.' They said it several times, so there wasn't any doubt in anybody's mind that they knew it."
>
> Kirby, now 86 and retired in Texas, said the transcripts were "something that's bothered me all my life. I'm willing to swear on a stack of Bibles that we knew they knew."

The planes involved in the attack reported directly to the Commander of the Israeli Air Force, Major General Mordechai "Moti" Hod (1966-1973). Hod (a.k.a. Mordechai Fein) was from Kibbutz Degania, like Moshe Dayan, the defense minister he served under.

Hod left the military in 1975 and created CAL, an Israel air cargo company. After only two years, he left the company and became chief executive of El Al airlines from 1977 to 1979. In 1985, he founded an un-named security company, according to his June 2003 obituary in the *Guardian* (UK). From 1987 until retirement in 1993, he was the chairman of Israel Aircraft Industries (IAI).

ICTS, the Israeli airport security company, was a key defendant in the 9-11 tort litigation. The ICTS website says this about the company: "ICTS International N.V. was founded in 1982 by a select group of security experts, former military commanding officers and veterans of government intelligence and security agencies."

An employee of ICTS told me in 2001 that Huntleigh USA, their wholly-owned airport security subsidiary, had handled passenger screening at Boston and Newark airports on 9-11. As a matter of fact, the Mossad-linked company probably had people at every one of the airports involved in the attacks of 9-11. The ICTS company website says: "In 1998, ICTS International N.V. made a strategic decision to focus on the US market. The following year, it acquired Huntleigh USA Corp., which provides airline passenger screening services at 47 US airports, including all the international aviation gateways in the USA."

The ICTS company developed out of El Al (the state airline of Israel) security. The Israeli airline security firm went through a number of name changes as it began providing "security" to European and American airports.

Cover-Up

The U.S. government, military, and media all went along with the cover-up of the deliberate attack on the USS *Liberty* to avoid blaming Israel for the murder of 34 American servicemen, 26 of whom died from a torpedo blast, and the wounding of some 173 others. Shimon Peres, the Israeli president, certainly knows who made the decision to attack the U.S. vessel in 1967.

Moshe Dayan, defense minister during the Six-Day War, was a close associate and political ally of Shimon Peres. In 1965, former prime minister Ben Gurion and his closest followers, including Shimon Peres and Moshe Dayan, broke away from the ruling labor party, Mapai, and formed a separate minority faction, the Rafi or Workers' List.

The Crewdson article reveals that the Israelis knew very well that the USS *Liberty* was an American vessel in international waters – before they fired the torpedo that killed twenty-six U.S. servicemen:

> Twenty minutes later, after the *Liberty* had been hit repeatedly by machine guns, 30 mm cannon and napalm from the Israelis' French-built Mirage and Mystere fighter-bombers, the controller directing the attack asked his chief in Tel Aviv to which country the target vessel belonged.
>
> "Apparently American," the chief controller replied.
>
> Fourteen minutes later the *Liberty* was struck amidships by a torpedo from an Israeli boat, killing 26 of the 100 or so NSA technicians and specialists in Russian and Arabic who were working in restricted compartments below the ship's waterline.

"Sink the Target – No Survivors"

Lt. James M. Ennes, Jr., an officer on the bridge of the USS *Liberty*, wrote his first-hand account of the Israeli attack in a 1979 book entitled *Assault on the Liberty*. Lieutenant Ennes' book provides evidence that the Israeli attack was deliberate and not an accident of war. Ennes describes how Israeli torpedo boats repeatedly machine-gunned *Liberty* sailors fighting the napalm fires on deck and shot her life rafts in the water while an oversize U.S. flag flew from its mast.

The shooting of the life rafts indicates that the Israelis did not want anyone to survive the assault and intended sinking of the U.S. vessel. Steve Forslund, an intelligence analyst for the 544th Air Reconnaissance Technical Wing in 1967, saw the transcripts from the Israeli pilots and their ground control as they came off the teletype machine at Offutt Air Force Base in Omaha.

"The ground control station stated that the target was American and for the aircraft to confirm it," Forslund recalled. "The aircraft did confirm the identity of the target as American, by the American flag. The ground control station ordered the aircraft to attack and sink the target and ensure they left no survivors." Forslund said he clearly recalled "the obvious frustration of the controller over the inability of the pilots to sink the target quickly and completely." "He kept insisting the mission had to sink the target, and was frustrated with the pilots' responses that it didn't sink," he said.

Chief Petty Officer Stanley W. White, president of the *Liberty* Veterans Association, said, "The Israeli planes and gunboats spent more than one hour hitting us with rockets, napalm bombs, torpedoes, cannon and machine-gun fire. They machine-gunned our firefighters on deck and they shot our life rafts out of the water...I don't know of a single member of our association who believes that attack was an accident."

There are three reasons that have been given as to why the Israelis wanted to sink the U.S. electronic reconnaissance vessel:

1. To prevent the U.S. from knowing that Israel was planning to seize the Golan Heights from Syria;

2. To prevent the U.S. from obtaining evidence that Israeli troops were slaughtering some 1,000 Egyptian prisoners of war near Gaza;

3. To destroy the U.S. vessel that was capable of discerning that Israel was sending false communications to Jordan and Egypt to prolong the war until the Israeli military achieved its territorial goals.

"U.S. intelligence documents indicate the Israelis attacked the *Liberty* deliberately. They feared she would monitor their plans to attack the Golan Heights in Syria - a move the United States opposed for fear of provoking Soviet military intervention," Ennes wrote.

Wilber Crane Eveland, an author formerly with the CIA in the Middle East, wrote that the *Liberty* had intercepted messages that "made it clear that Israel had never intended to limit its attack to Egypt."

Israeli Massacre

The *Tribune* article of 2 October 2007 about the new revelations concerning the attack on the *Liberty* reported that the NSA's deputy director at the time, Louis Tordella, speculated in a recently declassified memo that the attack "might have been ordered by some senior commander on the Sinai peninsula who wrongly suspected that the *Liberty* was monitoring his activities." The activities that needed to be hidden included the slaughter of some 1,000 Egyptian POWs.

Aryeh Yitzhaki of Bar Ilan University, who worked in the Israel Defense Forces (IDF) history department, said in an August 1995 interview with Israel Radio that a reconnaissance unit, known as Shaked (Almond), headed by Binyamin Ben-Eliezer, had killed hundreds of Egyptians who had abandoned their weapons and fled into the desert during the 1967 war.

Yitzhaki said he had investigated six or seven separate incidents, in which approximately 1,000 unarmed Egyptian prisoners of war had been killed by Israeli forces.

The U.S. Marine Barracks – Beirut 1983

Sixteen years later, 241 U.S. Marines died when a Mercedes truck packed with explosives demolished their barracks at Beirut International Airport on October 23, 1983. A similar explosion occurred nearly simultaneously at the French military barracks a few kilometers away, killing 56 French troops.

In the wake of the 1982 Israeli invasion of Lebanon, President Ronald Reagan sent 1,800 marines to Beirut to act as "peace keepers." Ariel Sharon and the Israeli leadership, however, resented the interference and used the U.S. presence to commit a false-flag operation that killed 241 marines, according to Victor Ostrovsky in his book on the Mossad, *By Way of Deception*.

Ostrovsky, a former Mossad officer, reported that Nahum Admoni, the Mossad director at the time, had very specific information about the truck being prepared for the attack on the U.S. Marines, but had intentionally withheld this crucial information from the U.S. military. "No, we're not there to protect Americans. They're a big country. Send only the regular information," Admoni reportedly said.

Admoni, the son of Polish immigrants, was director of the Mossad from 1982 to 1989. In 1947-48, Admoni had served in the Shai, the Haganah intelligence branch headed by Isser Harel, and later in the newly created IDF intelligence agency, Aman. After the 1948 war, Admoni studied at the University of California, Berkeley, until 1954.

The purpose of the false-flag terror bombings in Lebanon was to create U.S. animosity toward the Arab world and align the U.S. with Israel, according to Ostrovsky. There had been an earlier car bomb at the U.S. Embassy in Beirut on April 18, 1983, which had killed seventeen Marines. The truck bombing compelled the Marines to move offshore and President Reagan ordered them to be withdrawn from Lebanon on February 7, 1984.

Israeli intelligence is suspected of having been involved in the 1983 bombing of the Marine barracks, the deadliest single-day death toll for the United States Marine Corps since the Battle of Iwo Jima.

"War on Terror"

The Israeli strategy of using terrorism to instigate U.S. animosity toward the Arab world, which began with the Lavon Affair in 1954, reached its goal of bringing the United States into a fraudulent "War on Terror" with the false-flag attacks of 9-11. With its U.S.-led invasions and occupations of Afghanistan and Iraq, the "War on Terror" was the fulfillment of a key strategic goal for Israeli military planners.

To have the armies of the U.S. and European nations occupying Iraq, the most powerful and advanced Arab nation, has long been the dream of Zionist strategic planners. Benjamin Netanyahu, for example, has explicitly called for such a global "War on Terror" since 1980, when his first book, *International Terrorism: Challenge and Response*, was published by the Yonatan (Netanyahu) Institute. Netanyahu's appeal for the Western democracies to wage war against Israel's foes was repeated and amplified in his 1986 book, *Terrorism: How the West Can Win*.

Although it is never mentioned as such in the controlled press, it needs to be understood that the pre-planned invasions of Afghanistan and Iraq are, in fact, wars of aggression. To prepare for and carry out a war of aggression is a serious war crime under the Nuremberg Principles of 1950. The United States and its allies convicted and literally strangled to death dozens of senior Nazis at the Nuremberg trials for having committed such war crimes.

In the aftermath of 9-11, the U.S. government failed to prove that the terror attacks had been planned, sponsored, or executed by members of the ruling Taliban regime prior to invading Afghanistan. Ten years later, the U.S. government still had not proven a connection between the Taliban regime and 9-11.

On June 5, 2006, author Ed Haas contacted the Federal Bureau of Investigation headquarters to ask why, while claiming that Bin Laden was wanted in connection with the August 1998 bombings of U.S. embassies in Tanzania and Kenya, the "most wanted" poster did not indicate that Bin Laden was wanted in connection with the events of 9-11. Rex Tomb, Chief of Investigative Publicity for the FBI responded, "The reason why 9-11 is not mentioned on Osama bin Laden's Most Wanted page is because the FBI has no hard evidence connecting bin Laden to 9-11." Tomb continued, "Bin Laden has not been formally charged in connection to 9-11."

Likewise, there is no evidence of involvement in 9-11 by any member of the regime of the former Iraqi leader Saddam Hussein. Furthermore, allegations that the Iraqi regime had obtained weapons of mass destruction, trumpeted by senior officials of the Bush administration and Judith Miller of the *New York Times*, turned out to be lies crafted solely for the purpose of deceiving the public and provoking another illegal invasion. The passage of time does not make a war of aggression any less criminal.

Decades of Planning

The same key people who were involved in the 1954 Israeli terror bombings of the U.S. Information Agency libraries in Alexandria and Cairo were holding high-level positions in the Israeli government in 2001. There are other Israelis, with long histories of terrorism and strategic planning, who revealed having very specific prior knowledge of 9-11 long before 2001.

The highest Israeli intelligence official at the time of the Lavon Affair, Isser Harel, was evidently aware of the long-term planning of 9-11 — more than twenty years before it happened. In 1980, twenty-one years before the attacks, Isser Harel, the former director of Haganah intelligence, the Shin Bet, and the Mossad, predicted with uncanny accuracy the events of 9-11 to Michael D. Evans, an American Zionist supporter of the Likud.

On September 23, 1980, Evans visited Harel at his home in Israel and had dinner with him and Dr. Reuven Hecht, a senior adviser to prime minister Menachem Begin. In an editorial entitled "America the

Target," published in the *Jerusalem Post* of September 30, 2001, Evans
related what Harel had told him twenty-one years earlier in 1980:

> I sat with former Mossad chief Isser Harel for a con-
> versation about Arab terrorism. As he handed me a
> cup of hot tea and a plate of cookies, I asked him, "Do
> you think terrorism will come to America, and if so,
> where and why?"

> Harel looked at his American visitor and replied, "I
> fear it will come to you in America. America has the
> power, but not the will, to fight terrorism. The terror-
> ists have the will, but not the power, to fight America
> - but all that could change with time. Arab oil money
> buys more than tents."

> As to the where, Harel continued, "New York City
> is the symbol of freedom and capitalism. It's likely
> they will strike the Empire State Building, your tall-
> est building [he mistakenly thought] and a symbol of
> your power."

In another article on his Jerusalem Prayer Team website, entitled
"Jimmy Carter: Radical Islam's Ally," Evans relates the same story
about Harel:

> My last question was would terrorism ever come to
> America. "You have the power to fight it," he said,
> "but not the will. They have the will, but not the
> power. All of that will change in time. Yes, I fear it will
> come to New York and your tallest building, which is
> a symbol of your fertility."

In 2004, Evans published a book entitled *The American Prophecies, Terrorism and Mid-East Conflict Reveal a Nation's Destiny*. In a subsequent interview, published under the title "Is America in Bible Prophecy?" Evans explained what Harel meant about fertility symbols:

Question: So extrapolating from the scenarios of the Bible, what do you believe is our nation's future, based on prophecy?

Evans: The story of prophecy that has to do with the Jews goes all the way through to the end of the Book of Revelation. Jesus prophesied in Matthew 24. The disciples said, "What shall be the signs of the coming of the end of the age?" And he said, "The first sign would be deception." Now, there's never been greater deception then what happened on September 11, 2001.

Question: Why do you say that America's story is contained within biblical prophecies?

Evans: America stepped into the eye of a prophetic storm when it took covenant with both Ishmael and Isaac, the sons of Abraham, the Arab and the Jew... Most of the Bible talks about this battle between these two brothers, and we're right in the middle of that.

             On September 23, 1979, the founder of Israeli intelligence over dinner told me that America was developing a tolerance for terror. The gentleman's name was Isser Harel, the founder of Mossad Israeli intelligence — he ran it from 1947 to 1963.

             He told me that America had developed an alliance between two countries, Israel and Saudi Arabia, and that the alliance with Saudi Arabia was dangerous and would develop a tolerance for terror among Americans. He said if the tolerance continued that Islamic fundamentalists would ultimately strike America.

I said "Where?"

He said, "In Islamic theology, the phallic symbol is very important. Your biggest phallic symbol is New York City and your tallest building will be the phallic symbol they will hit." Isser Harel prophesied that the tallest building in New York would be the first building hit by Islamic fundamentalists 21 years ago.

The interview with Evans is published on-line on Beliefnet, a Zionist propaganda network disguised as a religious website. Steven Waldman is CEO, Co-Founder and Editor-in-Chief of Beliefnet. Previously, Waldman was National Editor of *US News & World Report*, National Correspondent for *Newsweek*, and editor of *Washington Monthly*. One of Beliefnet's directors is Michael S. Perlis, the former President of the *Playboy* Publishing Group.

Think about this for a minute. The founder of Israeli intelligence tells an American Zionist in 1980 that Arab terrorism will come to America and that the terrorists will strike the tallest building in New York City. His bizarre prediction, which makes no sense, then comes to pass thirteen years later with a fake terror bombing in 1993, evidently set up by the FBI. The FBI-coordinated false-flag terror event is then followed, eight years later, by a spectacular, well-planned, and extremely lethal attack which kills thousands. So, how did Isser Harel know what Arab terrorists had planned more than two decades before 9-11?

Isser Harel – Mossad's Master Terrorist

Under David Ben Gurion, Isser Harel was the former chief of Haga-nah intelligence (Shai) from 1944, the Shin Bet from 1948, and the Mossad until 1963. Admoni, the Mossad director who refused to warn the U.S. Marines in 1983, had served under Harel. Given his unique position and penchant for terrorism as a means of coercion, the uncanny accuracy of Harel's prediction says more about the years of Israeli planning that went into 9-11 than it does about any criminal plots of alleged Arab origin.

After nearly two decades as the head of Israeli intelligence, Ben Gurion reportedly asked Harel to resign in 1963 because of his use of terror bombings as a means of coercion against the West. Harel, as director of the Mossad, had initiated "The Damocles Operation" of the early 1960s, which was a terror bombing campaign to threaten German scientists and prevent them from helping Egypt develop its defense systems.

Two Mossad agents were arrested and jailed in Switzerland for us-ing terror bombs against German scientists. The wife of one scientist was killed in a mysterious explosion, a second scientist disappeared, and the secretary of a third scientist was blinded and mutilated by a mail bomb in Cairo. As Ian Black and Benny Morris, authors of *Israel's Secret Wars: A History of Israel's Intelligence Services*, wrote:

> Dr. Heinz Krug, director of a Munich-based Egyptian front company called Intra, had disappeared mysteri-ously and was presumed murdered in September 1962.

> On 7 October Harel [Isser Harel, Mossad head] left for Europe 'to personally supervise authorized op-erations and the special collection programme.'

In November, Aman [IDF intelligence] sent several letter bombs to the rocket installations in Egypt and one of them, a large parcel that had been mailed by sea from Hamburg, killed five Egyptians. Someone with a black sense of humour dubbed the campaign 'post mortem.'

It is interesting to note that Yosef Goell, a columnist with the *Jerusalem Post*, published an editorial entitled "Isser Harel and the German Scientists" on February 22, 1991, in which Israel's English-language newspaper delivered a thinly-veiled threat of Harel-type terrorism to European scientists and companies doing business with Arab nations:

> The directors and managers of those firms and the experts who work for them should be reminded that they are playing with their lives and the welfare of their families. It would be well if they went back and studied the episode of Isser Harel and the German scientists in Nasser's missile program of the 1960s.

The Lavon Affair

The Lavon Affair, or "the shameful affair" (*Esek Habish*) as it is known in Hebrew, was an Israeli false-flag terror bombing campaign against the United States and Britain that was carried out in Egypt in 1954. Israeli military intelligence had set up a terror cell of sleeper agents in Egypt, which was activated in July 1954 to blow up U.S. and British targets. The Israeli operation was code-named "Susannah." The false-flag terrorist bombings were meant to be blamed on Egyptians in order to alienate the U.S. and Britain from President Gamal Abdul Nasser and prevent Egypt from nationalizing the Suez Canal.

The Lavon Affair is seldom discussed in the media or in university courses on Middle Eastern history. Strict censorship in the Israeli media even prevented the Israeli public from knowing about the affair for many years. Only in 2005, fifty-one years after the bombings, did Israel finally admit responsibility for its 1954 false-flag terrorist bombing campaign in Egypt. The bombings were carried out between July 2 and July 27, 1954, by a covert terror cell composed of about one dozen Egyptian Jews under the command of Israeli intelligence agents.

The Israeli-run terror cell was discovered and broken up on July 27, 1954, when one of its members was caught in Alexandria after the bomb he was carrying exploded. An Israeli terrorist cell, Unit 131, was reportedly responsible for the bombings. At the time of the incident, Unit 131 is said to have been the subject of a dispute between Aman and Mossad over who controlled it.

The Egyptian operatives had been recruited several years earlier, when an Israeli intelligence officer named Avram Dar went to Cairo posing as John Darling, a British citizen from Gibraltar. Dar recruited Egyptian Jews, who had helped the Mossad with illegal emigration to Israel, and trained them for covert operations. The Israeli terror cell went to work in the summer of 1954. On July 2, a post office in Alexandria was firebombed. On July 14, the U.S. Information Agency libraries in Alexandria and Cairo, and a British theater were bombed. The bombs contained nitroglycerine and were placed on the shelves of the libraries. After the terrorist cell was discovered, three of the Israeli terrorist commanders succeeded in fleeing Egypt and the fourth committed suicide. After the trial in Cairo, two of the accused Egyptians were condemned to death and executed, and eight were condemned to long terms of imprisonment.

Moshe Sharett

The Israeli prime minister and foreign minister at the time, Moshe Sharett, was evidently unaware of the intrigue, which had been carried out by disciples of David Ben Gurion, namely Isser Harel, Moshe Dayan, and Shimon Peres.

Sharett (born Shertok in Ukraine) was Israel's first foreign minister (1948–1956) and second prime minister (1953–1955). Sharett held both positions at the time of the Israeli terror campaign. Sharett, who appears to have known nothing about the terror ring, only became informed of the facts afterwards.

In October 1953, shortly before Ben Gurion took a two-year hiatus in the Negev Desert leaving Sharett in charge, he appointed Pinhas Lavon, a staunch supporter of the "retaliation" [i.e. terrorism] policy, as minister of defense, and nominated Moshe Dayan as chief of staff of the armed forces. When Sharett was told of Ben Gurion's decision to nominate Dayan as chief of staff, he penned this note in his diary: "The new chief of staff's immense capacity for plotting and intrigue-making will yield many complications."

Lavon – Terrorize the West

Pinhas Lavon, Israel's minister of defense at the time of the bombings, was part of a group of military leaders who advocated the use of terrorism against the Western nations, particularly Britain and the United States. This group included the Polish-born immigrants David Ben Gurion and Shimon Peres (Szymon Persky), and Moshe Dayan, the *kibbutz*-raised son of Ukrainian immigrants.

In January 1955, Sharett wrote about Lavon to Aharon Barkatt, secretary general of the Mapai party:

He [Lavon] inspired and cultivated the negative adventuristic trend in the army and preached the doctrine that not the Arab countries but the Western Powers are the enemy, and the only way to deter them from their plots is through direct actions that will terrorize them.

When the Israeli terrorist plot against Britain and the U.S. was exposed, Ben Gurion blamed Lavon, who, in turn, blamed Col. Benjamin Givli, another Ben Gurion protégé and the head of Aman, Israeli military intelligence. Lavon said that Givli had organized the covert operation behind his back.

Sharett and Israeli Terrorism

Prime Minister Sharett, however, had "no doubts about the guilt of the Dayan-Peres-Givli clique," according to the late Israeli historian Livia Rokach, the daughter of Israel Rokach, the former mayor of Tel Aviv and minister of internal affairs in the Sharett government:

> For him [Sharett], the question of who gave the order was secondary to the necessity of pronouncing a judgment on the ideology and politics of Israel's terrorism. Therefore, while he had no doubts about the guilt of the Dayan-Peres-Givli clique; to him Lavon's political responsibility was also inescapable.

As Sharett wrote about Lavon on January 10, 1955:

> [People] ask me if I am convinced that "he gave the order?"... but let us assume that Givli has acted without instructions... doesn't the moral responsibility lie all the same on Lavon, who has constantly

preached for acts of madness and taught the army
leadership the diabolic lesson of how to set the Middle East on fire, how to cause friction, cause bloody
confrontations, sabotage targets and property of the
Powers [and perform] acts of despair and suicide?

As a "moderate Zionist," Sharett believed that Israel's survival would
be impossible without the support of the West, Rokach wrote, but
that Western "morality" and interests in the Middle East would not
support a Jewish state which "behaves according to the laws of the
jungle" and "raises terrorism to the level of a sacred principle."

Shimon Peres – "Frighten the West"

In May 1947, Ben Gurion drafted Shimon Peres into the Haganah
high command, where he was initially put in charge of manpower and
later became involved in arms procurement and production. Peres
served as chief of the naval department in 1948 and was sent to the
United States in 1950 on an arms procurement mission. Peres was
instrumental in acquiring weapons for the Haganah and establishing
the Israeli defense industries, especially the aircraft and avionics industries, according to his biography. He is also known as the godfather
of the Israel's high-tech defense industries and illegal nuclear arsenal.

Peres built an alliance with France that secured a source of arms,
and was responsible for the program to develop nuclear weapons for
Israel, convincing the French to help Israel build a secret nuclear reactor at Dimona in the Negev Desert in 1957. It was Peres who acquired the French advanced Dassault Mirage III jet fighters that the
Israeli air force used to attack the USS Liberty in 1967.

About Shimon Peres, whom Sharett considered to be one of the key planners of the terror bombing campaign of U.S. institutions in Egypt, he wrote this note in 1955: "Peres shares the same ideology [as Lavon]: he wants to frighten the West into supporting Israel's aims."

Two years later, in 1957, Sharett wrote even more critically about Peres:

> I have stated that I totally and utterly reject Peres and consider his rise to prominence a malignant, immoral disgrace. I will rend my clothes in mourning for the State if I see him become a minister in the Israeli government.

Sharett's terrorist adversaries: Ben Gurion, Dayan, and Peres, however, prevailed and dealt "a crushing blow" to "the very hypothesis of moderate Zionism," Rokach concluded:

> In the final analysis the West, and in particular the U.S., let itself be frightened, or blackmailed, into supporting Israel's megalomaniac ambitions, because an objective relationship of complicity already existed and because once pushed into the open this complicity proved capable of serving the cause of Western power politics in the region.

The immense profits that have flowed into the coffers of Western drug and oil cartels as a consequence of the Anglo-American control over the opium production of occupied Afghanistan and the oil of occupied Iraq illustrate Rokach's point that Israeli false-flag terror is "capable of serving the cause of Western power politics in the region."

As Rokach concluded in her study of Sharett's diary and documents:

Just as Zionism, based on the de-Palestinization and the Judaisation of Palestine, was intrinsically racist and immoral, thus the West, in reality, had no use for a Jewish state in the Middle East which did not behave according to the laws of the jungle, and whose terrorism could not be relied on as a major instrument for the oppression of the peoples of the region.

By April 1957, Sharett realized that the hard-line terrorist faction headed by Ben Gurion and his protégés Dayan and Peres had won – and that he, and his vision of moderate Zionism, had lost:

I go on repeating to myself nowadays, "Admit that you are the loser!" They showed much more daring and dynamism...they played with fire, and they won...The public, even your own public, does not share your position. On the contrary...the public now turns even against its "masters" and its bitterness against the retreat [from Sinai and Gaza] is developing into a tendency to change the political balance in this country in favor of [the former Irgun terrorist leader Menachem] Begin.

"His [Sharett's] defeat in internal Israeli politics reflected the ascendancy of the positions of Ben Gurion, Dayan, and others [Peres] who were not reluctant to use force to attain their goals," Noam Chomsky wrote in his forward to Rokach's book:

His diaries give a very revealing picture of the developing conflict, as he perceived it, and offer an illuminating insight into the early history of the state of Israel, with ramifications that reach to the present, and beyond.

9-11 and the "War on Terror" are clearly two "ramifications" of the victory of the terrorist Zionists that "reach to the present."

Had Moshe Sharett, the Israeli prime minister, "spoken frankly" and torn up "the mask of secrecy" surrounding the Israeli terror bombings, he could have changed the history of the Middle East, as Rokach wrote:

> At this point, Sharett could have changed the history of the Middle East had he spoken frankly and directly to public opinion, which was deeply troubled by the events in Egypt: the arrests, the trial, the executions, the contradicting rumors, the climate of intrigue surrounding the "Affair." [By] tearing up the mask of secrecy, denouncing those who were responsible, exposing his true convictions in regard to Israel's terroristic ideologies and orientations, [and] proposing an alternative, he could have created for himself the conditions in which to use the formal powers that he possessed to make a radical housecleaning in the security establishment. The impact of such an act would have probably been considerable not only in Israel itself but also in the Arab world, especially in Egypt. The downfall of Lavon on one hand and of the Ben Gurionist gang, headed by Dayan and Peres, on the

other hand might have blocked Ben Gurion's return to power, and in the longer range, the Sinai-Suez war. Events since then would have taken a different course.

Unfortunately, "the Ben Gurionist gang, headed by Dayan and Peres" came to power. Peres, who had been appointed to high-level positions, was elected to the Knesset in the 1959 elections. Peres, the former Director General of the Ministry of Defense under Moshe Dayan, then became the Deputy Defense Minister, a position he held until 1965 when he was implicated, with Dayan, in the Lavon affair.

On June 5, 1967, Israel started the Six-Day War when it launched a pre-emptive attack against Egypt and its air force. Yitzhak Rabin was chief of staff and Moshe Dayan was minister of defense during this crucial war that reshaped the Middle East. Ben Gurion and his gang of Dayan and Peres had formed a new party in 1965, Rafi, partly due to their involvement in the Lavon Affair. Dayan and Peres had worked closely together since their days in the Haganah.

Shimon Peres: Terrorist-in-Chief

Shimon Peres, a most unsuitable recipient of the Nobel Peace Prize in 1994, has a long history of terrorism, which is not well known in the West. Peres, the octogenarian president of the State of Israel, has a record of involvement in terrorist crimes over a period of more than five decades.

Peres is a survivor of the struggle among Zionists between the militant hard-liners, who promoted the use of violence and terrorism, and the "moderates," who opposed terrorism and advocated the use of diplomacy. Shimon Peres is a hard-liner. Born Szymon Persky in Poland on August 2, 1923, Peres is the first cousin of Lauren Bacall, the Brooklyn-born Betty Joan Persky. This relationship is a good example of how Zionist Jewish families from the Pale of Settlement often established branches in Israel and the United States in the early 1900s.

In 1947, the Polish-born Zionist leader David Ben Gurion (born David Grün) met Shimon Peres, then age twenty-three, at Haganah headquarters and made him responsible for manpower and arms purchases for the underground Zionist militia Ben Gurion commanded in Palestine.

Peres became a protégé of Ben Gurion. After the bombing of the King David Hotel and other terror killings by the Haganah and other Zionist terror groups, the British withdrew from Palestine. The armed gangs of Zionist immigrants and veterans of the Red Army then turned their skills of terrorism, which some had gained during World War II, against the indigenous population of Palestine. Nearly 400 Palestinian towns and villages were completely obliterated or "ethnically cleansed" during the 1947-48 Zionist conquest of Palestine.

Peres was also the chief of the Israeli navy, whose main task at the time was the illegal smuggling of men and arms for the Zionist forces in Palestine. Peres "assumed the position of Director of the Defense Ministry's procurement delegation in the United States," after the 1947-1948 war, according to his biography. As director of arms procurement in the United States, Peres was responsible for organizing illegal arms smuggling. Transfers of weapons and planes to Zionist forces in Palestine violated the U.S. Neutrality Act. Much of the Haganah arms smuggling activity was run from an office above the "syndicate-owned" Copacabana Club in New York City, where Peres and Teddy Kollek, the Hungarian-born son of the director of the Rothschild bank in Vienna, worked closely with the "crime syndicate" headed by the leading Jewish gangsters of the time.

After World War II, Kollek had been sent to New York to serve as the Haganah representative and head of its weapons purchasing team in New York. Also deeply involved in the Zionist arms smuggling were the American Jews, Adolph "Al" Schwimmer and Hank Greenspun. Greenspun, the Las Vegas-based publicist for mobster Benjamin "Bugsy" Siegel, was eventually pardoned for his crimes by President Bill Clinton, a close friend of the Greenspun family. In 1951, at the request of Ben Gurion, Schwimmer and Peres founded Bedek, the military's aviation firm that became Israel's largest company, Israel Aircraft Industries (IAI).

In 1952, the same year Ben Gurion made Isser Harel the head of the Mossad, he appointed Peres to be Deputy Director General of the Ministry of Defense. The next year, at the age of twenty-nine, Peres became the youngest ever Director General of the Defense Ministry, a position he held until 1959. It is interesting to note that Peres never attended university or served in the army, according to the Israeli daily *Ha'aretz* of June 14, 2007.

As Director General, Peres was a founder of Israel's military and its subsidiary, Israel Aircraft Industries. Ben Gurion, Israel's first prime minister, put Peres in charge of the establishment of the Israel's unlawful nuclear program and secret reactor at Dimona in the Negev Desert.

Peres has never been popular with Israeli voters. Although he served twice as prime minister, he was never elected to that position. In 2000, he even lost a parliamentary election for the presidency to Moshe Katsav, an Iranian Jewish immigrant. Peres served as Israel's foreign minister under the Likud right-wing Ariel Sharon from early 2001 until November 2002. In July 2007, at nearly 84 years of age, Peres finally won the presidency, but only after Katsav was forced to leave office under a storm of allegations of rape and sexual misconduct.

One might wonder why an eighty-four-year-old man would want to be president. Is this an example of the maxim, "no rest for the wicked?" Is Peres still working because he needs to protect the critical secrets about 9-11 and the war agenda it launched? Oddly, prior to 9-11, Peres, a politician from the left, held the most powerful positions of Deputy Prime Minister and Foreign Minister in a government led by a prime minister from the extreme right, Ariel Sharon. Peres held these positions in the Israeli government from March 3, 2001, until November 2, 2002. Sharon, who reportedly became comatose in January 2006, is a well-known Israeli terrorist and war criminal with a long record of committing atrocities in Palestine and Lebanon.

Peres, godfather and chief architect of Israel's high-tech military and unlawful nuclear arsenal, is a person who has always supported the use of terror to coerce the West to support Israel's strategic goals. He has been involved, at the highest level, in numerous covert false-flag terrorist operations, such as the Lavon Affair, which was even kept secret from the Israeli prime minister at the time. Did Peres use his senior position in a government of like-minded terrorists to launch the false-flag terror attacks of 9-11 in order to coerce the United States and the West into the Zionist-planned "War on Terror?"

Shimon Peres has the credentials of a Zionist arch-terrorist. Furthermore, he has the record, the worldview, and the capability to be an architectural level planner of 9-11. Is Peres one of the masterminds behind the terrorist crime of the century? Were Isser Harel and Mordechai Hod also involved in the planning of 9-11?

To help identity the architectural level planners behind the false-flag terrorism of 9-11 we need a better understanding of how such terrorist attacks can be carried out within the context of anti-terrorist exercises. One military exercise being conducted on 9-11, for example, simulated a passenger plane crashing into a military building near the Pentagon. Was there a connection between the simulated attack and the real one?

The easiest way to carry out a false-flag attack is by setting up a military exercise that simulates the very attack you want to carry out.

Captain Eric H. May,
former U.S. Army military intelligence officer

Chapter IV

The Terror Drills
That Became Real:
9-11, the London Bombings
and the Sinking of *Estonia*

The past two decades have been marked by a large number of terror events which remain unsolved to this day. Several of these events involved heinous crimes of mass murder and are similar in a remarkable way. These are the disasters which occurred during security drills or military exercises in which the scenario was incredibly similar, if not identical, to the real-life terror attack. Understanding the nature of the exercises that formed the background and framework for these attacks is essential to understanding how the attacks were carried out.

The fact that these real-life terror events occurred within the context of virtually identical exercises has been completely ignored by the media — as if the exercises had never happened. Of the major terror events that occurred during such exercises, we will look at three specific examples: the aerial attacks of 9-11, the bombings of the London Underground and a bus in 2005, and the sinking of the Baltic ferry *Estonia* in 1994.

While there certainly have been other major disasters that occurred within the context of military exercises, such as the sinking of the Russian submarine *Kursk* in 2000 and the 1988 downing of Iran Air Flight 655 by the *USS Vincennes* in the Persian Gulf, the three events being discussed here involved attacks on civilian transportation systems far from any war zone. The three disasters were all handled in the same way by their respective governments and media. In each case, before a proper investigation could begin to establish the facts and examine the evidence, a politically acceptable explanation was put forward by government officials and repeated, without question, by the mass media. Evidence that contradicted the "official" version of events was confiscated, destroyed, or simply ignored.

The extremely hasty and improper destruction of the steel from the World Trade Center, for example, must rank as the most egregious case of destruction of evidence from a crime scene in American history. In late September 2001, officials uncovered a criminal scheme to divert metal to dumps in Long Island and New Jersey. Some 250 tons of scrap metal were found at unofficial dump sites. In November 2001, the trucks carrying steel from the World Trade Center were outfitted with a Global Positioning System (GPS) device monitored by an Israeli named Yoram Shalmon of PowerLoc Technologies of Toronto, a subcontractor in the clean-up project. Shalmon was then able to track nearly 200 trucks in real time as they carried the crucial steel evidence to the scrap yards that destroyed it using PowerLoc's Vehicle Location Device (VLD). Each VLD unit cost about $1,000.

"We were able to start identifying patterns of behavior. If a driver arrived late, the traffic analyst would look at why. Maybe the driver stopped for lunch, or maybe he ran into traffic," Shalmon told Jacqueline Emigh of SecuritySolutions.com. "Ninety-nine percent of the drivers were extremely driven to do their jobs. But there were big concerns, because the loads consisted of highly sensitive material. One driver, for example, took an extended lunch break of an hour and a half. There was nothing criminal about that, but he was dismissed. There were also cases where trucks did little detours from their routes," Shalmon said.

Likewise, during the official dive for evidence to the wreck of *Estonia*, on which more than 852 people are known to have died, the crucial locking bolt from the bow visor, which officials say caused the catastrophe, was thrown back into the sea. The bolt had been removed by divers and brought to the surface for investigation only to be thrown back by Börje Stenström, the Swedish navy commander who was the head of the technical group of the international investigation commission. According to German investigators, Stenström threw away the bolt, which according to his own explanation of the sinking, was "one of the most important pieces of evidence."

The first rule in managing a criminal cover-up is to control access to the evidence. The second rule is to destroy any and all evidence that contradicts the official version of events.

The fact that these three disasters all occurred during exercises that simulated similar terror scenarios has been ignored by the mass media, which has treated these extremely uncanny coincidences as complete non-issues. Information about the exercises has been kept from the public. The government cover-ups have been facilitated by the compliant mass media which has consistently ignored the fact that these disasters occurred within the context of strikingly similar terrorism exercises.

The terrorist attacks, for example, that struck New York and

Washington on 9-11, and the London bombings of July 7, 2005, were the realization (i.e. the making real) of computer-based scenarios that were being staged in the same place at the same time. Would a truly free press ignore the fact that these terror atrocities occurred within the context of terror exercises?

"The easiest way to carry out a false flag attack is by setting up a military exercise that simulates the very attack you want to carry out," Captain Eric H. May, a former military intelligence officer from the U.S. Army wrote in an article entitled "False Flag Prospects, 2008 - Top Three U.S. Target Cities."

"This is exactly how government perpetrators in the U.S. and U.K. handled the 9-11 and 7/7 'terror' attacks," May writes, "which were in reality government attacks blamed on 'terrorists.'"

False flag terror attacks are designed and carried out with the intention of having a targeted foe wrongly blamed in order to manipulate public opinion and foment war.

Captain May certainly knows what he is talking about. He is an expert in military exercises involving simulations. May completed advanced courses at the U.S. Army's school for military intelligence officers at Fort Huachuca, Arizona, and served five years with the U.S. Army's 75th Division as an Opposing Forces Controller, where he ran "contrarian scenarios."

May's aim, he says, as a former military intelligence officer who spent five years conducting war games, is to warn the public that the "'next 9-11' — constantly promised by officials and the media — is likely to be carried out under the guise of future military exercises.

"If the American people are aware of pending exercises and the danger they represent," May says, "then the exercises cannot 'go live' and effect the very terror events that they are supposed to be rehearsing against."

9-11 and the July 7, 2005, bombings in London "have smoking guns proving that the mass murderers were not foreign terrorists but domestic tyrants," May writes. The "smoking guns," he says, are the terror exercises that simulated the attacks that actually occurred.

While the terrorism/security drills created the "contrarian scenario" framework within which the real terror attacks occurred, it does not necessarily follow that the agency running the exercise is the actual terrorist. The true culprit may be a foreign agency, who is covertly, but intimately aware of the planning of the exercise. By having access to the critical computer networks involved in the exercise this outside agency has the ability to hijack the drill and make it "go live."

While the real terrorists could be from any agency that is involved in the drill, they could also be from a foreign intelligence organization that has gained "back door" access to the computer networks on which the exercise is planned and carried out. Israeli military intelligence, for example, which has long been engaged in supplying enterprise software, such as Ptech, and network security personnel and programs to the U.S. government and military, undoubtedly has "back door" access to these sensitive computer networks.

As May says, the "smoking gun" terror drills disprove the official fairy tale that "Islamic terrorists" are responsible for these false flag terror attacks. The Arabs and Muslims who have been wrongly blamed for 9-11 and the London bombings have simply been framed, like Lee Harvey Oswald, as part of the deception.

London – July 7, 2005

At the exact time of the terror bombings of the London Underground and a bus at Tavistock Square, a man named Peter Power and his crisis management company, Visor Consultants Ltd., was conducting a terrorism drill for a mysterious un-named client. The Visor exercise was precisely identical to the bombings that occurred. How likely is such a coincidence?

Peter Power had previously worked at Scotland Yard, the Anti-Terrorist Branch, and as a police superintendent in West Dorset, England. In 1993, Power was the subject of a criminal investigation which led to his suspension and retirement from the police in April 1993.

Superintendent Power was suspended following an internal police inquiry, which resulted in a file being submitted to the Director of Public Prosecution. Oddly, the details of the Power investigation have been kept classified. After a five-month investigation, Power retired from the police force in September 1993, at the age of forty-two, "on health grounds."

"This Is the Real One"

Just hours after the London bombings, Power explained the incredible coincidences with the drill his company was conducting in a radio interview with Peter Allen on BBC 5:

Power: At half past nine this morning we were actually running an exercise for a company of over a thousand people in London based on simultaneous bombs going off precisely at the railway stations where it happened this morning, so I still have the hairs on the back of my neck standing up right now.

Peter Allen: To get this quite straight, you were running an exercise to see how you would cope with this and it happened while you were running the exercise?

Power: Precisely, and it was about half past nine this morning, we planned this for a company and for obvious reasons I don't want to reveal their name but they're listening and they'll know it. And we had a room full of crisis managers, for the first time they'd met, and so within five minutes we made a pretty rapid decision, "this is the real one" and so we went through the correct drills of activating crisis management procedures to jump from slow time to quick time thinking and so on.

"We Chose a Scenario"

Peter Power appeared in a television interview on ITV News on the day of the bombings and revealed more details about the terror drill he was involved in:

Power: Today we were running an exercise for a company - bearing in mind I'm now in the private sector - and we sat everybody down, in the city - 1,000 people involved in the whole organization - but the crisis team. And the most peculiar thing was we based our scenario on the simultaneous attacks on an underground and mainline station. So we had to suddenly switch an exercise from 'fictional' to 'real'. And one of the first things is, get that bureau number, when you have a list of people missing, tell them. And it took a long time.

ITV Host: Just to get this right, you were actually working today on an exercise that envisioned virtually this scenario?

Power: Er, almost precisely. I was up to 2 o'clock this morning, because it's our job, my own company Visor Consultants, we specialize in helping people to get their crisis management response. How do you jump from 'slow time' thinking to 'quick time' doing? And we chose a scenario — with their assistance — which is based on a terrorist attack because they're very close to, er, a property occupied by Jewish businessmen, they're in the city, and there are more American banks in the city than there are in the whole of New York - a logical thing to do. And it, I've still got the hair....

One would think that such astounding revelations of a British terrorism expert about how the terror bombings were "almost precisely" like the exercise he had been conducting for a mysterious company would be of great interest to the media. That has, however, not been the case. There has been virtually no discussion in the "mainstream" media that the London bombings, or other terror atrocities and disasters like 9-11 and the sinking of *Estonia*, occurred within the context of security drills that were very similar to what actually happened. Why has this crucial background information been censored?

Astonishing first-hand accounts, like Peter Power's, from people engaged in these exercises were reported shortly after the events occurred, yet these important stories were confined to local news outlets and not reported in the major national and international news outlets, in newspapers like the *New York Times*, for example, whose motto is: "All the news that's fit to print."

BBC and the "Series of Explosions" at the World Trade Center

Power's comments about the amazing coincidences with his security drill were censored by the BBC in the same way as the eyewitness report of Stephen Evans, their reporter at the World Trade Center on 9-11. Evans was on the ground floor of the South Tower when planes struck the complex. When he appeared on BBC World television shortly after the collapse of the twin towers, Evans repeatedly described a "series of explosions" he had witnessed at the base of the tower before it was demolished.

From the first minute Evans spoke, however, it was quite obvious that his eyewitness report was being censored by the higher powers at the BBC. When the BBC later revisited the events of 9-11 with Evans, there was absolutely no mention of the "series of explosions" he had talked about on the morning of the attacks. How can that be? Such blatant and intentional omissions are properly defined as censorship. Evans' astonishing eyewitness account from 9-11 was evidently dropped into the "memory hole" at the BBC. Peter Power's revealing comments about the London bombings met the same fate.

The BBC has a very peculiar history regarding the events of 9-11. Not only did the British network censor Evans' reports of explosions at the World Trade Center, it also reported that the building known as WTC 7 had collapsed about 30 minutes before the 47-story tower mysteriously fell into its foundation. Jane Standley, a BBC World television reporter in New York City on 9-11 reported at about 4:54 p.m. (21:54 GMT) that the Salomon Brother's building owned by Larry Silverstein (WTC 7) had collapsed. Silverstein's building, however (which he later admitted had been "pulled"), did not collapse until 5:20 p.m. (22:20 GMT).

BBC news editor Richard Porter subsequently wrote on the BBC website in February 2007: "We no longer have the original tapes of our 9-11 coverage (for reasons of cock-up, not conspiracy)." But, why would the BBC destroy its original tapes of 9-11? (This was the same excuse for destroying evidence given by the corrupt Hoffman Estates, Illinois, police who said they had "recycled" the video tapes they had made of their three-man undercover tactical squad assaulting me at my house in August 2006.)

For independent journalists to question the controlled-media's version of events, from which such significant first-hand accounts have been censored, is to risk being branded a "conspiracy theorist."

The public is now told that eyewitness reports from people who were actually in the disaster or saw it with their own eyes can no longer be considered reliable testimony. How very odd. Such was the case with the downing of TWA Flight 800 off Long Island, New York in 1996, when more than a hundred eyewitnesses reported seeing what appeared to be a missile streak from the surface of the ocean, strike the aircraft, and cause an explosive fireball.

I attended the final presentation of the official TWA 800 report by the National Transportation Safety Board (NTSB) in 2000, when David Mayer, whose only credential as a panel member was a Ph.D. in Applied Experimental Psychology from Rice University, audaciously dismissed the reports of more than one hundred eyewitnesses as the collective hallucinations of intoxicated New Yorkers, based solely on the fact that it was a summer evening! At that point, it was abundantly clear that there was something seriously wrong with the NTSB and their investigation of the downing of TWA 800. The cover-up could not have been more obvious.

The "Plane-into-Building" Drill of 9-11

On 9-11, an agency of the Department of Defense and the CIA was conducting a terror simulation in which an imaginary airplane from Washington's Dulles International Airport were to crash into one of the four towers of the suburban campus of the National Reconnaissance Office (NRO) in Chantilly, Virginia, just a few miles from the Pentagon. The plane that allegedly crashed into the Pentagon, American Airlines Flight 77, departed from the same airport at 8:20 a.m. on 9-11.

When the terror scenario became real in New York and at the Pentagon, the NRO exercise was cancelled and nearly all its three thousand employees, the people who operate the nation's "eye in the sky," were sent home.

The government said it was a "bizarre coincidence" that the NRO, a military intelligence agency working under the Department of Defense and the CIA, had planned a simulated exercise with a mock "plane-into-building" crash on the morning of 9-11. "It was just an incredible coincidence that this happened to involve an aircraft crashing into our facility," spokesman Art Haubold told the Associated Press in August 2002. "As soon as the real world events began, we canceled the exercise."

As the agency that operates the nation's spy satellites, the NRO personnel come from the military and the CIA. When the attacks occurred, however, most of the three thousand people who work at the agency were sent home. Why would they do that?

The fact that the spy agency had planned such a drill was casually leaked in an announcement for a Homeland Security conference in Chicago in 2002. In a promotion for speaker John Fulton, a CIA officer assigned as chief of NRO's strategic gaming division, the announcement said:

> On the morning of September 11, 2001, Mr. Fulton and his team . . . were running a pre-planned simulation to explore the emergency response issues that would be created if a plane were to strike a building. Little did they know that the scenario would come true in a dramatic way that day.

Critical Failures

The most pressing questions about why the U.S. military air defense system failed to intercept the four hijacked planes on 9-11 are obviously of crucial importance. Captain May writes that "even official apologists call [9-11] the greatest defense failure in American history." How could the most modern and expensive air force in the world fail to intercept four airliners, three of which roamed wild for hundreds of miles before striking landmark buildings in New York and Washington? Why was the U.S. air defense system unable to intercept several large, slow-moving planes before they struck the nation's largest city and its capital?

These crucial questions have never been raised by the government-appointed commissions or the media, which have all avoided discussing the military exercises of 9-11. It's not that these drills were not reported, but rather that their connection to the disasters has not been openly discussed and investigated.

Four months after 9-11, the *Post-Standard* of Syracuse, New York, published an article by Hart Seely that featured first-hand accounts of the military radar operators of the Northeast Air Defense Sector (NEADS) at the former Griffiss Air Force Base in Rome, New York. These radar operators were the eyes of the U.S. air defense system for the eastern part of the nation on 9-11. In Seely's article, the NEADS personnel explained how a North American Aerospace Defense (NORAD) exercise called Vigilant Guardian, which they were participating in, had caused systemic confusion which prevented an effective military response to the real emergency.

The confusion at NEADS was evident from the moment Boston Flight Control informed them that a plane had been hijacked. At 8:38 a.m. an air traffic controller telephoned Sergeant Jeremy Powell at NEADS to inform him that one of their planes had been hijacked and was headed to New York:

> "Is this real-world or exercise?" Powell asked.
>
> "No. This is not an exercise; not a test," Powell was told, according to the transcripts of the 9-11 Commission report.

Seely's article described the context — and the confusion — at NEADS:

> 6 a.m.: WAR GAMES
>
> Lt. Col. Dawne Deskins figured it would be a long day.
>
> Sept. 11 was Day 2 of "Vigilant Guardian," an exercise that would pose an imaginary crisis to North American Air Defense outposts nationwide. The simulation would run all week, and Deskins, starting her 12-hour shift in the Operations Center as the

NORAD unit's airborne control and warning officer, might find herself on the spot. Day 1 of the simulation had moved slowly. She hoped the exercise gathered steam. It made a long day go faster.

8:40 a.m.: REAL WORLD

In the Ops Center, three rows of radar scopes face a high wall of wide-screen monitors. Supervisors pace behind technicians who peer at the instruments. Here it is always quiet, always dark, except for the green radar glow. At 8:40, Deskins noticed senior technician Jeremy Powell waving his hand. Boston Center was on the line, he said. It had a hijacked airplane. "It must be part of the exercise," Deskins thought. At first, everybody did. Then Deskins saw the glowing direct phone line to the Federal Aviation Administration. On the phone she heard the voice of a military liaison for the FAA's Boston Center. "I have a hijacked aircraft," he told her. American Airlines Flight 11, headed to Los Angeles, had veered off course, apparently toward New York. The liaison said to get "some F-16s or something" airborne.

Forty-one minutes earlier, Flight 11 had left Logan Airport with 81 passengers. For the last 27 minutes, it had not responded to ground control. Deskins requested Flight 11's latest position, which an operator put up on the screen. Flight 11 wasn't there. Someone had turned off its transponder, the device that identifies the plane to ground control. Boston Center could still track it on primary radar, but the operators in Rome would be hard-pressed to find it amid the jumble of blips on their screens. "We'll direct the intercept," the liaison told Deskins. "Just get something up there." Deskins ran up a short flight of stairs to the Battle Cab and reported the hijacked plane - real world, not a simulation.

"Not a Simulation"

What is most peculiar is that Seely's informative article about the confusion among the critical military radar operators at NEADS was never published or referenced by any national newspaper in the United States. The *New York Times,* for example, has never even mentioned "Vigilant Guardian," the air defense exercise that contributed to the confusion behind the military's failure to protect New York City on 9-11.

Oddly, among the national newspapers and news magazines of the United States, "Vigilant Guardian" was only mentioned once, very briefly, in a *Washington Post* book review of the 9-11 Commission report. The review began: "If the 9-11 report had been written as a novel, nobody would believe it. The story is too far-fetched."

The *Post* mentioned "Vigilant Guardian" when it quoted "a little-noticed footnote" from the report:

When FAA officials realize (late) that planes are being hijacked, they can't monitor them - or decide what to do. The vice president thinks he has issued orders to shoot down civilian planes, but the pilots in the air don't get the word. The military's air-defense command isn't sure whether it's dealing with an exercise or a real event. Incredibly, according to a little-noticed footnote in the report, "On 9-11, NORAD was scheduled to conduct a military exercise, Vigilant Guardian, which postulated a bomber attack from the former Soviet Union."

"Vigilant Guardian" obviously confused the military because simulated hijackings and false "injects," radar indications of non-existent planes, were reportedly part of the exercise. This is why Deskins and others were initially uncertain whether the reports of hijacked planes were "real world" or simulation.

"First thing that went through my mind was, 'Is this part of the exercise?" Air Force Maj. Gen. Larry Arnold, who was at a command center at the Tyndall Air Force Base in Florida, told ABC News. "Is this some kind of a screw-up?'"

The military's inability to respond effectively to the rogue aircraft of 9-11 was evidently caused, at least in part, by the NORAD exercise. The fact that a similar exercise, involving a plane striking a military facility near the Pentagon, was being staged on the morning of 9-11, indicates that the computer-based exercises played key roles in the actual terror attacks that occurred.

What role the military exercises played in the 9-11 terror attacks and how they could have been hijacked, and by whom, are questions that need to be answered and which will be addressed in a later chapter.

The *Estonia* Catastrophe

The unexplained sinking of the Baltic ferry *Estonia* on its way to Stockholm from Tallinn in late September 1994 is the third catastrophe (not chronologically) that occurred within the framework of a military exercise. The day before it sank, *Estonia* had been the scene of a terrorism exercise in which the simulation was a terror bombing of the ferry. Looking at the NATO military assets that were assembled nearby and the terrorism drill that had just been conducted on the ship, the stage was set and the actors in place for what turned out to be a real disaster. The *Estonia* catastrophe is Europe's worst maritime disaster since World War II.

Tragically, 852 people are known to have died when *Estonia* sank in the early hours of September 28, 1994. More than 1,000 may have perished if the report is true that some 150 Iraqi Kurds were being smuggled to Sweden in a truck. Scores of people died in the frigid water of the Baltic Sea waiting for rescue boats and helicopters that came too late. More than ninety lifeless bodies were retrieved from the life rafts.

NATO's "Search & Rescue" Exercise

Although it is seldom mentioned, the *Estonia* catastrophe occurred on the first day of a 10-day NATO naval exercise called "Cooperative Venture 94", in which more than fifteen ships and "a number of maritime aircraft" were prepared to conduct "humanitarian and search and rescue operations" in nearby waters. The NATO exercise, which involved ten NATO member states and the Baltic "partner" nations of Russia, Sweden, Poland, and Lithuania, was to be staged in the Skagerrak, between Denmark, Sweden, and Norway, and the Norwegian Sea, according to the NATO press release about the exercise from September 16, 1994.

The NATO nations who participated in the exercise were Belgium, Canada, Denmark, Germany, Italy, the Netherlands, Norway, Spain, United Kingdom, and the United States. Many other allies and partners sent observers to the exercise, according to the NATO press release.

The fact that *Estonia* sank as the submarines, ships, planes, personnel, and satellites from the navies of fourteen nations were preparing to begin their ten-day "search and rescue operations" exercise off the coast of Sweden raises several obvious questions that deserve to be answered: If NATO had fifteen ships and a number of aircraft assembled nearby, prepared to conduct a "search and rescue" exercise, why did they stay away? The Swedish rescue helicopters were ill-prepared and ill-equipped, which resulted in a fatal delay for those waiting to be rescued. Of the 989 people aboard *Estonia,* only 137 survived.

"Were there specially-equipped rescue helicopters or other aircraft that could have assisted?" Drew Wilson, author of *The Hole* (2006), a book about the *Estonia* catastrophe, wrote. "Survivors who didn't die from hypothermia while floating on upturned boats or flotsam in the biting water waited four to six hours for rescue. NATO search-and-rescue personnel and equipment could have saved some lives. Flying time was under 1 hour. Why didn't they respond to the distress traffic? What happened?"

The evidence indicates that the Mayday signals from *Estonia* had been jammed, as were all radio communications in the area. "A series of comprehensive malfunctions in regional communication systems all at once, and all at the exact time the ferry had sunk suggest involvement by a military or intelligence services," Wilson writes in *The Hole.* "Was a distress call intentionally blocked? If so, why?

"Communications throughout the Northern Baltic Sea were disrupted during the time of the accident." As Wilson documents, VHF Channel 16, the international Mayday channel, and Channel 2182 were blocked. "Signal jamming of all radio communications apparently occurred on the Southern coastline of Finland as the accident unfolded.

"Werner Hummel, the German investigator, said that his Group had documentation showing that the regional telephone network servicing the catastrophe site failed just as it was needed most. The malfunction was truly a startling coincidence. The telephone company stated its entire radio communications network, for unknown reasons, had been down from 1:03 to 1:58 a.m. – almost exactly the time the *Estonia* first encountered trouble until the time it disappeared from radar."

Didn't the NATO communications units prepared for the "search and rescue" exercise overhear the distress calls coming from *Estonia*? NATO, with state-of-the-art satellite and airborne surveillance assets in place over the Baltic Sea certainly must know who was blocking the SOS calls. Why has this information been kept secret since 1994?

Blocking SOS calls and jamming distress signals is a violation of international law. Why has this crime not been investigated? The intentional blocking of the Mayday signals from *Estonia* points to complicity in mass murder.

"Naval exercises are meant to be as realistic as possible," Olivier Schmidt, author of *The Intelligence Files: Today's Secrets, Tomorrow's Scandals*, writes. What was the "search and rescue" scenario of NATO's Cooperative Venture 94 exercise, which was commanded at sea by the Dutch submarine commander Gijsbert Goofert Hooft?

I sent a series of questions to Robert Pszczel, NATO's press officer for Baltic issues, about NATO's response to the *Estonia* catastrophe:

> Did NATO have any naval assets in the Baltic Sea on the night of September 27-28, 1994 and what actions did NATO take in the immediate aftermath of the *Estonia* disaster?
>
> Did NATO pick up the Mayday signals being sent (and jammed) from *Estonia*?
>
> Why didn't NATO assist, given the urgent need to retrieve hundreds of freezing people from life rafts?
>
> What was the scenario of NATO's search and recovery exercise?

Despite telephone calls and email exchanges with the press office at NATO headquarters, Robert Pszczel failed to respond to a single question about NATO's failure to respond to the *Estonia* catastrophe. Drew Wilson met the same wall of silence at NATO when he asked questions about *Estonia* for his book *The Hole*. NATO had fourteen ships, submarines, aircraft, and personnel from the United States, Europe, Sweden, and Russia assembled near the scene of the sinking of *Estonia*. If NATO has a reasonable explanation for its failure to respond to Europe's worst maritime disaster since World War II, why is it unwilling to provide it?

Estonia's Bomb Drills

The *Estonia* ferry had been the object of bomb threats and had participated in at least two terror bomb exercises in 1994, one in February and another just the day before it sank.

On February 2, 1994, *Estonia* was the subject of a major mock bomb exercise conducted with RITS, Sweden's maritime fire and rescue agency, and the Stockholm police. The Stockholm police had requested to take part in the exercise and used bomb-sniffing dogs to find explosives. The terror simulation involved a scenario in which "bombs" had been placed in the sauna and swimming pool area on the lowest deck, below the waterline in the bow of the ship. A second "bomb" was placed in the sleeping quarters on the first deck, also below the waterline.

In the *Estonia* terror scenario, the explosives in the sauna were to be found by the dogs, while the second "bomb" was to explode. The purpose of this terrorism drill was to train with the ship's crew and include shore-based terrorism experts and police with bomb-sniffing dogs, brought to the ship by helicopter. In the simulation, the "bombs" were set to explode about halfway between the Estonian and Swedish coasts, which is where the ship actually sank in September 1994 after a similar mock bomb exercise.

When *Estonia* sank, a bomb drill on the ship had just been concluded. Survivors from the sinking actually reported hearing two huge explosions immediately before the ship listed to starboard. Several crew members testified to having heard the coded fire alarm "Mr. Skylight to No. 1 and 2" over the ferry's public address system at about 1:02 a.m. after the vessel had listed severely. This is the message for the crew that was used during the previous bomb drill in February 1994. "Mr. Skylight" was a signal for the firefighters to go to fire stations 1 and 2 and prepare for damage control. The coded alarm indicates that there was damage caused by a fire or explosion that required immediate attention. The massive ferry, 150 meters in length, sank in less than thirty minutes.

The fact that the ship sank extremely quickly and the eyewitness reports from survivors suggest that explosives had torn a large hole in the hull below the waterline, as in the drill. Swedish policemen who had just conducted training involving a mock bomb threat on the ferry were returning home when *Estonia* sank. Of the seventy policemen, only seven survived.

According to survivors, *Estonia* sank after two explosions rocked the ship in the middle of the night. A drill of a bombing simulation on the ship had just been completed the day before. It is now known that the passenger ferry was being used to transport Soviet military contraband when it sank. The highest officials in Swedish customs, government, and military were aware of the sensitive and illegal shipments that put the ferry and her passengers at risk. Is this why they have been so dedicated to protecting the lies about the sinking?

P tech was with Mitre [Corporation] in the basement of the FAA for two years prior to 9-11. Their specific job is to look at interoperability issues the FAA had with NORAD and the Air Force in the case of an emergency. If anyone was in a position to know that the FAA, that there was a window of opportunity or to insert software or to change anything, it would have been Ptech along with Mitre.

Indira Singh, IT and risk consultant with JP Morgan Chase and DARPA, 9-11 Citizens' Commission Hearings, New York City, September 9, 2004

Chapter V

Why Did Crucial
Computer Systems Fail?

The dependence of the U.S. government and military on computer systems, which often run software provided by outside vendors, is an Achilles' heel of the world's most powerful nation. The failure of crucial computer systems on 9-11 is proof of that fundamental weakness and vulnerability. Apart from being a monstrous crime of mass murder and false-flag terrorism, 9-11 was also a sophisticated computer crime, carried out through long-term foreign infiltration of the most sensitive U.S. military and government computer networks. This infiltration gave the perpetrators "real-time" access to all the data on the computers of the U.S. government and military. On 9-11, this "super-user" access gave the people behind the terrorist attacks the ability to thwart a military response to the emergency as it developed.

Ptech and 9-11

The subject of computer sabotage in relation to the aerial attacks of 9-11 was first raised by Indira Singh, who spoke at some of the early 9-11 conferences. During these 9-11 "truth" events, Singh talked about a small Massachusetts-based software company called Ptech, which she said was linked to Arab "terrorists". Ptech was said to be a start-up company from Quincy, Massachusetts, whose software was running on the most sensitive computer systems of the U.S. government, including those of the Federal Aviation Administration (FAA) and the U.S. Air Force, two agencies whose computer systems evidently failed on 9-11.

Singh, a senior risk and IT consultant with JP Morgan Chase in 2001, is described as a "whistle-blower" because of her revelations about Ptech's involvement with the critical computer systems that failed on 9-11. "Ptech was with Mitre Corporation in the basement of the FAA for two years prior to 9-11," Singh said. "Their specific job is to look at interoperability issues the FAA had with NORAD and the Air Force in the case of an emergency. If anyone was in a position to know that the FAA — that there was a window of opportunity or to insert software or to change anything — it would have been Ptech along with Mitre."

Mitre Corporation

The Mitre Corporation has provided computer and information technology to the FAA and the U.S. Air Force since the late 1950s. Mitre is a Federally Funded Research and Development Center (FFRDC) for the Department of Defense, the FAA, and the Internal Revenue Service. Mitre is a major defense contracting organization headed by the former Director of Central Intelligence (DCI), Dr. James Rodney Schlesinger. Schlesinger, who was reportedly made DCI at the request of Henry Kissinger in 1973, later served as Secretary of Defense. Schlesinger, a former director of strategic studies at the RAND Corp., was described in a 1973 biography as a "devout Lutheran," although he was born in New York in 1929 to immigrant Jewish parents from Austria and Russia.

Mitre's Command, Control, Communications, and Intelligence

(C3I) FFRDC for the Dept. of Defense was established in 1958. The C3I "supports a broad and diverse set of sponsors within the Department of Defense and the Intelligence Community. These include the military departments, defense and intelligence agencies, the combatant commands, and elements of both the Office of the Secretary of Defense and the office of the Joint Chiefs of Staff," according to Mitre's website. "Information systems technology," it says, "coupled with domain knowledge, underpin the work of the C3I FFRDC."

The U.S. Air Force maintains its Electronic Systems Center (ESC) at the Hanscom AFB in Bedford, Massachusetts. The ESC manages the development and acquisition of electronic command and control (C2) systems used by the Air Force. The ESC is the Air Force's "brain for information, command and control systems," according to Charles Paone, a civilian employee of the ESC. It is the "product center" for the Air Force's Airborne Warning and Control System (AWACS) and Joint Surveillance Target Attack Radar System (J-STARS), Paone said. Asked about Mitre's role at the ESC, Paone said, "Mitre does the front-end engineering. It's basically our in-house engineer." Mitre employees operate the computer systems at Hanscom AFB, Paone said. MIT's Lincoln Laboratories, the parent of Mitre, is located on Hanscom AFB.

A second FFRDC, the Center for Advanced Aviation System Development (CAASD) provides computer engineering and technology to the FAA. Mitre's support of the FAA began in 1958, when the company was created. The FAA's Airspace Management Handbook of May 2004, for example, was written and published by the Mitre Corp.

Jennifer Shearman, Mitre's public relations manager for "corporate identity" in Bedford, said that Mitre is a "trusted mentor" for the FAA and is a "unique" provider of "objective and independent" information for the U.S. civil aviation authority. Mitre's Bedford headquarters are located near Boston's Logan airport where the two planes that struck the World Trade Center supposedly originated. Bedford lies directly under the flight path of westbound flights leaving Logan. Mitre developed the technology "to aid controllers in solving problems while keeping aircraft close to their route, altitude, and speed preferences." Shearman was unable to say why the Mitre technology failed on 9-11.

Ptech

In her speeches about Ptech, Indira Singh talked about Ptech's alleged connections with Saudi Arabia but said little about Mitre. Here is an extract from an interview she did with Pacifica Radio in 2005:

> Maybe those organizations don't fully know who their masters are. And Ptech is the one thread, the one golden thread you pull on and all of this is unraveled, because it goes into the corporations, it goes into these government entities, it goes into the terrorism financing entities that were, that none of which have been, by the way, taken to task. There are just so many questions about what does this all mean. And as we investigated, as I investigated further, we found that the origins of Ptech were very interesting – where did this company come from obviously is the first question. And how did they get to be so powerful, who were the people, who were the organizations that brought them in, who knew, who gave them the power?

Ptech software "is utilized at the highest levels of almost every government and military and defense organization in this country,"

Singh said, "including the Secret Service, the FBI, the Department of Defense, the House of Representatives, the Treasury Department, the IRS, the U.S. Navy, the U.S. Air Force, and, last but not least, the Federal Aviation Administration."

I found it hard to believe that the most sensitive government and military computers would run enterprise software from a Lebanese-owned start-up company called Ptech. All the talk about the Saudi-financier behind Ptech being linked to Osama Bin Laden seemed fishy. It simply did not make sense that the most secure computer systems of the U.S. government would be running software written by a Lebanese Muslim immigrant financed by a Saudi who happened to be on the most-wanted list of global terrorists.

Oussama Ziade, a Lebanese immigrant who came to the U.S. in 1985, founded Ptech in 1994. After 9-11, Ptech was said to be connected to "the Muslim Brotherhood" and Arab financiers of terrorism. The firm's suspected links with terrorism resulted in a consensual examination by the FBI in December 2002. The media reports of the FBI "raid" on Ptech soon led to the demise of the company.

When I turned my attention to Ptech in early 2005, I discovered that a key person involved in the development of the company was a Zionist Jewish lawyer named Michael Goff from Worcester, Massachusetts. Here is what Goff Communications website said in 2005 about his work with Ptech:

> Michael was marketing manager at Ptech, Inc., a leading provider of business process modeling, design and development software. In this capacity, Michael managed various marketing programs and activities including public relations, direct mail, Web develop-

ment, collateral, trade shows and seminars. Additionally, Michael worked closely with the Ptech sales organization to perform competitive analysis as well as manage lead tracking and fulfillment activities.

When Michael first joined Ptech, he shared responsibilities between marketing and information systems for the company. As information systems manager, Michael handled design, deployment and management of its Windows and Macintosh, data, and voice networks. As part of this effort, Michael developed Lotus Notes-based systems for sales and marketing lead tracking and IS service and support requests. Michael also performed employee training and handled all procurement for software, systems and peripherals.

At the time (March 2005) Goff's website said that he was working for an Israeli-run computer security company called Guardium. Goff's relationship with a Mossad-funded database security company raised my suspicion that Ptech was probably an Arab false front that was actually controlled by Israeli intelligence. Goff would have been their primary agent inside the company.

Guardium is less than 5 miles from Hanscom AFB, site of MIT's Lincoln Labs and about the same distance from Boston's Logan Airport. Guardium, a "database security" firm, was clearly a Mossad funded operation. This was evident by the three Israeli venture capital firms that financed Guardium: Cedar Fund, Veritas Venture Partners, and StageOne. A closer look at the key personnel of these firms revealed that they were all manned by high-level agents of Israeli military intelligence.

Michael Goff has solid Zionist credentials, which explains why Israeli intelligence would use him as a "sayan", i.e. a "helper" who is willing to perform a necessary function for the Mossad. Goff's father and grandfather were highest-level Masons in the Worcester lodge of B'nai B'rith, the secret Masonic organization of Zionist Jews that was established in New York City in 1843. Goff got involved with Ptech in 1994. When I asked him how he wound up working with Ptech, he told me that he had left his law firm and been placed with Ptech through a temporary agency, although he could not name the agency. I found that rather hard to believe. Why would a young American Jewish lawyer working with a good law firm in his home town suddenly leave the practice to start working with a dodgy start-up software company owned by a Lebanese Muslim and financed by a Saudi? Why the abrupt career change?

With this discovery it seemed clear to me that the Israeli hidden hand behind Ptech had been exposed. My revelations about the Zionist connections at Ptech were published in a newspaper based in Washington, D.C. in April 2005.

Singh, however, seemed to ignore the evidence of an Israeli connection to Ptech and continued to talk about the company being linked to Saudi sponsors of terror. In any case, Singh and I were asking the same questions: How did Ptech get to be so powerful? Who gave them the power? Who were the people that brought them in? Who knew?

After 9-11, the crucial question was how did Ptech software get onto the critical U.S. government networks – particularly those of the FAA, the U.S. Air Force, and NORAD? Who would have allowed Ptech personnel access to the FAA's core air traffic control system computers in Herndon, Virginia?

During my research about the military exercises that were ongoing when 9-11 occurred, I read documents about how the FAA and NEADS computer systems failed. The FAA in particular was extremely slow to contact the military about the rogue aircraft of 9-11. In one case, one of the rogue aircraft had been allowed to fly without communication for nearly thirty minutes before the military was notified.

"The Heart of the Matter"

The flawed and delayed FAA procedures and communications with the military are "the heart of the matter," as 9-11 relative Kristen Breitweiser said:

> You know, it is very upsetting that the 9-11 Commission had to subpoena the Federal Aviation Administration [FAA]. According to news reports, there are 150,000 documents that were left out of what the FAA sent to the commission. Those documents went toward the time line of when the FAA notified the North American Aerospace Defense Command [NORAD], when the fighter jets were scrambled and the communications between air-traffic control and the pilots. These are threshold issues that go to the heart of the matter. How did the FAA overlook 150,000 documents pertaining to these issues? It is more than mildly upsetting that they would leave out these documents.

Monte Belger at the FAA

In the documents about the FAA failures on 9-11, I came across the name of a Monte R. Belger, acting deputy administrator of the FAA at the time. A long-term FAA official who began his career with the FAA in Chicago, Belger was the senior official who oversaw the upgrading of the FAA air traffic computer systems that began in the late 1990s and which was ongoing in 2001.

Belger, as Acting Deputy Administrator for Air Traffic Services and System Operations, was the key man at the FAA making the executive decisions about these computer upgrades. As the *New York Times* of June 7, 2001, reported:

> The aviation agency is installing a computer system that controllers can use to determine whether airplanes can depart from established traffic lanes and fly long distances, and whether they will conflict with other airplanes by doing so.

Belger was the key decision maker at the Federal Aviation Administration, responsible for the software and computer upgrades that involved Ptech, the suspicious upgrades which were being done prior to 9-11. Documents and reports from the Mitre Center for Advanced Aviation System Development in McLean, Virginia, show that Ptech was working with Mitre on FAA computer systems.

As his on-line biography says, Belger, a thirty-year veteran of the FAA, was Acting Deputy Administrator for the FAA for five years, from 1997-2002, leading the 49,000-person team and in charge of operating the world's safest aviation system.

During his tenure with the FAA, Belger was the Associate Administrator for Air Traffic Services, responsible for day-to-day operations of the nation's airspace system, and supervised the FAA's modernization plan aimed at improving aviation capacity, safety and service to airlines. Belger played a pivotal role in assisting in the transition of aviation security responsibilities from the FAA to the new Transportation Security Administration, and he co-chaired the FAA's successful efforts to adopt acquisition and personnel reform. Belger retired from the FAA in September 2002.

U.S. Aviation Technology LLC

After he left the FAA, Belger became the "Vice President, Government Connection" of a small Israeli-run company based in the Fort Lauderdale area called U.S. Aviation Technology. The company was founded by Ehud "Udi" Mendelson, who described himself as "a captain in the prestigious Army Intelligence Unit of the Israel Defense Force."

"Ehud received his BS Degree in Business and Economics from the Bar-Elan [sic] University in Tel-Aviv, Israel. He holds a computer Network Engineer certification from Microsoft and Novel," his webpage said.

Company documents and information from the Israel Venture Capital Research Center website also named Monte Belger of Centreville, Virginia, as a Vice President and "Government Connection" of U.S. Aviation Technology LLC.

Mendelson, age 51, was Chief Technology Officer of U.S. Aviation Technology, which was apparently based out of his apartment in Parkland, Florida. Mendelson's company promoted a remote-control system that allows a "ground pilot" to monitor and adjust the computer flight systems on aircraft. As his company presentations say, "We put the ground 'pilot' in the cockpit."

The software and system promoted by Mendelson is designed to obtain real-time data from the aircraft's computer recorders (black box, FDR) in order to monitor flight systems — and make corrections — if necessary. The possibility to remotely hijack a plane with this system is obvious. Mendelson also promoted a Flight Data Animator, which he said gives the ground pilot all of the data and the visuals that the pilot in the aircraft has. In the two on-line presentations of this equipment it was stated that corrections could be made by the ground pilot to avoid an accident or situation.

The data is sent via satellite to an antenna on the top of the aircraft. This software and equipment allow a remote "pilot" to fly the aircraft. Mendelson was apparently promoting this software and system before 9-11 and hoped to have it on the market in November 2001, according to a document in his company presentation.

I called Monte Belger to ask about his relationship with Ehud Mendelson and his remote-control aviation company. I found it very disturbing that a senior administrator with the FAA would be associated with such a business project, especially after 9-11. I reached Belger at his home on Eagle Tavern Lane in Centreville, Virginia at about 9 a.m. on January 24, 2008, and asked him about his relationship with U.S. Aviation Technology and Ehud Mendelson. He denied knowing or having anything to do with either the man or the company and asked me to call back later to his office at Lockheed Martin Corporation where he was a vice president responsible for Transportation Systems Security. When I called Belger at his office he put me on the speaker phone, he said, in order to try and access the websites where he was named as a vice president of U.S. Aviation Technology. He continued to deny knowing anything about the company or its founder, a member of Israel's Army Intelligence Unit.

Peter Goelz of the NTSB

Peter Goelz, the former managing director of the NTSB, the federal agency that investigates air crashes, was also named along with Monte Belger as "Vice President, Corporate Strategy" of U.S. Aviation Technology. Goelz, at the NTSB from 1995 until 1999, personally supervised the investigations of TWA Flight 800, Egypt Air 990, the ValuJet crash in Miami, and the mysterious crash of the young John F. Kennedy's plane off the coast of Cape Cod. There are many outstanding questions about what really happened to the aircraft involved in several of the high-profile cases that Goelz was involved in.

Peter Goelz, former managing director of NTSB, also oversaw the seriously flawed TWA 800 and Egypt Air 990 investigations. Prior to being appointed to the NTSB during the Clinton administration Goelz had been a political advisor in New Hampshire and a lobbyist for gambling interests in Kansas City but lacked any real expertise in accident investigation. I found nothing in his resume that would make him a suitable candidate to oversee aviation accident investigations.

I called Peter Goelz at his home on January 25, 2008, and asked him about his relationship with Ehud Mendelson and U.S. Aviation Technology. Goelz immediately recalled Mendelson, saying that he had been based in Miami, and said he had met with the Israeli captain from Israeli military intelligence "two or three" times in Washington, D.C.

When asked if his relationship with Mendelson had begun before or after 9-11, Goelz said that he did not remember. He did, however, have a very clear recall what Mendelson's company was all about: real-time access to all the data from the computer system on an aircraft. Goelz said he had a hard time understanding what was proprietary about Mendelson's U.S. Aviation Technology. He asked me to send him an email with my questions and the scope of my article.

In my email, I explained that as he was listed as a Vice President of U.S. Aviation Technology on the company's website and on that of Israel Venture Capital, and asked how and when he had gotten involved with Mr. Mendelson. He wrote back on January 26 and asked me to "enlighten" him "a little more on the focus of [my] work in this matter." It is worth noting that Goelz did not deny being a Vice President of the company, but he was not forthcoming with information about his relationship with Ehud Mendelson.

If Goelz was confused about Mendelson's system, he certainly does not show it in his comments that are found on the testimonial page of U.S. Aviation Technology, where he wrote (as found on the company's website, with corrections in brackets):

> I have reviewed your proposed integrated aircraft early warning system and believe it has considerable technical merit. During my years at the National Transportation Safety Board we were greatly concerned about the increasing complexity of airplane accidents. Advance[s] in safety (ground proximity warning devices, TCAS, etc.) have virtually eliminated certain type[s] of accidents and have forced a greater reliance on the flight data recorder (FDR).

In a number of accidents, particular[ly] those over open water (TWA Flight 800, Egypt Air, Swiss Air) the investigations were seriously hindered until the boxes were recovered. In the tragic events of September 11th, three of the four FDR's were destroyed so no data (or voice recordings) was recovered.

Your system of real time downloading of aircraft data meets a very real and pressing problem. Not only is it important from a safety and security standpoint it also has applicability for navigation and flight management. A robust two-way data pipe from the aircraft to the ground and back could revolutionize the industry.

The key to your system is it[s] initial simplicity, relying on tested, almost off the shelf, components. That your concept is well on the way to securing a patent further strengthens your proposal.

I look forward to working with you on this project and believe that with the appropriate backing it will be successful.

Peter Goelz, Former NTSB Managing director.

Note – After contacting Belger and Goelz, the incriminating webpages were taken down from the Internet. This included the removal of the U.S. Aviation Technology documents. A warning message appeared when trying to access these documents. Some links can only be found using the Internet Archive tool (Way Back Machine).

Terror is theatre ... Theatre's a con trick. Do you know what that means? Con trick? You've been deceived.

John Le Carré, *The Little Drummer Girl,* 1983

Chapter VI

The Florida Connection

Florida was the central networking base and staging area for the "false flag" terror attacks of 9-11. Fifteen of the nineteen Arabs allegedly involved in the hijackings lived and had their base of operations in South Florida.

A "false flag" crime is one which is designed to be blamed on others in order to achieve a strategic or political goal for the real perpetrator of the crime. To understand how Israelis have used this tactic of terrorism I recommend reading *The Little Drummer Girl* by John Le Carré and watching the movie by George Roy Hill. Victor Ostrovsky's books about Mossad operations are also recommended reading.

The Little Drummer Girl was written with input and advice from many Mossad officers, including a former head of Israeli military intelligence. Much of the book deals with the way Mossad created a completely false history for a Palestinian "terrorist" by leaving a trail of traces across Europe. This is what was done in Florida with the 15 Arabs "hijackers" whose identities were used to create a false history prior to the attacks of 9-11.

That a false history was being laid was quite clear from published reports: "At least six of the suspected terrorists had two sets of driver's licenses issued by Florida, which would have allowed two or more people to use the same identity," the *Sun-Sentinel* (Florida) reported on September 28, 2001. "Many of the suspected terrorists, it is becoming increasingly clear, swapped identities as part of their preparations for the Sept. 11 attacks on the World Trade Center and the Pentagon, according to a *Sun-Sentinel* review of documents, interviews and published reports." But why, and by whom were the "hijackers" identities being swapped? Were the Arab suspects even aware that their identities were being used by others?

"These guys were just committed zealots and willing to give it up for the cause without really being key members of the network," Larry Johnson, former deputy-director of counter-terrorism for the U.S. State Department, said. "They were told what to prepare for, what to train for. They were not the ones calling the shots."

"They were, however, extremely well organized," Johnson said. If the Arab suspects in Florida were only the "working level" and part of the deception, who were their managers? Who were the architectural level planners "calling the shots"? Are we supposed to think that Osama Bin Laden or Khalid Sheikh Mohammed were truly the brains behind this organization?

"We don't have anything in history to compare with this," Johnson said. "The only thing that comes close to it is a former Soviet intel [intelligence] operation."

So who was really running the terrorist network in Florida that resembled a Soviet intelligence operation? A preponderance of evidence indicates that it was Israeli military intelligence that was the master planner behind the "Arab" terrorist network based in Florida.

My discovery that Ehud Olmert, then mayor of Jerusalem, made a secret visit to New York City on the eve of 9-11 led to more discoveries about the Israeli intelligence network in Florida and its role in the terror attacks.

Wings of Sunny Isles Beach

I have experienced several remarkable coincidences related to the events of 9-11. The first was my wife's vivid dream about our family being attacked by airplanes, which she experienced a few days before the attacks. What is most remarkable about this coincidence is that Helje related her dream to me as we drove through New York City in the early morning hours of September 11, 2001, about 7 hours before the first plane struck the North Tower.

Another remarkable coincidence happened during a visit to Miami in February 2006. My family and I had flown in from Germany and were staying at the Monaco Hotel on Collins Avenue. The Monaco is in a part of North Miami Beach that is now called Sunny Isles Beach. We had arrived at night and simply driven north on Collins Avenue until we found a suitable hotel.

The Monaco Hotel is one of the few old fashioned low-level hotels that remain in that area. The surrounding buildings are monstrous 55-story skyscrapers built right on the beach, the tallest oceanfront condominium towers in the United States. These are the Trump Palace, the Trump Royale, the Trump Grande Ocean Resort, and the Trump International Sonesta Beach Resort in Sunny Isles.

At the time, these awful skyscrapers were still under construction and the fences around the site were plastered with posters of the developers, or "the visionaries" of Sunny Isles Beach: Donald Trump and his Israeli partners, Michael and Gil Dezer. Michael Dezer is a veteran of the Israeli Air Force who immigrated to the United States in 1962. The Dezers and the "Florida Friends of the Israel Defense Forces" hold annual poker tournaments "to benefit the soldiers of Israel."

We went for a walk along Collins Avenue the next evening and stopped in a large beach store called Wings about a block north of our hotel, looking for a bathing suit for my daughter. The logo for the store reminded me of the "wings" an Israeli pilot wears on his chest. My wife noticed that the screen saver on a computer on the back counter, facing into the store, was an Israeli flag that covered the entire screen.

While my family browsed around the huge store, in which we were the only shoppers, I talked to the young Middle Eastern-looking man behind the counter. I asked him in Hebrew if he was from Israel, which he was, and then asked him if the store was Israeli-owned. That also turned out to be the case.

Having visited Florida, California, and the Caribbean, I have seen all kinds of surf and beach stores but the Wings store was unusual. The store on Collins Avenue was a very large free-standing building with a high ceiling and a huge windowless storage space behind the store. There were two trucks parked in the store's parking lot on the side of the building. The large warehouse space behind the store seemed out of proportion for a simple beach store. How much space is required to store bikinis, Tee-shirts, and suntan lotion? Most beach stores get by with very little storage space, but not Wings.

Every time we walked by the Wings store we never saw any customers; the store was always empty. This seemed odd because they must have had very high overhead costs. Nothing about this store made sense. It seemed to me more like a logistics base that operated a beachwear store as a front, not unlike the shuttered Urban Moving Systems (UMS) outfit I had visited in Weehawken, New Jersey. UMS was the fake moving company, across the river from the World Trade Center that was exposed as an Israeli intelligence (Mossad) front.

Apart from the young man working inside the Wings store, there always seemed to be an Israeli man of military age coming or going near the store. This seemed very strange for a beach store in a quiet part of town. Most beach stores in Miami are small boutiques run by women or retired people. The staff is usually female. Young military age men from Israel are the last people one would expect to find running a bikini store in Miami. It turns out that Wings has a whole chain of stores in Florida and up the East Coast, as well as in Texas and on the West Coast.

What is most interesting about my experience at Wings is that this chain of beach stores is owned by the two Israelis that met with Ehud Olmert in New York City on the eve of 9-11 on September 10, 2001. The founders of L&L Wings are Shaul and Meir Levy, two Israelis of Syrian origin.

I learned that Ehud Olmert had made an undisclosed visit to New York City on the eve of 9-11 from an article in the *Jerusalem Post* about the Likud football club, Betar. Buried deep in the sports section of July 23, 2004, I discovered this very significant bit of information:

> Three years ago, Betar was sold to a four-man consortium (US businessmen Meir and Shaul Levy, local businessman Meir Finegel, and Jerusalem real estate agent Sasson Shem Tov, who pulled out a few weeks ago), following a meeting in New York with then-

mayor Ehud Olmert on September 10, 2001. There
were no other potential buyers.

The day before 9-11, the men that own the L&L Wings chain of beach
stores met with Ehud Olmert, then mayor of Jerusalem, in New York
City. Other than what I have written, this significant fact has not been
reported or discussed in the media, mainstream or alternative.

According to the website of Wings, the company's corporate office and warehouse are on the second floor at 2800 NW 125th Street
in Miami, where Shaul Levy is the registered agent. What's interesting
about this address, very near the Opa-Laca Airport, is that it is also
the location of a company called Empire Art Products, Inc.

Why would a multi-millionaire Israeli businessman, who owns
spacious properties on both coasts of Florida, New York, Texas, and
California, share a low-rent building in an industrial park with a company that deals in art products? Is Shaul Levy involved in selling art
products? Was he the source of the paintings that Israeli intelligence
agents posing as art students tried to sell at U.S. government offices
from 1999 to 2001?

To understand how the 9-11 false-flag operation was set up requires an understanding of the extensive network of Israeli companies in the United States and how Israeli military intelligence sets up
companies disguised as Arab-owned companies. The two men that
Ehud Olmert met in New York City on September 10, 2001, are
linked to an Israeli network that ran such a false-front company in the
Fort Lauderdale area during the years prior to 9-11. Is this the reason
why Olmert's pre-9-11 visit to New York has been kept secret?

When I discovered that Ehud Olmert had visited New York City on the eve of the 9-11 terror atrocity, I suspected that his visit was connected to the false flag attacks. Why else would the visit by the well-known mayor of Jerusalem to his "sister city" have been kept secret? Visits by high-level Israeli politicians are usually front page news in New York City.

If Olmert's visit to New York City was innocent and only involved the transfer of an Israeli soccer club, why was it kept under wraps? Why did Rudy Giuliani and the New York Police Department conspire to keep it out of the press? It is impossible that the authorities in New York City did not know that Ehud Olmert, Israel's deputy prime minister at the time, was in their city on September 10, 2001. Mayor Olmert's visit was certainly not unknown to the federal authorities. Why wasn't his visit reported in the media?

The American journalist Wayne Madsen reported in March 2010 that a full El Al Boeing 747 had departed from New York's John F. Kennedy Airport on the afternoon of September 11, 2001, bound for Tel Aviv's Ben Gurion International Airport. Although all civilian flights had been grounded since 9:45 in the morning of 9-11, an exception was made for the Israeli flight. According to Madsen's report the Israeli flight departed JFK at 4:11 pm. The El Al flight to Tel Aviv was authorized by the direct intervention of the U.S. Department of Defense. U.S. military officials were on the scene at JFK and were personally involved with the airport and air traffic control authorities to clear the flight for take-off, Madsen reported. Was Ehud Olmert on this plane? Why did the U.S. government make an exception made for this flight?

Olmert, who was raised in the Betar militia in a founding family of the Irgun (the Zionist terror group of the 1930s and 40s which later became the Likud party), became the prime minister of Israel after Ariel Sharon fell (or was put) into a coma.

The secrecy surrounding Olmert's pre-9-11 visit suggests that it had something to do with the terror events which befell the city the following day. With so much evidence of Israeli prior knowledge and involvement in 9-11, Olmert's undisclosed visit raises obvious questions: Were the people that Olmert met with part of the network behind the false-flag terror attacks of 9-11? Are they connected to the network of Israeli agents who posed as art students?

From a tip that I received, I found that Shaul and Meir Levy are connected to an extensive Israeli network in Florida (and across the U.S.) that included a suspicious art graphics business that disguised itself as an Arab-owned company. Mossad operations in the United States are usually carried out under the guise of a legitimate business, such as Urban Moving Systems of Weehawken, New Jersey.

An Israeli-owned firm will only disguise itself as an Arab-owned company when it is playing a part in a false-flag operation, like 9-11. The purpose of the Arab disguise is to put up a false front to hide the real people involved in the operation. This is, for example, exactly the kind of disguise that was used by Ptech, the enterprise software company that loaded spy and control software onto the most sensitive computer networks in the U.S. government.

The Tip

I received this very interesting email at the end of 2007:

Dear Mr. Bollyn,

Something has been bothering me for some years. I feel it may be insignificant, but the event is so out of place, that I had to share it with someone like you who investigates 9-11 earnestly.

My wife and I run a small gift shop selling seashells, t-shirts, and Florida gifts. I print my own Florida t-shirts using heat transfers, which I buy from a company called Next Graphics in Fort Lauderdale. One day just before September 11, 2001, I went to their plant to get some transfers. Normally there is a secretary sitting in her cubicle, and she calls to a salesman who takes my order.

This time it was different, there was no secretary and nobody in attendance, so I went along the corridor to my left towards the end where I knew there was a large conference room, something like you would use for presentations, and just before entering the room I was accosted by an Israeli (I knew by accent) who started to ask me about my business and expressed an interest in buying it.

It was obvious that he was trying to engage me in conversation so I would not go into the room. I ignored him and went straight in. I saw about 10-12 Israelis sitting around this very large conference table.

I engaged some of them in conversation, because some spoke Russian, the language I speak fluently. We spoke about the business, but I soon discovered that they knew nothing about graphics. It is only after 9-11 that I put two and two together and realized the significance of the Israelis being there: Next Graphics is owned by a Palestinian family, which recently purchased their building in a high-profile industrial area.

After receiving this interesting tip, I looked into Next Graphics and found that it was not truly Palestinian or Arab-owned at all. While the company was registered under the names of Nabil and Nidal Alif, the "principal" person behind the company was actually a Sephardic (Spanish or Arabic Jew) Israeli named Samuel Anidjar. The Anidjar name originated with a Jewish family in Moorish Spain that was expelled in 1492 to Morocco. Israelis and Palestinians do not usually set up companies together. Many Sephardic Jews came to the New World, particularly the West Indies and South America. They were often involved in the slave trade and owned many slaves.

A Samuel Anidjar from Hollywood, Florida, is the president of the B'nai Sephardim synagogue. Samuel Anidjar is also a business partner in a Boca Raton-based company called The Big Apple Corp., whose website says this about Mr. Anidjar:

> Samuel Anidjar is a merchandising consultant for The Big Apple and the principal of Next Graphics, Inc., based in Fort Lauderdale, Fla. The firm specializes in the design, manufacture and sales of high-tech transfers used in the garment industry. Mr. Anidjar is also an owner of Next Authentic, Inc., an upscale

fashion boutique in the Art Deco district of Miami's South Beach. He recently completed a remodeling and expansion of the location to accommodate its continued growth. A graduate of College Technique in Deromans, France, Mr. Anidjar moved to the United States with his family in 1972. After settling in Wildwood, N.J., he developed and operated a chain of beachwear stores. After several successful years in operation, Mr. Anidjar selected partners to operate the seasonal shops and relocated to Florida. He continued in the retail business with five new beachwear and souvenir stores, which he sold after a decade of profitability. Mr. Anidjar also owns several commercial properties along the eastern coast of Florida, which he leases to well-established proprietors. His tenants include franchises of Häagen-Däzs and Edy's Gourmet Ice Cream; and Mezzaluna, a popular restaurant and bar on Ocean Drive in Miami Beach.

Samuel Anidjar worked with another Israeli named Dror Levy on the Big Apple scheme. The Big Apple website provided this sketch about Dror Levy:

Dror Levy (age 28) is Vice President of Research and Development for The Big Apple. Currently, Mr. Levy provides consulting services to sportswear manufacturers in the South Florida area. He offers comprehensive solutions and creative recommendations for apparel design, logo and image development, manufacturing, fiscal planning, personnel and distribution.

For several years, Mr. Levy also operated La Flame Fashion, Inc., a Hollywood, Fla.-based firm he joined in partnership. His knowledge and application of computer systems integration, financial and operational strategies, marketing and staff retraining brought considerable increases in production, revenues and profits. Mr. Levy is the principal of Dror Inventions, Inc. He holds United States and Canadian patents for a revolutionary automobile cupholder; the device can be fitted to any vehicle, supports most beverage containers, and eliminates spillage during adverse driving conditions. As a result of his invention, Mr. Levy has been selected as a member of Who's Who of American Inventors and International Who's Who of Entrepreneurs. He was nominated as Inventor of the Year for 1997 by Intellectual Property Owners, a non-profit association founded in 1972. Its membership includes Fortune 500 companies, small businesses, universities, attorneys, independent inventors and others who own patents, trademarks, copyrights and trade secrets. Mr. Levy is also an active member of the Israel Economic Development Council, a professional association committed to enhancing international trade and commerce between Florida and Israel. Mr. Levy is a graduate of the Amal Institute of Engineering in Tel Aviv, Israel. Immediately following the completion of his formal education, he served four years in the Israeli armed forces as a computer systems analyst and researcher. His responsibilities included computer-aided design (CAD) for defense equipment and supplies, and cost and feasibility studies for various military operations. Mr. Levy also developed and conducted extensive studies on human behavior; specifically, methods of improving soldier morale, motivation and performance during combat.

(Note: Some of the places or institutions in these biographical sketches do not exist, at least not the way they were spelled on the website, for example Deromans and the Amal Institute of Engineering. The information was about 10 years old, which would have made Mr. Levy about 38 in 2011.)

Dror Levy, Anidjar's partner at the Big Apple, has long been a business partner with Shaul and Meir Levy, the Israelis who met Ehud Olmert in New York City on the eve of 9-11. Dror Levy and another Israeli, Eliezer Tabib, are the registered heads of several companies that were started by Shaul and Meir Levy, the 1000 Highway 98 East Company, for example, which is also the address of the Wings store in Destin, Florida.

Dror Levy was described as "vice president and marketing director for Miami-based Marco Destin Inc., parent of Wings" in the *Mobile Register* (AL) and *Naples Daily News* (FL) of January 7, 2004. Marco apparently stands for Marco Island where the company also owns property. "Marco Destin Inc. is led by Eliezer 'Eli' Tabib, who took over Wings in Florida and on the Gulf Coast when the L&L Wings partnership was amended in 1998. Marco Destin has 23 stores, including 10 in the Panhandle," the *Naples Daily News* reported.

I wrote back to the person who provided the tip and told him that

Next Graphics appeared to be an Israeli-owned business operating behind the false front of being an Arab-owned company. He then responded:

Amazing, amazing, amazing. Next Graphics is out of business. I used to buy transfers from them via phone for years between 1996 and 2001. At that time they were at a different location. Sometimes I had a rush job when someone ordered a dozen shirts or something so I used to go there...

I am puzzled by the behaviour of these people. If you entered Graphics waiting room, they had a small altar on your left with and elaborate "kursi", an Islamic prayer on the wall, and several very beautiful Islamic inscriptions, small table with a gold trimmed Holy Quran on it, and several other Islamic mementos.

I am a Muslim and was happy to see display of their faith, but we are not that showy, and very few Muslims have things hanging on their walls. If you go in my house, you will see very little besides The Quran and some scenes from old Cairo on the walls. So this also made me suspicious, since this waiting room is a place where all kinds of people come in, maybe even with drinks, dogs and obscenities, so that it is not a place where a Muslim would display the Quran. It was an obvious attempt at flaunting their nonexistent Islamism...

I know that they bought this warehouse around 1999, when they moved from another Lauderdale location at 5600 NW 12th Ave., 33309. Their last location was 2131 Blount Road.

You mention that you would like to know how far their location was from the phony hijackers. You will find that it is not that far. "Atta" lived in one of those two story motel type buildings in Fort Lauderdale, near the beach, there are hundreds of such structures near the water there. The distance would be about 1.5 to 2 miles at most, and the Delray location would be about 4 to 5 miles.

Interestingly, at that time there was a mosque in an industrial park near FAU, that was operated by a fellow called Ibrahim Bedali, very nice guy, ocean geologist by profession; many of us attended the place, he also taught martial arts, but we never saw a single one of these "hijackers" there. Maybe they attended a synagogue, instead!

Why was Anidjar running the false front Next Graphics business in the Fort Lauderdale area in the years prior to 9-11? Is this business or the people involved in it connected with the fake Israeli art students who infested U.S. government offices from 1999-2001? Was it a base of operations to monitor the Arab patsies who were being cultivated to be the suspects of 9-11?

Why were these Israeli art students, with backgrounds in bomb and demolition units, targeting Drug Enforcement Agency offices? Was this elaborate false front part of the operation controlling and monitoring the 9-11 suspects? Was this an intelligence operation to infiltrate the DEA in order to protect an Israeli drug-running operation?

Was this part of an Israeli intelligence "Arabesque," which happens to be the name of another of the "Nabil Alif" fake front operation at the 2131 Blount Road location, along with the adjacent stores Next U.S.A. and Next Factoring? Nabil and Nidal Alif were certainly a couple very busy and enterprising Arabs.

Did Shual (or Shaul) and Meir Levy become multi-millionaires by selling beach towels and bathing suits? Could there be another reason why they own so many "free-standing" warehouses along the coast of the United States? Have their beach-side business locations been used by Israeli intelligence as logistic bases for drug smuggling or other operations, such as 9-11? Why was Ehud Olmert meeting these men in New York City on the day before 9-11 and why was this visit by a senior Israeli politician ignored by the media?

What we need to stand up and say is not only did they attack the *USS Liberty*; they did 9-11. They did it. I have had long conversations over the past two weeks with contacts at the Army War College, at its headquarters, Marine Corps, and I made it absolutely clear in both cases that it is 100 percent certain that 9-11 was a Mossad operation. Period.

Dr. Alan Sabrosky, former Director of Studies, Strategic Studies Institute, U.S. Army War College, March 14, 2010

Chapter VII

The Architecture of Terror: Mapping the Network Behind 9-11

Thomas Paine was the most popular and inspirational writer of the American Revolution. "The cause of America," Paine wrote in *Common Sense* (1776), "is in a great measure the cause of all mankind." In 1787, having "stood out the storm of one revolution" (i.e. the American) and with "no wish to embark in another," Paine returned to Europe and wound up playing a role in the French Revolution – and nearly losing his head.

"To the Citizens of the United States" is a series of letters written by Paine in 1802-03, when he returned to America after an absence of almost fifteen years. In the first letter, Paine wrote:

> But while I beheld with pleasure the dawn of liberty rising in Europe, I saw with regret the luster of it fading in America. In less than two years from the time of my departure some distant symptoms painfully suggested the idea that the principles of the Revolution were expiring on the soil that produced them.

"A faction, acting in disguise, was rising in America; they had lost sight of first principles," Paine wrote. "They were beginning to contemplate government as a profitable monopoly, and the people as hereditary property." Two hundred years later, as an American student of history, I made the same observation: A faction, acting in disguise, was rising in America. This faction also viewed government as a profitable monopoly, which they sought to control. The rising faction I noticed taking control in the 1980s was primarily Jewish by ethnicity, and Zionist by ideology.

After spending several years in Europe, Israel, and the Middle East, I returned to the United States in the late 1970s and found the discourse in the media about Zionism to be extremely one-sided and distorted. Zionism, a nationalist ideology based on race, was misrepresented in the U.S. mass media as being a progressive and democratic movement while the state of Israel was depicted as being a kosher slice of America in the Middle East. It was very clear though that the people providing the distorted view of the Middle East were themselves devoted to Zionism, the violent and chauvinistic nationalism of Eastern European Jews who have occupied Palestine since 1948.

Honest and unbiased coverage of Israel and the Middle East became increasingly difficult to find in the U.S. in the 1980s and 1990s. The sale of Ted Turner's progressive Cable News Network (CNN) to Gerald M. Levin of AOL Time Warner, and the transformation of the previously informative *Christian Science Monitor* marked the end of the two independent unbiased news outlets covering the Middle East. An ethnic minority with a foreign agenda – Zionism – was gaining monopoly control over the U.S. mass media while the United States was being drawn more deeply into the Arab-Israeli conflict as the primary supporter, financier, and political ally of Israel.

As an American raised with traditional Christian values, I came to realize that the culture I had grown up in was under attack and being reduced to a subculture. Through the media, a distinctly foreign and anti-Christian culture of pornography, perversion, and violence was being promoted. A diet of perverse entertainment and un-American values was being pushed onto the unsuspecting American population through the mass media.

Concurrent with the rise of the Zionist faction in the U.S. media there was a significant increase of Zionist influence in the government. This could be seen in the way the U.S. government and federal courts unfairly prosecuted innocent people, including the president of Austria, on unfounded allegations of having committed crimes against Jews during World War II, while more recent crimes committed by Jews in the United States and the international arena went completely unpunished.

The Israeli Architects of 9-11

The false-flag terrorism of 9-11 is a monstrous Zionist crime of our time. The true culprits of this heinous crime are clearly being protected by a gang of like-minded Zionists in the government, particularly in the U.S. Department of Justice and the federal court system where justice for the victims of 9-11 has been obstructed.

The media deception about 9-11 has been accepted as truth by millions of Americans. Based on lies and fabrications, the fraudulent "War on Terror" has been waged with wars of aggression in Afghanistan and Iraq. Thousands of lives have been lost and hundreds of billions of dollars wasted on this criminal enterprise, yet there is no end in sight to the madness. The "War on Terror" has also been accompanied by a massive assault on our American liberties.

The controlled media has completely ignored the evidence of Israeli involvement in 9-11 and refused to investigate any of the unanswered questions about what really happened. Likewise, the media has avoided any serious investigation of the official version of events. As a result, the public has been left with a confusing mixture of fact, fiction, and disinformation from which the truth is very hard to discern. It is unacceptable for a baseless fairy tale to pass for truth while the real history is suppressed. *Solving 9-11 - The Deception that Changed the World* is my attempt to clarify this muddled history by discovering and exposing the true culprits.

"But let them go on," Thomas Paine wrote about the rising faction of his time, "give them rope enough and they will put an end to their own insignificance. There is too much common sense and independence in America to be long the dupe of any faction, foreign or domestic." Paine was, however, writing long before television became the most pervasive and powerful thought-control device on the planet.

The Zionist faction controlling the media and government has done immense damage to our republic and national prestige. Today, America is in dire straits economically, politically, and morally. Absent a revolution or sea change in political thinking, it is unlikely that the real culprits of 9-11 will ever be held accountable in a U.S. court. Finding the truth of 9-11 is, in any case, of the utmost importance. We need to know who did it and how they did it.

The Israeli Thesis

Although the available evidence and facts are sufficient to disprove the official version, 9-11 remains an unsolved crime. The version pushed by the government and media has not been proven for one simple reason: it is not provable. To help solve 9-11 we can use the Socratic method of developing a thesis by asking questions to find the truth.

I have been asking questions about Israeli involvement in 9-11 since September 2001 because of the evidence of prior knowledge shown by the five dancing Israelis and the warning messages sent on the Odigo messaging network. From the beginning I considered the possibility that 9-11 was an Israeli-produced false-flag terror spectacle. The Zionists, after all, have a long history of carrying out such attacks. My research found a great deal of evidence to support this thesis. I discovered that agents of Israeli military intelligence or people devoted to the Zionist cause occupied every key position in the 9-11 cover-up. This consistency led me to believe that the Israeli thesis is correct.

Andreas von Bülow, the former head of the parliamentary commission that oversaw the financing of the German intelligence agencies, told me that a sophisticated false-flag operation like 9-11 has an organizational structure with three basic levels: architectural, managerial, and working. Atta and the nineteen Arabs blamed as the "hijackers" of 9-11 were part of the working level, von Bülow said, and were part of the deception. That is, he explained, how false-flag terror works. Von Bülow said that he believed that the Mossad was behind the terror attacks of 9-11. These attacks, he said, were designed to turn public opinion against the Arabs, and to boost military and security spending. With more than one trillion dollars wasted on the fraudulent "War on Terror" and the disastrous and costly wars in Afghanistan and Iraq, there is no question that 9-11 was used to push military and security spending through the roof.

"You don't get the higher echelons," von Bülow said, referring to the "architectural structure," which masterminds such false-flag terror attacks. At this level, he said, the organization doing the planning, such as Mossad, is primarily interested in affecting public opinion. The mass media must be tightly controlled in order for such a large-scale deception to succeed. "Ninety-five percent of the work of the intelligence agencies around the world is deception and disinformation," von Bülow said, which is widely propagated in the mainstream media creating an accepted version of events. "Journalists don't even raise the simplest questions," he said, adding, "Those who differ are labeled as crazy."

Terror as Deception

"Terror is theatre and theatre is illusion" is the theme of *The Little Drummer Girl* by John Le Carré, the realistic novel about Israeli false-flag operations. "On the old reality we impose the new fiction," said Joseph, the Israeli agent who was creating a false history for a Palestinian "terrorist" in the same way false histories were created for the 9-11 "hijackers".

Le Carré gave a "sincere thanks" to "certain past and serving officers" of Israeli intelligence in his preface to the book. He expressed "special gratitude" to General Shlomo Gazit, the former chief of Israeli military intelligence. The Israeli characters in *The Little Drummer Girl* come through without a scratch as Palestinians and Europeans are blown to bits in acts of false-flag terrorism. In one scene, a kidnapped Palestinian is put into the trunk of a car, which is exploded at a rest area on the German *Autobahn*. Similar Israeli techniques have long been used in "suicide bombs" in occupied Palestine, Iraq, and Afghanistan to kill and maim thousands of innocent people and instigate sectarian violence. The controlled media routinely blames these terrorist bombings on "suicide bombers" – without any independent examination of the evidence.

"Of the Palestinians," whose real-life stories informed the plot of *The Little Drummer Girl*, "some are dead, others are taken prisoner, the rest presumably are for the most part homeless or dispersed," Le Carré wrote in July 1982. He wrote as the Israeli military, led by the Zionist terrorist and war criminal Ariel Sharon, carried out new atrocities in Lebanon on a daily basis.

Sharon, a *genocidaire* from the extreme right-wing Likud party became prime minister of Israel in early 2001 as George W. Bush entered the White House as an un-elected president from the Republican Party, creating the same dangerous political and ideological conjunction that had produced the disaster in Lebanon in 1982.

The "Fixed Frame" of 9-11

If one considers Eckehardt Werthebach's expert judgment that "the magnitude of planning" behind 9-11 required the "fixed frame" of a state intelligence organization, then there should be evidence of such an organization connecting the key players of the network behind the crime. If we can discern some elements or identify some of the key people in this network, we should be able to discover other key people through their mutual connections.

In order to carry out the sophisticated terror attacks of 9-11, the architects would have had to create an organizational structure in the United States over a period of years, or even decades. This structure was needed to connect the key individuals at crucial points of the crime, including those involved in the "non-investigation" and cover-up. All the bases had to be covered.

The organizational structure is required to provide secure channels for the criminal organization, the conduits through which the terror operation is set up and carried out. A secure conduit could be a company, a group of people, or even a single individual. Complete loyalty and wholehearted devotion to the cause are the most essential qualities for the people involved in the criminal network. When the structure for the 9-11 operation was in place, the switch was thrown and the long-planned terror atrocity became real.

There is no evidence whatsoever that "Al Qaida" or any such Islamic terrorist structure ever existed in the United States, or that any Muslim or Arab organization was interested in, or capable of carrying out such a sophisticated attack. There is, on the other hand, a great deal of evidence that an Israeli military structure, which employs Arab disguises when necessary, is behind 9-11. This network connects the highest officers and veterans of Israeli military intelligence with the key players, companies, and funding entities involved in the 9-11 attacks.

There is evidence of an Israeli military intelligence network connecting every key player and entity behind 9-11. At the most crucial position in U.S. law enforcement, for example, where executive decisions were made concerning the federal investigation, sat Michael Chertoff, an Israeli whose mother was one of the first agents of Israeli intelligence. Having a dedicated Zionist agent in the key position as Assistant Attorney General controlling the criminal division of the Department of Justice, gave the Israelis the operational security to carry out this massive crime without fear of exposure or prosecution. It should be noted that Chertoff also played a key role in the prosecution of the 1993 false-flag terror bombing at the World Trade Center.

Likewise, two federal judges, Alvin K. Hellerstein and Michael B. Mukasey, both dedicated Zionists, have overseen virtually all the litigation related to 9-11 and the 1993 false-flag bombing at the WTC. Small wonder that of the ninety-six families who chose to seek justice through the courts rather than accept the government pay-out for the loss of their loved ones, not one wrongful death case from 9-11 went to trial.

Judge Alvin K. Hellerstein waged a war of attrition against the ninety-six families that chose to litigate. By the 7th anniversary of 9-11 fewer than seven families remained. One year later, in 2009, there were only three cases left. In 2011, with only one case left, Judge Hellerstein imposed an arbitrary time limit of one month for a trial. He also dismissed the key Israeli defendant, ICTS, the parent company of Huntleigh USA, who was responsible for passenger screening operations at Boston's Logan Airport on 9-11. Faced with such restrictions and obstacles, the last 9-11 family gave up their hope of finding the truth through the court and accepted an out-of-court settlement.

The absence of a proper investigation, the confiscation and criminal destruction of evidence, the escape or dismissal of all Israeli suspects, and the use of unwarranted secrecy measures to block discovery in the 9-11 tort litigation all point to an Israeli-based terror network being protected from exposure.

It stands to reason that the terror network being protected by high-level Zionist agents is itself a Zionist structure. If it were truly an Arabic, Islamic, or even American criminal network, it would have been exposed long ago. The fact that the terror network behind 9-11 has been protected by Zionist agents and the controlled media strongly suggests it is an organization to which they are dedicated.

Michael Goff, Ptech & Guardium

My discovery in 2005 that the Ptech software company from Quincy, Massachusetts, was actually a disguised Israeli intelligence operation is key to understanding the Israeli role in 9-11. This discovery helped reveal other key people in the Israeli network behind the crime. Through Michael Goff's connection to Guardium we can trace an Israeli military intelligence network linking the key players of 9-11. This connection explains how Israeli enterprise spy software wound up on critical U.S. government and military computer networks. By 2002, Ptech software was on the networks of eighteen federal agencies, including the FBI, U.S. Treasury, Customs Service, Secret Service, Department of Energy, Army, Navy, Air Force, Federal Aviation Administration, the U.S. Postal Service – and even NATO.

Goff, who had procured all software for Ptech and who had been responsible for marketing Ptech's enterprise software, went on to work for Guardium, a company that is a branch of the research and development department of the Israeli Air Force. What does this connection tell us?

Guardium is a spin-off of Log-On Software, an Israeli military intelligence company based in Ramat Gan, Israel. Log-On Software was founded by Major Gil Migdan and Joseph Segev, the former head programmer and telecommunications officer for the Israeli Navy. The vice president of the company is Danny Zeitouny, the head of logistics programming for the Israel Defense Forces (IDF). One of the directors of Guardium is Gill Zaphrir (a.k.a. Zafrir), an Israeli colonel who "headed the research and development department of the Israel Air Force." In its "Executive Profile" about Col. Zaphrir, *Business Week* says:

Mr. Gill Zaphrir is a Partner at Veritas Venture Partners. He joined Veritas in 1999 and has been actively managing the funds of Veritas. Mr. Zaphrir has research and development and management experience in Israel's air force and aerospace industry. Prior to joining Veritas in 1999, he headed the research and development department of the Israel Air Force. In 1987, Mr. Zaphrir served as System Engineer on the first Israeli satellite project, under the auspices of IAI-MBT.

Mr. Zaphrir is a Director of Bamboo Mediacasting Inc., and Guardium Inc. He was a Director of eShip-4u Inc. He was born and raised in Israel, served as a military navigator in the Israel Air Force and is a Colonel (reserve). Mr. Zaphrir holds a B.Sc. in Aeronautical Engineering from the Technion in Haifa and an M.B.A. from Bar-Ilan Business School in Israel.

Another founder and director of Guardium is Amit Yoran, an Israeli who went to West Point and became the manager of computer network security for the Pentagon and Secretary of Defense. Yoran went on to serve as the "czar" of cyber security for the U.S. Dept. of Homeland Security. *Business Week* says the following about Yoran:

> Dr. [Amit] Yoran is a Co-Founder of Guardium, Inc. and also served as the Chief Executive Officer and President. He was the President and Chief Executive Officer at Riptech Inc., which Dr. Yoran co-founded in 1998.
>
> He was appointed by George W. Bush as the administration's Cyber Chief, responsible for coordinating

the nation's activities in cyber security. Prior to this, Dr. Yoran served as a Vice President for worldwide-managed security services at Symantec Corp. and was primarily responsible for managing security infrastructure in 40 countries.

Before working in the private sector, he served as a Network Security Manager at the Department of Defense and [was] responsible for maintaining operations of the Pentagon's network. Dr. Yoran also served as an officer in the United States Air Force [as the Director of Vulnerability Programs for Dept. of Defense's Computer Emergency Response Team]. He designed security architecture for the Pentagon and Office of the Secretary of Defense networks' backbones.

Dr. Yoran served as a Director at Guardium, Inc. and Director of the Vulnerability Assessment and Assistance Program for the U.S. Department of Defense Computer Emergency Response Team. As a Director, he worked with national and international law enforcement and intelligence organizations to prevent and respond to security breaches of national infrastructure networks.

He serves as a Member of the Adjunct Faculty at George Washington University. Dr. Yoran has conducted a Doctoral research in the area of Intrusion Detection Technologies.

Michael Goff's working relationship with Amit Yoran and the Israeli intelligence operation known as Guardium, Inc. is an excellent example of a high-level Israeli military intelligence "channel" in the United States. I don't have specific information about when Goff's relationship with Israeli military intelligence began, but I would assume it began sometime prior to 1994 when he suddenly left his law practice and began working at Ptech. Goff's father and grandfather were both highest-level Freemasons in the International Order of the B'nai B'rith, an exclusive Jewish-Zionist order of Freemasons founded in New York City in 1843.

The B'nai B'rith is a secretive, powerful, and influential order of Freemasonry. It is, for example, the parent organization of the Anti-Defamation League of the B'nai B'rith (ADL), which has a great deal of influence with legislators and law enforcement agencies across America. It is also the parent of Hillel, an organization for Jewish students at colleges across the United States. The *New York Times* can be called a B'nai B'rith newspaper due to its ownership by the Sulzberger family, one of the leading families of B'nai B'rith Lodge No. 1 in New York City.

Goff's relationship with the Israelis at Guardium appears to have been the channel through which Israeli spy software was provided to Ptech. The Ptech enterprise spy software was then installed onto the most critical computer networks of the U.S. government in the years prior to 9-11. "The boy's job in this operation is to play cut-out," the Mossadnik in *The Little Drummer Girl* says. "That's all he does. He breaks the circuit." In real life, Goff was the connection between the Israeli military programmers and the crucial computer networks of the U.S. military.

At the time that Goff worked for Ptech, Yoran was Network Security Manager at the Department of Defense designing computer security for the Pentagon. In this position, Yoran was ideally situated to arrange the installment of Ptech software onto the critical computer systems of the U.S. military. The Israeli nexus between Michael Goff, Ptech, Guardium, and Amit Yoran provides a logical explanation for how Ptech enterprise "spy" software wound up on the critical computer networks of the U.S. government and military.

Guardium is closely connected with other companies of the Israeli military intelligence network in the United States. Some of the key Israeli-run companies linked to Guardium are Amdocs, ViryaNet, Nice Systems, and CreoScitex. Like Guardium, these companies are all run by senior officers of Israeli military intelligence. Amdocs and Nice Systems are especially noteworthy because these two companies were involved in the espionage network of computer programmers and demolition experts from the Israeli military who posed as art students as they tried to infiltrate offices of the U.S. Drug Enforcement Agency (DEA) in 2000 and 2001.

The "most activity" of the Israeli operation aimed at infiltrating offices of the DEA was "reported in the state of Florida," according to the leaked DEA report. "The Hollywood, Florida area seems to be a central point for these individuals with several having addresses in this area," the report said. Hollywood is also the area which connected fifteen of the nineteen Arab "hijackers" of 9-11. If the "art student" operation is connected to 9-11, as it seems to be, then Amdocs and Nice Systems are also involved.

"A majority of those [Israeli "art students"] questioned has stated they served in military intelligence, electronic signal intercept, or explosive ordnance units. Some have been linked to high-ranking officials in the Israeli military. One was the son of a two-star general, one served as the bodyguard to the head of the Israeli Army, one served in a Patriot missile unit. That these people are now travelling in the U.S. selling art seems not to fit their background," the U.S. DEA investigators concluded.

One of the Israeli agents was 27-year-old Lt. Peer Segalovitz, a platoon leader with Israeli special forces 605 Battalion in the Golan Heights. Segalovitz and the eighty-man platoon he commanded specialized in demolition. "Segalovitz acknowledged he could blow up buildings, bridges, cars and anything else that he needed to," according to the report.

If the Israeli "art student" intelligence operation is connected to 9-11, then the prevalence of military computer programmers and demolition experts among the agents would make sense given the evidence that the terror attacks of 9-11 required expertise with computer networks and explosives.

Nice Systems

Nice Systems, Inc., the wholly-owned U.S. subsidiary of an Israeli company with the same name, was headed by Brigadier General Shlomo Shamir from April 2001 when he became President and Chief Executive Officer. This is precisely the time when Israeli employees of Nice Systems and Amdocs were caught trying to infiltrate Drug Enforcement Agency and other U.S. government buildings posing as art students. General Shamir was certainly aware that Nice Systems employees had been arrested for illegal spying activity prior to 9-11.

General Shamir "built and led the planning division in the IDF [Israeli military] headquarters and served as Israel's military attaché to Germany" until 1994. Shamir went on to head Scitex America Corp. in 1997, which became CreoScitex America, Inc.

Avinoam Naor Aharonovich, one of the founders of Amdocs, was President and CEO of Amdocs Management Ltd., the company's management group from 1995 to 2002. As Chief Executive Officer of Amdocs Management Ltd., he had overall responsibility for the operations and activities of the company's subsidiaries. A number of senior corporate officers of Amdocs, all Israelis, moved between Nice Systems, ViryaNet Ltd., and Guardium. Sometimes a person would go to a company for a while and then return to the previous company. In some cases, such as with Gill Zaphrir, a person would be involved in an Israeli "venture capital" fund supporting a company while serving as a director of the company being funded. Elad Yoran, Amit's older brother, held similar positions at Broadview International and Riptech, a "security" software company that specialized in hacking into corporate computer networks.

Amit Yoran's "Ethical Hackers"

"Mr. [Amit] Yoran is chief executive of Riptech, a U.S. company that employs 'ethical hackers' to test vulnerability of networks, including those of utility companies," the *Irish Times* reported on October 5, 2001. "He [Yoran] says his teams have had success in disrupting utilities' power networks, in Europe particularly," according to the article, which was aptly titled, "Welcome to the Art of Electronic Warfare." The Yorans' company hacked into the computer networks of dozens of energy companies, the *Los Angeles Times* reported on August 20, 2001:

Riptech Inc., a security company in Alexandria, Va., has tested security for dozens of energy-industry clients. In every case, the firm penetrated Internet-connected corporate networks and often hopped from those networks into supposedly sealed grid-control systems, according to Riptech's president, Amit Yoran.

In February 2001, Amit Yoran, then chief executive of Riptech, told the Associated Press that hackers often break into a system through a computer that runs a Web site. "Once you break in (to the Web server), there are fewer protections between it and other parts of the network," Yoran said.

Riptech "was founded by Elad and Amit Yoran, two Israeli West Point graduates who claim years of security experience, and Tim Belcher, a Desert Storm veteran who serves as the company's chief technology officer," the *Washington Times* reported on December 11, 2000. "Amit Yoran reportedly helped design the Pentagon's computer security architecture," the *Times* reported.

"The threat changes every day. There has always been and always will be a criminal element out there. [The crooks] are not going away," said Elad Yoran, the company's chief financial officer. He should know. He was Riptech's chief marketing officer and vice president for business development at the time of 9-11.

"Riptech's specialty is in security management and monitoring of corporate computer networks," the *Washington Times* reported on October 23, 2000, when the Yoran brothers' private company of "ethical hackers" announced an infusion of $23 million in venture capital. Oddly, the *Washington Times* reported that Elad Yoran had "joined"

Riptech in August 2001, when he had already been the company's vice president for two years.

Elad Yoran was clearly performing two functions for Riptech: funding the company through his position as "vice president at Broadview International" and serving as "executive vice president" of the company he co-founded with his brother in 1998. It is through such secretive "venture capital" funding entities like Broadview and Veritas Venture Partners that the hand of Israeli military intelligence can be seen running the computer network "security" companies they have spawned, like Guardium. Before becoming a director of Guardium, for example, Col. Gil Zaphrir was "actively managing the funds of Veritas," which funded Guardium. Prior to joining Veritas in 1999, Col. Zaphrir "headed the research and development department of the Israel Air Force."

Security Growth Partners

Elad Yoran is also the CEO and founder of a funding company called Security Growth Partners (SGP). The SGP website says this about the company's mission:

> Security Growth Partners' (SGP) mission is to support companies that provide security solutions for the security market. SGP serves a large and diverse industry including, among others, information technology (IT) security, Critical Infrastructure Protection (CIP), homeland security and their related markets.
>
> SGP is more than a fund or typical venture capital organization. We identify desirable opportunities

and become extensively involved in the strategy and operations of each company with which we work.

Rather than simply invest, we capitalize on both our extensive expertise and experience in the security sector and our strong network of contacts to help management grow their businesses.

The founder of SGP, Elad Yoran, "advises leading companies in the security market and helps guide emerging companies with innovative technology to rapid growth. Mr. Yoran also advises government and infrastructure organizations on security and business risk matters."

The list of Elad Yoran's advisors and partners at SGP is very interesting. It includes his brother Amit Yoran and previously included another Israeli named Ilan Juran, which is another spelling of the name Yoran. Ilan Juran works at the Polytechnic University in Brooklyn and is director of the US-Israel Civil Infrastructure Security Program, an initiative of the Urban Utility Center, of which he is "executive director." Juran's program is, "designed to foster collaboration, as well as knowledge and technology sharing, between the U.S. and Israel governments and critical infrastructure organizations."

Tim Belcher, a co-founder of Riptech, the company of "ethical hackers," is another advisor at SGP. As Belcher's biographical sketch says:

Mr. Belcher has also conducted security assessments of some of the nation's most critical infrastructure components, including the Federal Aviation Administration's Air Traffic Control Network. He has also worked with government organizations such as the National Aeronautics and Space Administration, the National Reconnaissance Office, the Office of the Secretary of Defense, and Space and Naval Warfare Command.

The Kroll Connection

It is interesting to note that Jeremy M. Kroll, the Managing Director of Marsh Kroll, is also on the "advisory board" of Elad Yoran's Security Growth Partners. This is a crucial connection in the Zionist network behind 9-11. Kroll, the son of Jules B. Kroll, has been an executive at Marsh Kroll, a division of Marsh & McLennan Co. (MMC), since 1996. Jeremy Kroll's connection with Elad and Amit Yoran through SGP reveals a key link between the American Zionist network and Israeli military intelligence.

Marsh & McLennan is headed by Jeffrey Greenberg, the son of Maurice Raymond "Hank" Greenberg. Maurice Greenberg, the former CEO of A.I.G., has been a business partner with Jules B. Kroll since 1993 when he bought twenty-three percent of Kroll Inc. for $15 million. In 2004, MMC acquired the rest of Kroll for the hugely inflated price of $1.9 billion. Jules Kroll reportedly retired in July 2008. The first plane on 9-11 flew directly into the secure computer room of Marsh & McLennan, where Jeffrey Greenberg was CEO. What an amazing coincidence - or was it?

Kroll Security at the World Trade Center

Kroll Associates was responsible for "revamping security at the World Trade Center after the 1993 terrorist bombing," Douglas Frantz of the *New York Times* reported in 1994. This is a crucial point because those who controlled security at the WTC are prime suspects in the demolition of the Twin Towers. It was directly into the computer room of Marsh (Kroll) USA in the North Tower that the first plane struck, or was precision-guided, on 9-11.

John O'Neill, the former chief of counter-terrorism with the FBI who had investigated Al Qaida, was the head of security for the World Trade Center complex and was killed on his first day of work on 9-11. O'Neill had been appointed to this position by the managing director of the Kroll security company, Jerome M. Hauer. Kroll evidently continued to manage security for the WTC complex from 1993 until 9-11.

Prior to joining Kroll, Hauer, a Zionist Jew, was the director of Mayor Giuliani's Office of Emergency Management (OEM), where he had been the driving force behind having the OEM command bunker built in Larry Silverstein's 47-story WTC 7, the tower which mysteriously fell into its footprint at 5:21 p.m. on 9-11. Testimony from Larry Silverstein and physical evidence strongly suggest that WTC 7 was demolished with explosives and Thermite.

History of Mossad Security at Port Authority

There is a very significant but little-known history of senior Israeli intelligence officers trying to get the security contract for the World Trade Center in the 1980s. Being in charge of security at the Twin

Towers was obviously crucial to the 9-11 operation. The explosive charges and Thermite that evidently demolished the three towers could not have been placed in the buildings without the perpetrators having complete control of security. Getting the security contract at the WTC was something senior officers of the Mossad had actively sought since at least 1987. This was clearly part of the Israeli master plan for 9-11, a plan first articulated in 1979 by Isser Harel, the former head of Israeli intelligence.

Harel, the director of Haganah intelligence in the 1940s, is seen as the founder of Israeli intelligence. The Haganah and Irgun were the largest Zionist militia/terrorist organizations in Palestine prior to the creation of Israel in 1948. Both organizations were involved in the bombing of the King David Hotel and other acts of terrorism. Harel was evidently involved in the long-term planning of 9-11. More than twenty years earlier he had told Michael D. Evans, an American Zionist, that terrorism would "come to America." Arab terrorists would strike the tallest building in New York City, "a symbol of your fertility," Harel said.

When Evans asked where the Arab terrorists would strike, Harel said: "In Islamic theology, the phallic symbol is very important. Your biggest phallic symbol is New York City and your tallest building will be the phallic symbol they will hit." How could Harel know in 1979 that "Islamic fundamentalists" would attack the World Trade Center if he was not part of the planning? "Isser Harel prophesied that the tallest building in New York would be the first building hit by Islamic fundamentalists twenty-one years ago," Evans said in a 2004 interview.

Seven years after Harel's bizarre prediction, a team of senior Israeli intelligence agents, men who had worked directly under Isser Harel for decades, obtained the security contract for the Port Authority, the agency that owned and operated the World Trade Center. The Israeli false-flag terror attacks of 9-11, designed to create the "War on Terror" and drag the United States military into the Israeli-Arab conflict on the side of Israel, were evidently planned decades in advance.

A team of senior Israeli intelligence veterans, men who had worked with Harel since the founding of Israeli intelligence, received the security contract for the Port Authority of New York and New Jersey (PA) in 1987, according to a *Washington Post* article from April 12, 1987. The Port Authority manages operations at New York's airports, as it did at the World Trade Center prior to the complex being leased to Larry Silverstein in late July 2001.

The security contract with Atwell Security of Tel Aviv, a company connected to the Mossad, was cancelled after the Port Authority learned that the firm was headed by Avraham Shalom Ben-Dor, the former head of Israel's General Security Service (GSS), a.k.a. Shabak or Shin Bet. The Atwell company appears to have been created only for the purpose of obtaining the security contract for the Port Authority and the World Trade Center. The Mossad needed to have control over the security at the Twin Towers in order for Isser Harel's prediction to come true.

Avraham Bendor, or Ben-Dor (a.k.a. Abe, Avrum, or Avram Shalom) had been forced to resign as head of the GSS, which he ran from 1980 to 1986, following the disclosure that he had ordered the execution of two detained Palestinian bus hijackers by having their skulls smashed with stones, and then lied about it. "Avrum lied and kept lying," a senior security official involved in the Bus 300 affair told the *Jerusalem Post* in 1995. "He failed because he was too sure of himself and too used to hearing how great he was."

Shalom, the head of the GSS, was identified by an Israeli Justice Ministry report in December 1986 as having ordered the murder and subsequent cover-up of the two Palestinians captured in 1984. Shalom and ten other Shin Bet agents were forced to resign, although President Chaim Hertzog subsequently granted them all pardons.

Shalom corrupted the GSS, as well: "Some of the vices of the Shalom regime still plague the GSS," the *Post* reported in 1995. "One problem … is the lack of parliamentary control over the GSS." This is an important observation because it indicates that the Shin Bet under Shalom had become a rogue agency. "The most disturbing trend is the recurring episodes in which GSS agents provide misleading information to officials and the courts," the *Post* reported.

"The head of Shabak [GSS] has an unusual personal relationship with Prime Minister Shamir, partly perhaps because of Shamir's own past in the espionage business," the *Jerusalem Post* wrote in June 1991.

Shalom had ordered the murders but tried to blame a senior army officer at the scene and later claimed that Shamir had given him a free hand. The former Irgun and Lehi terrorist Yitzhak Shamir (born Jaziernicki in Belarus) was the prime minister responsible for Shin Bet at the time. Shamir was a leader from the extreme right-wing Likud. After joining the Irgun terrorist group in 1935, he joined its most militant faction, Lehi, in 1940. He is reported to have personally authorized the assassination of the United Nations representative in the Middle East, the Swedish Count Folke Bernadotte, in September 1948.

Edward J. O'Sullivan, director of the office of special plans at the Port Authority of New York and New Jersey, simply said that the contract with Atwell Security of Tel Aviv had been terminated because "we are no longer satisfied with the agreement," the *Washington Post* reported in April 1987. O'Sullivan said the port authority's legal office told him not to comment on why he was killing the contract. O'Sullivan said he acted after a reporter inquired about the contract and Atwell's president, Avraham Bendor, acknowledged that he was also known as Avraham Shalom.

Atwell, a subsidiary of the Eisenberg Group [Shaul Eisenberg of the Mossad], had been chosen "largely on the basis of Bendor's credentials," O'Sullivan said. Use of such aliases in Israeli intelligence is common, the *Washington Post* reported. "One intelligence expert said that even Bendor may not be the former Shin Bet chief's real name." Had the contract with Atwell Security not been terminated in 1987 it is very likely that the false-flag terror attacks would have been carried out years earlier. The cancellation of the Atwell contract forced the Mossad to find other ways to get control of the security at the World Trade Center.

A New York-based senior Israeli intelligence officer, Peter [Zvi] Malkin, had acted as a New York representative for Atwell Security of Tel Aviv in the negotiations with the PA, O'Sullivan said. Malkin is famous for being the Mossad agent who grabbed Adolf Eichmann during the Israeli kidnapping in Argentina in 1960.

The executives running the Port Authority in 1987, the mayor, and his first deputy, certainly must have been aware of the PA's decision to hire a company run by a senior Mossad agent to provide security for New York's airports, ports, commuter trains, and the World Trade Center. The people who made the decision to give the security contract to Avraham Bendor's Atwell Security of Tel Aviv must have known that Zvi Malkin was a senior Mossad agent; they had negotiated with him, after all.

The executive director of the Port Authority in 1987 was Stephen Berger (1985-1990). Berger was described by Thomas J. Lueck of the *New York Times* in August 1987 as, "a man at the center of New York City's economy, deftly pulling strings in business and government alike." Today, Berger is Chairman of Odyssey Investment Partners, a private New York investment firm that specializes in private corporate transactions. Berger is a member of the board of New York's Citizens Budget Commission (CBC) with fellow Zionists Larry Silverstein and Felix Rohatyn.

Philip D. Kaltenbacher was the chairman of the Port Authority's Board of Commissioners from 1985 to 1990. Prior to becoming a PA commissioner in 1983, Kaltenbacher had been Chairman of the New Jersey Republican State Committee. Kaltenbacher's father, Joseph, was a founder of the New Jersey Chapter of the American Jewish Committee and a former member of the national board of governors of the AJC, a major Zionist organization.

Stanley Brezenoff, who later became executive director of the PA in 1990, was Deputy Mayor for Operations and First Deputy Mayor under Mayor Edward Irving Koch (1978-89) at the time the Port Authority's security contract was being negotiated with Zvi Malkin, a well-known senior Mossad agent. Brezenoff was "the second most powerful official in the Koch administration and was the government's chief operating officer, often serving as acting Mayor in Mr. Koch's absence," according to the *New York Times*. Brezenoff directed the day-to-day operations of city agencies, including police, fire, and transportation. It is hard to imagine that Brezenoff, whose Yiddish-speaking grandparents had immigrated to the United States in the early 1900s from Russia and Austria, was unaware of the deal to give the PA security contract to Atwell Security of Tel Aviv. Malkin was, after all, a legendary figure among Zionist Jews.

Malkin was one of the Israeli intelligence agents involved in the kidnapping of Adolf Eichmann in Buenos Aires in 1960 and wrote a book entitled *Eichmann In My Hands* about his role in the kidnapping. It was none other than Isser Harel, then head of the Mossad, who had sent Malkin and six others on the mission to kidnap Eichmann. Harel had also worked closely with Shimon Peres and Teddy Kollek in the pre-state Haganah militia of the 1940s when they had been responsible for procuring weapons and smuggling them to Zionist forces in Palestine.

Other agents on the Mossad team involved in the Eichmann kidnapping were Avraham Shalom Ben-Dor and Rafael "Dirty Rafi" Eitan, the senior Mossadnik [not the Chief of Staff with the same name], who ran the Jonathan Pollard espionage operation against the United States in the 1980s. Eitan later told the Israeli press that he had been made a scapegoat to cover for Shimon Peres and Yitzhak Shamir, Israeli politicians who knew about Eitan's espionage network in America, but defended themselves and the state by claiming it was "a rogue operation."

Eitan headed a special spying unit known as the Scientific Liaison Office and directed a team of agents working out of the Israeli Embassy in Washington when the Pollard spy operation was exposed in 1985. For Eitan, a minister in the Israeli government, the United States was considered "the enemy."

That Eitan, a member of the Israeli cabinet, would say to one of Israel's largest daily newspapers in 1997 that the United States is an enemy of Israel, and that his position would not be challenged, is something that would confound most Americans.

"I failed in the Pollard affair, just as I failed in other intelligence operations beyond enemy lines," Eitan told the newspaper *Yediot Aharonot* in June 1997. "That is the lot of an intelligence officer who runs complex intelligence operations. When you work a lot and do a lot, especially in the intelligence field, you win some and you lose some," he said. "Nobody knows either about your successes or your failures. It doesn't cause a fuss. But this was a big fuss. You take such a possibility into consideration, but there is nothing you can do about it."

"I'm surprised he would admit this," Joseph diGenova, the U.S. attorney who prosecuted the case, said. "But this is basically all stuff that the evidence in the case shows." DiGenova said Eitan's statement was unusual in that it contradicted the "official Israeli position" that the Pollard case had been an unauthorized "rogue" operation, and in that Eitan "does not refer to the United States as an ally, which is regrettable." Eitan's statement about the Pollard operation being an operation "beyond enemy lines" reveals how Israeli intelligence veterans view the Israeli-U.S. relationship, something DiGenova seemed unable to grasp or articulate.

Eitan said he has close relations with senior Cuban leaders, including Fidel Castro, and has helped develop Cuba's agricultural infrastructure with Israeli irrigation equipment, chemicals, pesticides and fertilizers, along with agricultural advisers. According to Eitan, the ten Israelis actively doing business in Cuba for the past five years [1992-97] "have more influence than Russia had in the last thirty years." The business has developed Cuba's corn, citrus fruit and tomato farming for export, and Eitan represented "a long list of Israeli companies in Cuba."

"We are changing agriculture in Cuba," Eitan said, adding that his business violated the U.S. embargo and had made U.S. officials "very angry." He declined to identify his business partners in Cuba, citing a U.S. law that penalizes foreigners doing business in Cuba who use confiscated American property. Eitan's revealing comments were published in the *Washington Times* of June 22, 1997.

Who is Zvi Malkin?

Peter Malkin (a.k.a. Zvi Malchin or Milchman) was born in Poland in 1928 and raised in British-occupied Palestine during the mandate period. At age twelve, Malkin joined the Haganah, the Zionist underground militia. In 1950, he joined the Shin Bet, the Israeli security agency. He became an explosives specialist and was known as a master of disguises. Malkin preferred international work and became chief of operations for the Israeli intelligence agency, the Mossad. "During foreign postings, Malkin posed as an artist," his March 3, 2005, obituary in the *New York Sun* said.

A very young Malkin "retired" as head of operations of the Mossad in 1976 and moved to New York, where he worked as "a security consultant" and "posed as an artist." His "security consultant" work involved getting the World Trade Center security contract for the Mossad. Malkin had clearly not retired from the Mossad; he'd gone undercover. Malkin's artist disguise may very well be the inspiration for the "art student" operation to infiltrate DEA offices. It is interesting to note that Michael Chertoff's mother, Livia Eisen, one of the first Mossad agents, owned an art gallery in Elizabeth, New Jersey, when Malkin was posing as a painter in nearby New York. These "retired" Mossadniks probably spent a great deal of time together.

Malkin, supposedly "retired" from the Mossad in 1976 – at the age of forty-eight. This is a very similar profile to that of Shalom Yoran, the former head of the IAI, Israel's aircraft industry, who retired at age fifty and moved to New York to write and speak about his days as a Zionist soldier. Malkin moved to New York, where he wrote, painted, and helped his friend, Manhattan District Attorney Robert M. Morgenthau, "on investigations." Morgenthau helped Malkin get a "green card" and to become a U.S. citizen.

Zvi Malkin, the Israeli intelligence agent who "will forever be known as the man who captured Adolf Eichmann," continued to work as "a security expert" in the United States. "I'm out of the secret service business for sure," he told Ralph Blumenthal of the *New York Times* in May 2003. "But I help."

The *Washington Post* revealed the serious nature of the crimes Malkin, Shalom, and Eitan had been involved in when it reported in 1986 that Rafi Eitan, posing as a chemist, had travelled in 1968 to the Pennsylvania nuclear processing plant that secretly diverted several hundred kilograms of weapons-grade uranium to Israel. A declassified FBI document shows that another Israeli, "Abraham Bendor, department of electronics," accompanied Eitan on that trip.

Malkin and Avraham Bendor were later named as the Mossad agents who obtained the security contract for the World Trade Center in 1987, only to lose the contract when Bendor's criminal past was discovered. Rafi Eitan, Zvi Malkin, and Avraham Bendor had been working together on secret Mossad missions for decades when they obtained the security contract for the Twin Towers.

The abrupt cancellation by the Port Authority of the Atwell security contract in 1987 forced the Mossad to rethink its tactics about how to get control of the security at the World Trade Center through other channels. They had to find another way.

The Role of Kroll and Greenberg in Getting the Security Contract

Rejected and exposed in 1987, the Mossad didn't give up on Isser Harel's prophecy, they simply changed tack and decided to work through Americans like Jules Kroll and Maurice Greenberg. Shalom went to work for Kroll, according to the online *9-11 Encyclopedia* entry for Maurice "Hank" Greenberg, the CEO of the American International Group (A.I.G.) insurance company. Using the companies controlled by Kroll and Greenberg as disguises, the Mossad continued their clandestine operation to carry out their master plan for 9-11.

Malkin, Eitan, and Abe Shalom/Bendor crop up frequently in reports from Miami in the 1980s and 1990s: "Israeli intelligence agent, author and artist Peter Z. Malkin", for example, addressed the Young Leadership Council of the Greater Miami Jewish Federation in October 1991 at the Hyatt Regency, according to the *Miami Herald*.

Amazingly, a "Rafi Eitan" and "Abe Shalom" even shared the same address in Miami in the 1990s. An "Abe Shalom" also shared a Miami address at 19707 Turnberry Way with a Morris (and Lillian) Saffati, a name very similar to that of the Miami-based Israeli agent who sold weapons to the Medellin drug cartel, Maurice (and Ilana) Sarfati, a.k.a. Moshe Tzorfati. "Abe Shalom" also lived in Deal, New Jersey, near Lillian Saffati, the wife of Morris. Are these mere coincidences or the tracks of the culprits?

Through Avraham Shalom Bendor, Kroll Associates bought Palumbo Partners, the Miami-based international security firm in August 1992, reportedly "to expand in key Latin American markets." "According to sources in the industry, Palumbo brought with him a personal history of involvement with the Medellin and other South American narcotics cartels; his business included helping relocate some of the capabilities of these cartels out of Colombia," the *9-11 Encyclopedia* says. "The deal to bring Palumbo into Kroll was worked out by Avram Shalom, the former head of Israel's Shin Bet secret police," the *9-11 Encyclopedia* says.

In 1993, Maurice Greenberg became a partner and co-owner of Jules Kroll's company when A.I.G. bought twenty percent of Kroll. Greenberg is very close to Henry Kissinger, who became chairman of A.I.G.'s International Advisory Board in 1987. Greenberg was deeply involved in China in the 1980s, where Henry Kissinger represented A.I.G. Through the China trade, Greenberg became close to Shaul Eisenberg, the leader of the Asian section of the Israeli intelligence service Mossad, and agent for the sales of sophisticated military equipment to the Chinese military. Eisenberg was the owner of Atwell Security of Tel Aviv.

Greenberg created a joint venture with the founder of Amdocs. Greenberg's insurance subsidiary in Israel, called A.I.G. Golden, is a joint venture with Morris Kahn's Aurec Group (the parent company of Amdocs), an Israeli private equity firm with cable and telecom investments. Kahn was an original investor in Amdocs Ltd., of which his Aurec Group is the parent company. Aurec is meant to signify "golden" from the Latin, hence the gilded name of the A.I.G. subsidiary.

Jules Kroll is connected with the key 9-11 players Kenneth Bialkin and Larry Silverstein through the Citizens Budget Commission of New York. Kroll's wife, Lynn Korda Kroll, the Vice Chairman of the United Jewish Appeal (UJA) Federation of New York, is likewise connected to Silverstein, former national chairman of the UJA, the biggest fund-raising organization for the State of Israel.

Maurice Greenberg and Jules Kroll are connected to the key players of 9-11 in so many ways that their connections would fill a book. For the purpose of this chapter, however, there are a few key connections that need to be underlined:

- Maurice Greenberg and Jules Kroll became partners in 1993, the same year Kroll Associates "was chosen over three other companies to advise the Port Authority on a redesign of its security procedures." "We have such confidence in them that I have followed every one of their recommendations," Stanley Brezenoff, the Port Authority executive director, told the *New York Times* in 1994.

- Kroll revamped security at the World Trade Center after the 1993 terrorist bombing. "Over the last two years, the Port Authority of New York and New Jersey has paid Kroll $2.5 million to overhaul security at the World Trade Center and evaluate procedures at the agency's bridges, tunnels and airports," the *New York Times* reported on September 1, 1994.

- Kroll controlled security at the World Trade Center complex in 2001 and was responsible for hiring John O'Neill, the former chief of counterterrorism for the FBI, who died on 9-11, reportedly his first day on the new job.

- Greenberg's son, Jeffrey W. Greenberg, became CEO of Marsh & McLennan (MMC) in 1999 and chairman in 2000. The first plane of 9-11 flew directly into the secure computer room of Marsh (Kroll) USA, part of Greenberg's company. Mark Wood, an eyewitness, said: "It looked like a mid-sized executive jet and the way it turned suggested it was being aimed deliberately at a target."

• Lewis "Jerry" Bremer, the U.S. proconsul who ran occupied Iraq until the end of June 2004, joined Marsh Kroll's crisis group shortly after 9-11. Bremer had worked closely with Kissinger since the 1970s and was managing director at Kissinger Associates in 2001.

• Jerome M. Hauer, the former director of Mayor Giuliani's Office of Emergency Management, was responsible for having the command bunker built in Larry Silverstein's WTC 7. Hauer was a managing director for Kroll in 2001.

• Kroll was hired by Kuwait in October 1990 to find the hidden wealth of Saddam Hussein.

• Kroll began profiting from the war in Iraq in April 2003 when it received contracts to provide protection and security for government agencies and companies in Iraq.

• Kroll's son, Jeremy M. Kroll, is the Managing Director at Marsh Kroll and has served as General Manager at Kroll's Information Security Group (i.e. computer security). He is responsible for business and strategic development, business intelligence, investigations, forensic accounting, and security services, such as those Kroll provided to the Port Authority and the World Trade Center prior to 9-11.

• Jeremy Kroll is on the board of the Israel-based Challenge Fund together with the top brass from the Israeli military, including the head of Israel's National Security Council, a former head of Shin Bet, a former commander of the Israel Air Force, the head of Boeing (Israel), and the son of Yitzhak Shamir. The Challenge Fund raises money through the Bronfman and Andreas (ADM) families to fund Mossad companies, like ViryaNet.

Kroll & the Challenge Fund

The Challenge Fund is an Israeli intelligence funding operation, based in Israel and also known as Etgar, which means "challenge" in Hebrew. This fund connects the biggest players in the Zionist funding network in North America with the most senior officers in Israeli military intelligence. This is one of the key funding entities for Israeli intelligence operations in the United States.

The Challenge Fund was founded in July 1995. A second fund was established in 1999. The funds claim to have a capital base in excess of $200 million, "making them one of Israel's leading sources of private investment capital." Challenge Fund investors include "a highly distinguished group of American and European investors," primarily members of the extended Bronfman and Andreas families. Charles de Gunzburg, for example, a Bronfman cousin, is on the funds' "investment committee." Bronfman, which means distiller in Yiddish, is the family behind Seagram's, the Canadian whisky company.

Andreas is the family behind the grain broker Archer Daniels Midland (ADM). The funds are managed by the "Challenge Partners," a small team of "experienced professionals," all Israelis of course, headed by Joseph Ciechanover, the president of the funds and member of the "Investment Committee". Ciechanover is a former chairman of state-owned El Al Israel Airlines. Living in New York, he is also a member of the NASDAQ Advisory Board. He previously served as President of PEC Israel Economic Corporation [P for Palestine], which was later merged into I.D.B. Holding [Israel Discount Bank], a private investment and holding company.

Ciechanover served as Chairman of the Board of Israel Discount Bank, Israel's third largest commercial bank, and was a member of the Bank of Israel Advisory Committee. He also served as Director General of Israel's Ministry of Foreign Affairs, Head of Israel's Defense Mission to the United States and Canada, and General Counsel to the Israel Ministries of Defense and Agriculture. Ciechanover's daughter, Tamar, is a "managing partner" of the funds.

Another partner of the Challenge Funds is Maj. General Ilan Biran, the Chairman of the Board of Rafael Armament Development Authority Ltd. (since June 2007), former Director General of the Israeli Ministry of Defense, and president and CEO of Bezeq, the Israel Telecommunication Corp. During his military service, Biran served as Commander of the Central Command and the Technology and Logistic Branch of the IDF.

On the "advisory board" with Jeremy Kroll sit some of the most interesting people involved in the Challenge Funds. One is David Ivry, president of Boeing [Israel]. Ivry has held several senior military and diplomatic positions, including Commander of the Israel Air Force

(1977-82), an unprecedented ten-year period as Director General of the Ministry of Defense (1986-96), and Israel's chief representative to the U.S.-Israel Strategic Dialogue. Ivry moved from the highest position in the Ministry of Defense to become the Minister of Strategic Affairs at the Prime Minister's office from 1996 to 1999, and Ambassador to the U.S. from January 2000 through 2002. Ivry has twice served as Chairman of the Board of Israel Aircraft Industries (IAI).

In 1962, David Ivry became the commander of the first Israeli squadron of the French Dassault Mirage fighter jet. During the six-day war of 1967, Ivry served as a Mirage pilot and the commander of the Mystère squadron. Ivry was either personally involved in the criminal Israeli attack on the USS Liberty with Mirage fighters or commanded those who were. Thirty-four American servicemen lost their lives in the Israeli attack. From October 1977 to the end of 1982 [i.e. during the period of Israel's criminal aerial bombings on Lebanon], Ivry commanded the Israel Air Force (IAF). Ivry also directed the IAF's criminal destruction of the Osirak nuclear reactor in Iraq. Ivry has a history of directing criminal actions using aircraft.

Another member of the Challenge Fund advisory board is Jacob Perry (a.k.a. Yaacov Peri). Perry is another former head of the Shin Bet (Director GSS, 1988-94). In 1995, Perry left the secret service and "joined the business sector" with his appointment as president and CEO of Cellcom Israel Ltd., Israel's largest wireless telephone service provider.

Avi Naor (Aharonovich) of the Aurec Group and president and CEO of Amdocs is another member of the Challenge Fund's advisory board.

In addition to Ciechanover, the Challenge Fund has been managed by Yair Shamir, the son of Yitzhak Shamir. During his term in the Air Force, Yair Shamir "attained the rank of colonel and served as head of the electronics department, the highest professional electronics position within the Air Force," according to his biography.

These are the high-level Israeli military agents that worked with Jeremy Kroll on the "advisory board" of the Challenge Fund. It was through this complex network of connections with Kroll and Greenberg that Mossad finally gained control of security at the World Trade Center and was able to carry out 9-11, as Isser Harel had predicted in 1979.

I have been told by reporters that they will not report their own insights or contrary evaluations of the official 9-11 story, because to question the government story about 9-11 is to question the very foundations of our entire modern belief system regarding our government, our country, and our way of life. To be charged with questioning these foundations is far more serious than being labeled a disgruntled conspiracy nut or anti-government traitor, or even being sidelined or marginalized within an academic, government service, or literary career. To question the official 9-11 story is simply and fundamentally revolutionary. In this way, of course, questioning the official story is also simply and fundamentally American.

Lt. Col. Karen Kwiatkowski (USAF ret.), *9-11 and American Empire: Intellectuals Speak Out, Vol. 1* (2006)

Chapter VIII

The Media Cover-Up

The cover-up of the evidence of Israeli involvement in 9-11 and of explosions in the World Trade Center by the media is indicative of a high-level connection between the perpetrators of the "false flag" terror attacks and the media moguls who control the major news networks in the United States.

As a longtime observer of Israel and the Middle East, I have observed how the U.S. media has become less impartial about the Israeli-Arab conflict. As Zionists extended their grip on American media networks, the outlets under their control were turned into propaganda tools to manipulate U.S. public opinion. The anti-Arab bias of Hollywood films and news programs became more noticeable as Zionists achieved greater control of the U.S. mass media.

It needs to be understood that the Zionist conquest of the U.S. mass media is the result of a long-term strategy to control the news and entertainment networks that inform the American view of the Middle East. The Zionists realized that if they could control what Americans read, see, and hear about the Middle East, they could control how Americans think about the region. Controlling U.S. public opinion is crucial to the Zionist agenda.

The Zionist dominance of the major media networks has resulted in Americans getting an extremely distorted and biased view of the Middle East, 9-11, and the "War on Terror." Understanding the strategy and the people behind the Zionist control of the American mass media is an essential step to recovering our national sovereignty.

As an independent journalist, I have seen how Zionist-controlled media outlets have avoided the evidence of Israeli involvement in 9-11 and the "War on Terror." I have also been subjected to slander and defamation from Zionist-controlled news outlets, such as CNN and FOX News, because I have investigated these subjects.

Today, the United States of America has the appearance of being an Israeli-occupied state. The U.S. Congress dutifully authorizes an annual payment to Israel, some three thousand million dollars a year. Like a subservient colony, the United States also provides hundreds of thousands of young men and women to fight in Zionist-planned wars in the Middle East. This dismal situation is, of course, not new. It has only become more obvious and extreme. By 2010, the United States had provided more than $109 billion in direct aid to the state of Israel since 1949. Israel receives more than $8.2 million per day from the U.S. taxpayer, and this amount is increasing every year.

Thousands of Americans have died as a result of serving on or near the front lines of Israel's wars. The 241 American marines killed in the Beirut bombing of 1983 and the 34 servicemen killed during the 1967 Israeli attack on the USS Liberty are the first that come to mind. More than 4,500 American men and women died during the two decades of war against Iraq. The U.S.-led invasion and occupation of Iraq, an illegal war of aggression, was a Zionist-planned war in which Americans and others did the fighting, and dying.

The obvious question is where is the outrage? Where is the spiritual, intellectual, and political resistance to this blatant exploitation of Americans and their national resources by a foreign state with a militant and racist ideology? Why do patriotic Americans tolerate this abuse?

While the power of the Israeli lobby may explain the lack of any significant political resistance in the U.S. Congress to Zionist demands, it cannot explain how the American population has come to accept this unhealthy relationship with a foreign state. How has this foreign agenda been foisted upon the American people?

Zionist Deceptions

Many Americans willingly accept the one-sided and abusive relationship with Israel because they have internalized three fundamental Zionist deceptions, which have been pushed into their brains by the controlled mass media.

The first deception is a religious fraud that equates the modern Zionist state with Israel of the Bible. This misrepresentation elevates modern-day Israelis, regardless of their ethnicity, to being the rightful heirs of the Promised Land. While this deceit is obvious to those who have read the history, it is believed by millions of naïve and misled Christian Zionists.

The second fundamental deception is that Israel is a "sister democracy" of the United States and that Israelis and Americans share the same "democratic" values. This lie is also quickly exposed by reading Palestinian history or visiting Israeli-occupied Palestine. The only Americans who share Israeli values are those who believe in Jewish supremacism, the central pillar of Zionism.

The third deception is that nineteen Arab Muslims under the

leadership of Khalid Sheikh Mohammed and Osama Bin Laden were behind the 9-11 attacks at the World Trade Center and the Pentagon. This deception was used to usher in the Zionist-planned "War on Terror," which brought U.S. troops into an extensive and long-term war in the Middle East. While the first two deceptions are subjective in nature, the 9-11 deception is very real and something we accept at our own peril.

Why hasn't the media interviewed the families of the nineteen suspected hijackers to learn more about them? Why has the media not supported an open trial for Khalid Sheikh Mohammed, the alleged "mastermind" of 9-11, who is supposedly held by the U.S. in Guantánamo? Why is the media coverage of the 9-11 suspects so shallow?

These Zionist deceptions have been carefully planted and cultivated in the minds of millions through the influence of the Zionist-controlled media. Zionist domination of the mass media and academia in the United States is so pervasive that Americans are subjected, like the protagonist in the film *The Truman Show*, to a constant barrage of multi-level deception, as if the entire population were living in a false construct.

Like the false world of Truman Burbank, the Zionist deceptions are so prevalent that even when we peel away the layers and expose the fraud, the show continues. For the criminals in high places, after all, the show must go on.

The first deception, the sleight of hand that equates the Zionist state with biblical Israel, is doctrine to television evangelists. The second and third deceptions have become "conventional wisdom" for the U.S. news media. Those who have accepted and internalized these Zionist falsehoods are unable to understand the realities of the

Middle East or the massive fraud behind the "War on Terror." The controlled media is careful to censor any information that might expose the falseness of the Zionist worldview.

The highly-regarded Israeli historian Avi Shlaim wrote an editorial titled "Is Zionism today the real enemy of the Jews?" Shlaim's comments were published in February 2005 in the *International Herald Tribune* (IHT), which is read in 180 nations, but not in the pages of the *New York Times*, IHT's parent newspaper published in the United States. Why would the *New York Times* censor the viewpoint of a renowned Israeli historian writing about anti-Semitism? What did Shlaim say that the editors at the *Times* thought was unfit for its American readers?

"Israel's image today is negative not because it is a Jewish state but because it habitually transgresses the norms of acceptable international behavior. Indeed, Israel is increasingly perceived as a rogue state, as an international pariah, and as a threat to world peace," Shlaim wrote. "This perception of Israel is a major factor in the recent resurgence of anti-Semitism in Europe and in the rest of the world. In this sense, Zionism today is the real enemy of the Jews."

When one understands that the primary function of the Zionist-controlled media is to keep Americans in the dark about the Middle East and Zionism, it becomes clear why Shlaim's article was not published in the *New York Times*. Shlaim's critical comments about Israel would have disturbed the worldview of American Zionists, both Jews and Gentiles.

The Media Cover-Up of 9-11

As an independent journalist I have seen many important stories covered-up or ignored by the controlled media. I have written about many of these suppressed subjects, such as the sinking of the *Estonia*, the downing of TWA 800, electronic vote fraud, and depleted uranium. At the top of my list is the criminal cover-up of 9-11.

After the London press conference during Jimmy Walter's European 9-11 Truth Tour in 2005, two reporters from the BBC asked to interview me. "Why are you the only journalist who does not believe the official explanation of what happened on 9-11?" was their first question. "If that is the case," I told them, "it is probably due to the fact that others who have questioned the official version have lost their jobs as a result."

When FOX News and CNN interviewed me on the pretense that they were interested in my 9-11 research and evidence, all they really wanted to do was to try to smear me as an anti-Semite. In both cases the interviewers were clearly not interested in discussing the evidence or my research.

"Ninety-five percent of the work of the intelligence agencies around the world is deception and disinformation," German intelligence expert Andreas von Bülow told me in December 2001. This deception is widely propagated in the mainstream media creating an accepted version of events. "Journalists don't even raise the simplest questions," he said. "Those who differ are labeled as crazy."

"The dissident cannot be taken seriously," the veteran British journalist Roland Huntford wrote about the mass media in his book *The New Totalitarians*. "There is a range of tolerated opinions, and a narrow one it is: woe betide him who departs from it." While Hunt-ford was writing about the controlled media of Sweden in the 1970s, his comments are true for the Zionist-controlled mass media in the United States today, particularly when the subject is 9-11 or Israel.

I have paid a high price for writing about the evidence that con-tradicts the government's version of what happened on 9-11. The first attack came from the Anti-Defamation League of B'nai B'rith (ADL) in November 2001. The ADL, an organization of Jewish Freema-sonry dedicated to supporting Zionist interests, first smeared the newspaper I wrote for, as a "conspiratorial and anti-Semitic weekly newspaper," which it said had "repeatedly turned to the subject of the 9-11 attacks as grist for its mill." The ADL then singled me out for my article, "Some Survivors Say Bombs Exploded Inside WTC," in which, the ADL said, "Bollyn suggests that the 'mainstream media' is ignoring eyewitness accounts of bombs that exploded inside the World Trade Center before the collapse of the Twin Towers."

I did indeed as the first line of my article from September 2001 said:

> Despite reports from numerous eyewitnesses and experts, including news reporters on the scene, who heard or saw explosions immediately before the col-lapse of the World Trade Center, there has been vir-tual silence in the mainstream media.

But the real question is why would an organization supposedly dedicated to defending Zionist interests attack a journalist for writ-ing about eyewitness reports of explosions in the World Trade Cen-ter? What did my writing about this subject have to do with Israel? What's the connection?

Had I continued with the BBC interview, I might have asked why the BBC had censored the comments of their own reporter, Steven Evans, who had been in the South Tower when it was hit and who reported having observed a "series of explosions." Shortly after the destruction of the Twin Towers, the BBC interviewed Evans on their television news program. Because Evans' observations were ignored by the BBC, I wrote about his description of the explosions he felt in the South Tower:

> Evans was asked what he had seen: "It's more what I felt really," Evans said. "I was at the base of the second tower - the second tower that was hit. There was an explosion – I didn't think it was an explosion – but the base of the building shook. I felt it shake ... then when we were outside, the second explosion happened and then there was a series of explosions ..." [At this point the London news anchor cut Evans off in mid-sentence rather than listen to Evans continue to describe the "series of explosions" that he saw and felt. Evans' microphone was turned down.] But in a minute Evans returns to the "series of explosions" that he witnessed: "We can only wonder at the kind of damage – the kind of human damage – which was caused by those explosions – those series of explosions," Evans said.

Evans is a professional journalist and his observations of explosions in the South Tower should be taken into account. Many eyewitnesses reported similar explosions, but these reports have been censored by the agencies who are supposed to be investigating the collapses. The same kind of censorship occurred with FOX News, CNN, and the leading U.S. news networks. First-hand reports of explosions at the World Trade Center from professional reporters were broadcast only once and never repeated, except by the much-despised "conspiracy theorists."

The news reports that five Middle Eastern men had been arrested in New Jersey after they had videotaped themselves celebrating in front of the burning towers were treated in the same way. The arrest of the five men, all Israelis, two of them known Mossad agents, was only reported in the *Bergen Record* (New Jersey) on September 12, 2001, and never discussed or investigated by the national news networks.

Israelis Forewarned

Likewise, the reports about the Odigo text message warning of the attack at the World Trade Center were dropped into the media's memory hole. The message of warning, sent two hours before it occurred and precise to the minute, was sent via the Israeli-owned Odigo text messaging service and had been received by Odigo employees in Israel. Although the story was reported in the Israeli press and picked up by Brian McWilliams of Newsbytes on September 27, 2001, it was never followed-up and discussed by the major news networks.

How did the news editors at the BBC, FOX, CNN, and the leading networks decide to censor certain aspects of 9-11? Let's look at this logically. The 9-11 attack was probably the biggest story these news editors had ever handled. Suffice it to say that the editorial decisions about how to cover 9-11 were made by the boss at the top. Any decision to omit or censor reports about explosions at the World Trade Center or indications of Israeli prior knowledge would have been made by the senior executive of each network. In the case of CNN it would have been Gerald M. Levin, the CEO of Time Warner who acquired Turner Broadcasting in 1997. (Levin unexpectedly announced his resignation in December 2001, less than three months after 9-11.)

At FOX News the top decision maker would have been Rupert Murdoch, CEO of News Corporation. At ABC News it would have been Michael D. Eisner, CEO of Disney, the network's parent company. Were the media moguls Murdoch, Levin, and Eisner involved in the 9-11 conspiracy? How did they know that certain aspects of the event needed to be suppressed? Their networks have continued to suppress important information about 9-11 since 2001. It can be said that they have been actively involved in a conspiracy to cover-up the truth. Who is behind this cover-up by the media? What hidden hand would be able to communicate with these men and influence them to suppress important reports and evidence from 9-11?

Arnon Milchan – Mossad's Man in the Middle

If one considers the evidence of Israeli prior knowledge of 9-11, the Odigo text messages and the five arrested Mossad agents, for example, as indicative of Israeli involvement in the crime, the nature of the cover-up is obvious. The "hidden hand" suppressing the information about 9-11 would have to be a high-level person in the Israeli political-military establishment who has very close relations with media kingpins like Murdoch, Levin, and Eisner. Arnon Milchan is such a person. Could Milchan be the hidden hand?

"Kingpins like Warner Brothers' Gerald Levin and Disney's Michael Eisner are quick to return his calls," the American journalist Ann Louise Bardach wrote about Milchan in her article "The Last Tycoon" in April 2000.

While millions of Americans have seen his films, such as *Pretty Woman* and *JFK*, very few know that Arnon Milchan is a "best friend" of Shimon Peres, the Israeli president and godfather of Israel's nuclear arsenal. Milchan's close friendship with Peres, the man who oversaw the illegal development of Israel's nuclear weapon program, is key to understanding Milchan's career as an undercover operative, weapons procurer, and film producer. The fact that Milchan, the Hollywood producer, has been Israel's "foremost weapons procurer" for decades, brokering deals for "everything from nuclear triggers to rocket fuel to guidance systems," is seldom mentioned in the U.S. news media.

This is probably due to the fact that Milchan is also a "best friend" and business partner of Rupert Murdoch. He is also a friend and business partner with Levin (Warner Brothers) and Eisner. "I consider him one of my best friends," Milchan said about Murdoch, "and I think vice versa. We're having a ball. He's a very cool guy."

In 1997, after a six-year relationship with Warner Brothers, Milchan became a partner with Murdoch, selling him twenty percent of his film company, New Regency Productions, for $200 million. Murdoch also invested another $30 million in Regency Television. Today, Murdoch's equity partnership with Milchan is close to fifty percent. "Milchan's deal with Fox also assures him a level of financial security," Bardach wrote. "With Murdoch's $200 million investment and a subsequent $600 million line of credit from a team of banks led by Chase Manhattan, Milchan is well into mogul territory. "Milchan's tony offices occupy most of Building 12, right next door to the Executive Building on the Fox lot," Bardach wrote. "And it is from this seat of power that Milchan is building an entertainment empire that could one day rival Murdoch's."

The Milchan Influence

The Israeli influence in films and news media has profoundly affected the quality of news reporting and entertainment. Israeli attitudes and ideas are now disseminated through national media outlets which reach the entire U.S. population on a daily basis. Israeli-made films often contain hints or clues about actual crimes or plots the Israeli producers are aware of.

One such project, *The Lone Gunmen*, produced by Milchan's business partner Rupert Murdoch, bore an uncanny resemblance to the 9-11 attacks on the World Trade Center. Was this Milchan's influence? The Milchan-Murdoch partnership in television production may be the key to understanding the genesis of the plot of the pilot episode of this short-lived television series. In the first episode a passenger airliner is hijacked by remote control and flown toward the World Trade Center. Disaster is narrowly averted at the last second by over-riding the computer program that has been used to hijack the plane.

Given the close and extensive collaboration between Murdoch and Milchan, it seems fair to ask: Was Arnon Milchan the source of the plotline for *The Lone Gunmen*? Why were the people involved in the production of this episode not investigated by the media? Why did the media ignore the uncanny prescience shown by *The Lone Gunmen* episode when it became real six months later? Was the similarity between the Murdoch-produced show and reality too close for comfort? Was it too uncomfortable to discuss the origin of the plot for the show?

It seems very likely that Arnon Milchan was the author of the plot for *The Lone Gunmen* episode that bore an uncanny resemblance to 9-11. Milchan's first film, in which he invested two million dollars, featured a scene in which a passenger airliner was flown into a high rise building. The British/French film, *The Medusa Touch*, was released in 1978. The Jewish Baron Lew Grade, born Lev Winogradsky in the Ukraine, bought the foreign rights for *The Medusa Touch* before it was produced for $5 million, putting Milchan ahead by a million dollars.

For the Israeli super-agent Milchan to have produced a film that depicts an airliner flying into a high rise in the same year that the head of Israeli intelligence predicted that Arab terrorists would attack the tallest building in New York City seems a most unlikely coincidence. This was the period, after all, when the former terrorists from the Irgun came to power in Israel as the Likud party. The evidence points to this being the time when senior Israeli terrorists began planning 9-11. Milchan's movie was probably useful in visualizing and planning the false-flag attacks that occurred 23 years later.

In Milchan's highly-controversial film *JFK* (1991), directed by Oliver Stone, the assassination of President John F. Kennedy is ascribed to conspirators within the U.S. military-industrial complex. Whose idea was this? Why was Arnon Milchan's personal connection with Yitzhak Rabin, who was in Dallas on the day Kennedy was shot, not an issue?

In Milchan's futuristic film *Brazil* (1985), directed by Terry Gilliam, terrorist explosions go off in cafes for no apparent reason, very much like the senseless terrorism that has plagued occupied Iraq and Afghanistan. Could this also be Milchan's influence?

"Milchan runs his company like a family business. Heading up New Regency Productions for him is his childhood friend David Matalon, whose parents were best friends with Milchan's," Bardach wrote. "Daughter Alexandra [Milchan-Lambert] is vice president of production in Los Angeles." Matalon has served as president and CEO of New Regency Productions since 1995.

In 1986, Matalon, an Israeli co-founder of Tri-Star pictures, released a film entitled *Iron Eagle*, in which the aerial combat scenes were filmed entirely with the Israeli Air Force. The plot of this film is about how a few teenagers are able to steal U.S. military codes, aircraft, and information from under the noses of the military brass and run an entire military operation in which they bomb Libya without the knowledge of the military command. This film gives some indication of the kind of projects and ideas the Israeli military has collaborated on with their fellow Israelis in Hollywood.

The Secretive Mogul

"Averse to publicity and little known outside Hollywood" is how one biography of Milchan begins. "My idea of a good profile is no profile," he told Bardach. Murdoch, Levin, and Eisner have obviously respected the Israeli's wish, but why would a Hollywood mogul not want to be known? "Arnon Milchan has kept his secrets to himself," Bardach wrote.

Indeed, very little is known about Milchan, Israel's mega-agent, except that he spends more time in Tel Aviv and France than he does in his office on the 20th Century Fox lot in Los Angeles, according to Bardach. Why would a Hollywood movie producer spend more time in Tel Aviv than in Hollywood?

Zionist Roots

Milchan was born on December 6, 1944, on the Zionist settlement of Rehovot, in what was then Palestine, according to his biography in *Current Biography* (2000). Rehovot, one of the earliest Zionist settlements, was founded in 1890 by Polish and Russian Jews, one of whom was Milchan's paternal grandfather. Rehovot has a street and a neighborhood named "Milchen", no doubt in memory of his grandfather.

"My family's been there for 500 years," Milchan told Bardach. "My grandfather was a very close friend of President [Chaim] Weizmann." Oddly, Bardach does not provide the name of his grandfather who was "a very close friend" of Israel's first president. Nor does she give the name of the ancestors Milchan proudly claims have lived in Palestine for five hundred years. "Milchan's father was an enviable success story himself, having laid the sprinklers that irrigated Israel," Bardach wrote. "Later, he would handle some of Israel's lucrative military contracts, according to his son."

Bardach continues:

> However, it was young Milchan who put the company on the map internationally, after his father's sudden death. Following a spot of schooling in London and Geneva, where he excelled in soccer and tennis, Milchan dropped out and returned to Israel. Soon, he struck gold. By marketing a newly discovered nutrient that quadrupled citrus production, he brought his company stratospheric sales throughout the world.

> "This is a man who made his fortune by screwing

with nature," says screenwriter Shawn Slovo, who began her career as Milchan's secretary in 1977. "He's
the Israeli who made the desert bloom. Amazing
when you think about it. He could have retired at the
age of 22."

Instead, like a kid racing around the Monopoly board,
Milchan gobbled up another half dozen businesses—
including electronics, chemicals, aerospace and plas-
tics. Still in his early twenties, he met the Shah of Iran
and reportedly talked the wily Persian into dozens of
contracts, one to build much of Tehran's airport.

When one considers that Arnon Milchan, in his early twenties, was
among the founders of Israel's Labor Party in the 1960s with Shimon
Peres, Moshe Dayan, and Teddy Kollek, then one can appreciate that
his contracts in Iran and his career in arms dealing and Hollywood
have been done with the active collaboration of the Mossad.

"I'm an Agent"

Milchan is a "go-between for American weapons manufacturers and
the Israeli government, thus playing a major role in the strengthening
of the Israeli military," according to *Current Biography*. "Throughout
the 1970s, 1980s, and even up until the Gulf War in 1991, Milchan
was Israel's foremost weapons procurer, brokering deals for such
prized superweapons as the Hawk missile and the famous Scud-foil
of the Gulf War, the Patriot," Bardach wrote.

"At different times in his career, his Israeli company, Milchan
Brothers, has represented arms manufacturers such as Raytheon,

North American Rockwell, Beechcraft, Bell Helicopter and Mag-navox. Or, as Milchan downplays it, 'there were a bunch of them.' Nevertheless, he bristles at being called an arms dealer. 'I'm their rep in Israel,' he says emphatically. 'I get a fee, a commission. I'm not even the buyer. I'm an agent.'

"What we do is send my people to the United States," Milchan told Bardach, "so we know what these guys are talking about, and you go back and say to the buyer, 'I think this guy has some interesting stuff. Would you meet with him?' And then you arrange a meeting with the head of the [Israeli] air force and the head of this and the head of that."

In 1992, Milchan was described by the *Jerusalem Post* as be-ing "among the handful of Hollywood moguls with the muscle and money to single-handedly give the go-ahead for a new movie project. The Mossad is undoubtedly the source of much of Milchan's "muscle and money."

Who pays Milchan's commissions? Whether the commission is paid by the weapon's vendor or by the state of Israel, the money going to Milchan is American money. He is paid either by the company or from the billions of U.S. taxpayer dollars provided to Israel for weap-ons every year. In this way, Milchan, Mossad's man in the middle, has been greatly enriched by U.S. weapons sales to Israel.

"Big Star" to Raytheon

In 1975, for example, Milchan reportedly received an improper $300,000 commission paid by a Raytheon subsidiary for the sale of Hawk missiles. Raytheon makes the Patriot and Hawk missile sys-tems and key components of the Global Hawk. Of particular interest is Raytheon's Unmanned Aerial Systems (UAS) which allow remote operators to pilot the Global Hawk from "thousands of miles away." This is the kind of technology that is thought to have been used in the terror attacks of 9-11.

Terry Gilliam told Bardach that he'll never forget a visit to the Paris Air Show with Milchan during the filming of *Baron Munchausen*. "It was wonderful to see how the whole arms business worked," Gilliam said. "Arnon was very psyched about the video games. He brought his son with him, who was then a teenager, to play the games, which can replicate the destruction of the planet. He took me to the Raytheon booth, and it was all showmanship. He was obviously a big star to Raytheon."

When one looks at Milchan's career as an Israeli agent who bought media outlets with dirty money one should consider that this may be the modus operandi he has employed to gain influence in the U.S. media market. Money laundering could explain his ability to make huge deals and control media networks - and his desire for secrecy.

"He's extremely powerful because he brings money to the table," journalist Anita Busch wrote. "He's unique in that way. He's got a credit line that's astronomical, like, you know, almost a billion dollars." Terry Gilliam, the director of *Brazil*, wondered where the money came from. "Arnon can be great, but when it comes to money there's something - I don't know - bits just don't seem to connect."

Charles McKeown, a film writer, had a hard time getting paid by the billion-dollar Israeli. "You just never know whether he was telling the truth or not," McKeown said. "The kind of deals he was in, the level of finance and the way he operated, seemed to me like a world upside down. I felt we were dealing with a sort of dangerous, shady quality."

Money Laundering

In 1975, the Israeli government headed by Yitzhak Rabin and Defense Minister Shimon Peres recruited Milchan to launder money from South Africa. Milchan "has admitted laundering some of the more than $100 million spent by the South Africans during the 1970s in an attempt to improve the white government's image abroad," according to the authors of *The Iran-Contra Connection*. Because both Israel and South Africa were ostracized in the 1970s, "The money laundering was part of the two countries' plan to buy newspapers and other media in various parts of the world," his biography reads. "The Rabin government recruited ... Milchan to launder cash ... to purchase influential publications," Andrew and Leslie Cockburn wrote in their book *Dangerous Liaison*.

Milchan told Bardach he was asked by "prominent Israelis if 'we can use your companies to make deals to buy newspapers.' I said, 'Sure. It sounds like fun.' Basically, I was used as a middleman." A citizen of both Israel and Monaco, he is said to control thirty companies in seventeen countries, profiting in everything from film production to the weapons trade.

But how does one man control thirty companies in seventeen countries? Clearly there must be an entire team behind these businesses. Milchan's team might be called Mossad. "I'll say it in my own words," Milchan told Bardach. "I love Israel, and any way I can help Israel, I will. I'll do it again and again. If you say I'm an arms dealer, that's your problem. In Israel, there is practically no business that does not have something to do with defense."

Milchan funds Christian Zionist movements and has reportedly contributed significantly to the Christian Coalition, an organization started by the Reverend Pat Robertson, a staunch supporter of Israel. He also underwrites the Israeli Network which transmits Israeli television programs to the United States and Canada via cable and satellite.

Milchan is an owner of the Israeli television station known as Channel 10. The other owners are Ronald Lauder, who like Milchan owned about twenty-five percent, and Josef (Yossi) Maiman, who owns fifty-one percent and who has been with Channel 10 since it was founded in 2003. Rupert Murdoch bought nine percent of Channel 10 stock from Milchan and Lauder in 2006.

Josef Maiman, a Mossad agent, owns and controls a great deal of the gas fields of Turkmenistan. One of the main goals of the occupation of Afghanistan is to build a pipeline to bring the Israeli-owned gas of Turkmenistan to India and China. (Maiman and Lauder are both linked to the Mossad and 9-11. For more on Maiman read my 2001 article, "The Great Game: The War For Caspian Oil And Gas." Information about Lauder can be found in "Mossad -The Israeli Connection To 9-11")

Smuggling Nuclear Triggers

Milchan should have been busted in 1985 for smuggling triggers for nuclear bombs, when a business associate, Richard Kelly Smyth, was indicted by a federal grand jury in Los Angeles on charges of smuggling 810 krytrons to Israel. Because krytrons are used as detonators or triggers for nuclear weapons, their export is tightly regulated.

In 1973, Smyth started a company called Milco International, Inc., financed, according to the *Washington Post*, by Milchan, hence its name. Up to eighty percent of Milco's business was reportedly with

Milchan and Israel. In 1980, the federal indictment asserted, Smyth and Milco sent 610 krytrons to Israel without the necessary licenses, plus another 200 in 1982.

The 1985 indictment identified the Israeli buyers of the nuclear triggers as Heli Trading Ltd. and Milchan Brothers, two of Milchan's Israel-based companies. Federal authorities told NBC News in 1993 that Milchan shared in the profits derived from the sales.

Announcement of the indictments came four days after the Israeli Defense Ministry, reacting to news of the grand jury probe, admitted that it had the devices, known as krytrons. The krytrons were shipped between 1979 and 1983 to an Israeli firm under contract to the government for defense work. The Israeli Ministry of Defense returned only 469 of the krytrons, and Smyth vanished a week before he was to appear for trial.

Robert C. Bonner, the U.S. attorney in Los Angeles, refused to comment on questions about whether the Israeli government had been involved in the illegal actions. State Department spokesman Edward Djerejian said, "I can only note that the indictment does not mention any Israeli citizen."

Djerejian added that the United States "has expressed its serious concern to the Israeli government about this alleged violation of U.S. law" and had been assured that Israel would cooperate with the continuing U.S. investigation "to the full extent permitted under Israeli law."

"Smyth's disappearance, and the unwillingness of Israeli officials to cooperate with U.S. investigators on the case, left federal authorities unable to proceed," Robert Windrem of NBC News reported in July 2001. Although Milchan is not mentioned in the indictment, a Milco employee, Gretel Siler, who identified herself as corporate treasurer of Milco, told the *Washington Post* that Milchan had been associated with Milco in various export transactions and had been involved in purchasing the krytrons from the manufacturer, EG&G, of Wellesley, Massachusetts.

Milchan denied being involved in the $60,000 krytron deal, but told "60 Minutes" (CBS) that he had allowed the Israeli government to use his companies as conduits for trading with the United States. "I'm not saying I'm an innocent person - but in this specific case, I knew nothing about it," Milchan told Frank Rose of *Premiere* magazine. He was never charged in the case.

Robert Mainhardt, a nuclear scientist and former director of Milco, told "60 Minutes" that he had resigned after Milchan had asked him to obtain advanced nuclear reactor designs and a supply of uranium hexachloride, which is used in the enrichment of bomb-grade uranium. Mainhardt's fellow directors at Milco, Arthur Biehl and Ivan Getting, began to feel uneasy sometime in 1982, according to the *Washington Post* which did a series of articles about the Israeli smuggling. The most important excerpts are the following:

> When they joined the board of directors of Milco International in 1980, Biehl and Getting recalled, they thought the company's primary business was developing aerospace software for U.S. military and space programs. They had been recruited by the company's owner, Richard K. Smyth, while serving with him on an influential panel that advises the U.S. Air Force on advanced technologies, work that required them to have top-secret clearances.

But they soon realized that Smyth, a California-based computer expert, spent most of his time trying to buy equipment with military applications, including a uranium byproduct known as "green salt" that can be processed into weapons-grade uranium, for the government of Israel. Often, they said, the sales were made through an Israeli middleman, Arnon Milchan, a flamboyant businessman who sold arms before becoming a producer of such popular movies as the recent *Brazil.*

"I didn't have any evidence there was anything improper," Biehl said. "I just thought it was a strange way to do business.... I wondered why the Israelis were paying fees to (Milco and Milchan) when they could get the same equipment directly" using U.S. foreign aid.

In late 1982, Biehl and Getting resigned from Milco's board of directors, in part because of their misgivings about Smyth's dealings with Milchan and Israel.

Asked why Israel didn't buy the krytrons through its 200-member procurement staff in New York, which buys military equipment with $1.8 billion in annual U.S. aid, Yossi Gal, spokesman with the Israeli Embassy in Washington, D.C., told the *Post* that Israel occasionally used "independent agents" to make purchases.

Under U.S. laws, Smyth needed a munitions license from the State Department to ship the krytrons overseas. If he had tried to obtain one, according to a knowledgeable State Department source, he would have been turned down because Israel has not signed the Nuclear Nonproliferation Treaty.

Smyth's relations with Israel began in the early 1970s when he was working for North American Rockwell as a chief engineer in its avionics division and traveled to Israel to help set up a subsidiary. There, he met Milchan, who was Rockwell's representative and "point man" with the Israeli government, according to an associate of Smyth from that period.

In January 1973, Smyth founded Milco while still working at Rockwell. His associate recalled Smyth once saying that Milchan provided money to start Milco; this associate said he believes that the name Milco was derived from Milchan.

At the time that Milco was founded, former U.S. intelligence officials said, the Central Intelligence Agency knew that Israel was working to perfect a solid-fuel tactical missile, known as the Jericho that could carry nuclear warheads. In late 1973, Smyth's associate recalled, he saw Milco order forms for several barrels of a butyl compound used to bind explosive powders into solid rocket fuel. Smyth said he was shipping the butyl to Milchan through another company he owned in Houston, the associate recalled.

Smyth's next known contact with Israel occurred in 1975, about a year after he left Rockwell to run Milco full time. On Oct. 30 of that year, Smyth applied for a munitions license to ship 400 krytrons to Heli Trading Inc., Milchan's company in Israel.

The application, which is filed in court records in Los Angeles, said that the "end user" would be Rehovot Instruments Ltd. and that the krytrons would be used as "remotely located intrusion detectors."

Smyth filed the application after being told by an official from an unnamed U.S. intelligence agency that a license was required, according to court records. Smyth met with the official and told him that "Arnon Milchan [had] requested that a certain number of krytrons be shipped to Israel," according to a letter filed by William Fahey, the prosecutor in the current case.

Internal Milco records, provided by former Smyth associates, show that the company struggled financially from 1975 to 1980. It landed several small contracts for less than $25,000 with the National Aeronautics and Space Administration and the Air Force for studies on computer software for avionics systems in advanced aircraft, the MX missile and a small ship defense missile called the Patriot.

It was also in 1980, the federal indictment alleged, that Milco sent 610 krytrons to Israel in 11 shipments without obtaining the needed licenses. Smyth bought them from EG&G in Salem, Mass., the sole producer of the switches in the United States.

In mid-1981, Smyth listed several contracts with Heli Trading to acquire training simulators for Hawk air defense missiles, a voice scrambler and lasers. He also cited "probable" contracts for a computerized flight control system for Israel's Lavi fighter plane, and thermal batteries and gyroscopes.

James Russell, vice president of Incosym Inc., a maker of gyroscopes in Thousand Oaks, Calif., said he sold Milco several $10,000 gyroscopes in that period. Smyth told him the navigation aids would be used on Israeli navy patrol boats. Milco also won a flight control contract for the Lavi in 1983, according to a listing in *Aviation Week* magazine.

Smyth's world started to crumble in early 1983 after someone broke into Milco's offices and took several thousand dollars worth of computer and software equipment. Because he was doing some classified U.S. government work and feared some records of it might have been stolen, Smyth wrote a lengthy report about the theft for the Pentagon and the Federal Bureau of Investigation, then-company attorney Brian R. Carter said.

Milco company records revealed that Milchan's companies had ordered large quantities of missile-related equipment and materials between 1977 and 1982. Among the nuclear items listed were the 810 krytrons, plus neutron generators, high-speed oscilloscopes and high-voltage condensers, according to a 1996 paper on Israel's Nuclear Weapon Capability by the Wisconsin Project on Nuclear Arms Control.

In August 1985, U.S. Customs subpoenaed the financial records linking Smyth and Milchan. The records were neither turned over nor found. Smyth and his wife disappeared just days before his scheduled trial, which almost certainly would have involved Milchan. "There were so many...indictments that they probably decided just to get out," Mainhardt, who operates a security business in Dublin, California, said. "If I had to make a guess, I'd say they're in Israel."

"Let's assume that there's nothing that Israel and the United States do separately," Milchan told Bardach. "Smyth, a U.S. fugitive for more than a decade, was last seen in Herzliya Pituach, an affluent suburb of Tel Aviv, where Milchan owns a home," Bardach wrote in 2000. In July 2001, Smyth was arrested in Malaga, Spain. Smyth pleaded guilty in December to one count of violating the Arms Export Control Act and one count of making a false statement to Customs agents. Proscutors dropped twenty-eight other counts.

On April 29, 2002, Smyth was sentenced to forty months in federal prison and fined $20,000 for illegally exporting to Israel the devices that are used as triggers for nuclear weapons. Smyth, 72, was immediately made eligible for parole at his sentencing.

Milchan and Peres

"In Israel, Milchan spends much of his time with best friend Shimon Peres," Bardach wrote. She continued, "Milchan's political connections would prove to be the foundation of his future empire. In addition to agriculture, there would be biotechnology, advertising, aerospace, and the biggest jackpot of them all — arms."

In 1953, at age thirty, Shimon Peres was appointed by Israel's first prime minister, David Ben Gurion, to become Director-General of the Ministry of Defense. Within three years, Peres had laid the foundation for Israel's nuclear weapon program, according to the Wisconsin Project on Nuclear Arms Control. Peres started Israel's program to develop nuclear weapons by convincing the French to help Israel build a secret nuclear reactor beginning about 1957. He chose France as the major supplier, arranged the sale of a nuclear reactor, and spent the next decade overseeing the construction of the Dimona nuclear weapon production complex.

An Israeli-written biography entitled *Confidential: The Life of Secret Agent turned Hollywood Tycoon - Arnon Milchan* was published in 2011. *Confidential* revealed that Milchan was the "most productive asset" for a super-secret cell, created by Shimon Peres, within the Mossad known as LAKAM:

> Immediately upon embarking on the massive, covert Israeli version of the Manhattan Project, Peres (who is today a Nobel Peace laureate) realized that he would have to deceive people on a large scale to avoid discovery... He also realized that the program would need to gain access to material and equipment that was not easily obtainable on the open market, and that few countries would be willing to sell such material to Israel.

> To overcome these complex and daunting problems, Peres decided to create a new top-secret agency, a unit so secret that even Israel's vaunted intelligence agency, the Mossad, would not be aware of its existence for years to come, even though it operated right under its very nose.

In the early 1970s, the unit would adopt the name Science Liaison Bureau, or LAKAM, its Hebrew acronym, and was nicknamed "Mossad II." Its original narrow mission was to secure the materials and the equipment that would make the production of nuclear bombs possible.

The close working relationship between Milchan and [Benjamin] Blumberg was exceedingly productive, and much of it will never be known... When Blumberg needed a thousand tons of ammonium perchlorate, Butarez, carbon-carbon, inertial-grade gyros and accelerometers, precision tracking radars, and other such basic material required by anyone seeking to develop a nuclear deterrent, it was Milchan he would call.

Milchan's constant movement between countries and continents make him an elusive target for any counterintelligence effort against him, and it made him the most productive asset for LAKAM and for the State of Israel.

In *Confidential*, the Israeli authors who are close to Milchan say that he and Shimon Peres are "strategic partners" and "holders of some of Israel's most significant secrets." Chief among these secrets would certainly be how Israeli agents carried out the false-flag terror attacks of 9-11.

Now it has emerged that Kuwaiti national Khalid Shaikh Mohammed did indeed perish in the raid, but his wife and child were taken from the apartment and handed over to the Federal Bureau of Investigation (FBI), in whose hands they remain.

Syed Saleem Shahzad, "A chilling inheritance of terror," *Asia Times*, October 30, 2002

David E. Klett, a retired professor of thermodynamics, had the real KSM in several of his classes. Asked about the photos of the person said to be the terror mastermind, Klett said, "I did not recognize that person. I never saw that face before."

Christopher Bollyn, "The Absence of Justice for 9-11 Victims", March 20, 2007

Chapter IX

The Secluded "Mastermind of 9-11"

In April 2011 the U.S. government said that Khalid Sheikh Mohammed (KSM), the alleged "Mastermind of 9-11", would not stand trial
in an open court in the United States but would face a military commission at Guantánamo, where he had reportedly been tortured 183
times in 2003. President Barack Obama was reneging on his campaign promises, but he has good reasons for not letting KSM face trial
in an open court. Putting KSM on trial would expose the pack of lies
behind 9-11 and the "War on Terror", which is something the administration's Zionist handlers would never let happen.

Six months earlier, on the ninth anniversary of the "War on Terror," the lead editorial of the global edition of the *New York Times*
had suggested that the accused "Mastermind of 9-11", Khalid Sheikh
Mohammed, would probably never be put on trial. These comments
from the *New York Times* were found in its editorial entitled "Military
Injustice", a piece that was published in the New York edition on October 6, 2010:

> There are more than 170 inmates left in Guantánamo.
> Only 36 have been referred for prosecution, some very
> dangerous men. Forty-eight are in a long-term deten-
> tion that is certainly illegal. Almost all the rest are in

limbo while the Obama team tries to figure out what to do. The chances are dimming every day that prisoners like Khalid Sheikh Mohammed, mastermind of the 9-11 attacks, will ever be brought to justice.

The only inmate on trial in Guantánamo is Omar Khadr, a Canadian who was accused at age 15 of killing an American soldier in Afghanistan. He has been held in extralegal detention for more than eight years, and the military has been attempting to try him since 2005. The thin evidence against him is tainted by his credible allegations of abuse.

This was the first time, to my knowledge, that a newspaper of record like the *New York Times* acknowledged what I had said for years: the U.S. government would probably never put the man they claim is the "Mastermind of 9-11" on trial. Go figure.

The editors of the *New York Times*, however, didn't give the real reason why the man accused of being the mastermind of 9-11 would not face trial in an open court. For that information one would have to read the articles I have written on this subject. The basic reason that there will never be trial is because the suspect being held at Guantánamo is neither Khalid Sheikh Mohammed nor the "Mastermind of 9-11", and the U.S. government and military are well aware of that.

The government's claim that it has the "Mastermind of 9-11" appears to be a hoax, as I explained in March 2007:

The person who is said to be Khalid Sheikh Mohammed (KSM) clearly does not appear to be the person who masterminded the attacks of 9-11. It does not appear that he has ever masterminded anything. He seems to be an imposter, a feeble-minded "fall guy," who has been tortured and whose mind has been manipulated in order to make these incredible claims.

In October 2010 the *New York Times* was floating the idea to prepare public opinion for the outcome I had predicted since March 2007. There would be no trial, I wrote, for the so-called "Mastermind of 9-11" because the U.S. does not have Khalid Sheikh Mohammed, who was reported to have been killed in Karachi, Pakistan on September 11, 2002:

> KARACHI - Ever since the frenzied shootout last month on September 11 in Karachi there have been doubts over whether Khalid Shaikh Mohammed, the self-proclaimed head of al-Qaeda's military committee, died in the police raid on his apartment...
>
> Now it has emerged that Kuwaiti national Khalid Shaikh Mohammed did indeed perish in the raid, but his wife and child were taken from the apartment and handed over to the Federal Bureau of Investigation (FBI), in whose hands they remain...
>
> But now it emerges that an Arab woman and a child were taken to an ISI safe house, where they identified the Shaikh Mohammed's body as their husband and father. The body was kept in a private NGO mortuary for 20 days before being buried, under the surveillance of the FBI, in a graveyard in the central district of Karachi.

The widow subsequently underwent exhaustive interrogation in the custody of FBI officials, during which she revealed details of people who visited her husband, and of his other contacts and plans. News of the death of Khalid Shaikh Mohammed was intentionally suppressed so that officials could play on the power of his name to follow up leads and contacts.
- "A chilling inheritance of terror" by Syed Saleem Shahzad, *Asia Times*, October 30, 2002

Nine years after 9-11, however, the U.S. government was still claiming that it had the "Mastermind of 9-11" and that he was in "legal limbo" in Guantánamo. Why would they do that? If they had a case against the man they claim to be Khalid Sheikh Mohammed, why didn't they make it? What were they waiting for? Why was the 9-11 criminal process being obstructed, just like the tort litigation had been?

When Attorney General Eric Holder was interviewed on *Face the Nation* on July 11, 2010, he gave poor excuses for the U.S. government's failure to hold a trial for the so-called "Mastermind of 9-11." Who does Attorney General Eric Himpton Holder really represent? Why is he unwilling to put the alleged mastermind of 9-11 on trial?

"After fourth grade, my schools were largely white, predominantly Jewish," Eric Holder said about his education. Holder not only studied with Jews at Stuyvesant High School, his family vacationed with the most elite Jewish Zionist families in the United States. Ancestry.com has records of the Holder family returning from Bermuda on a BOAC flight in April 1956 with the family of the mega-Zionist Edward Warburg. Warburg's mother was the only daughter of Jacob

Schiff. Eric Holder's close relationship with high-level Zionists may be behind his appointment to serve as U.S. Attorney General.

The Black Hole of Guantánamo

An Associated Press news story of July 31, 2010, entitled "U.S. Stalls on Sept. 11 Trial for 5 at Gitmo", reported on the "black hole" in which the alleged mastermind of 9-11 has been hidden. A black hole is a dark spot in the universe from which even light cannot escape. Why would the terror mastermind of 9-11 be held in a legal "black hole" created by the U.S. government?

> As the U.S. military prepares for the first war crimes trial under President Barack Obama, its most high-profile case against the planners of the Sept. 11 attacks is stuck in political and legal limbo.
>
> Canadian prisoner Omar Khadr, accused of killing an American soldier during a raid on an al-Qaida compound, is scheduled to go to trial Aug. 9 at the U.S. base in Cuba.
>
> But Khalid Sheikh Mohammed, the professed mastermind of the attacks, and four alleged accomplices are still sequestered at Guantánamo without charges. The Obama administration, after months of review, hasn't made a decision on whether to seek a military or civilian trial...
>
> "There's no case, there's no judge, there's nothing," said Navy Lt. Cmdr. Richard Federico, a military lawyer appointed to defend alleged plotter Ramzi

bin al Shibh. "They are back into the black hole."
– "U.S. Stalls on Sept. 11 Trial for 5 at Gitmo" by Ben
Fox, AP, July 31, 2010

This is a hoax I have written about for years. Quoting from news reports, I wrote about the resistance from Mayor Michael Bloomberg to having a 9-11 trial in New York City in February 2010:

On February 7, 2010, President Barack Obama acknowledged fierce opposition to his plans to bring accused 9-11 mastermind Khalid Sheikh Mohammed (KSM) to justice in New York, but would not rule out such a trial. The Obama administration said that it wants to prosecute Sheikh Mohammed and four co-defendants in a federal court in lower Manhattan, close to the site of the World Trade Center attack which killed nearly 3,000 people in 2001.

But the plan faced opposition from local lawmakers and authorities who have balked at the huge costs of such a trial, while others warned of perceived security implications.

"I have not ruled it out, but I think it is important for us to take into account the practical logistical issues involved," Obama said in a live interview from the White House on CBS. "If you have got a city that is saying no, and a police department that is saying no, and a mayor that is saying no, that makes it difficult," Obama said.

But he added: "we have not ruled out anything — we will make a definitive judgement based on consultations with all the relevant authorities." Mayor Bloomberg initially welcomed the idea of holding a September 11 trial in New York, but reversed his position last month, saying that a military base would make more sense as a venue.

"It's going to cost an awful lot of money and disturb an awful lot of people," Bloomberg said. "Can we provide security? Yes. Could you provide security elsewhere? Yeah, and I mean the suggestion of a military base is probably a reasonably good one."

"After a dinner in New York on Dec. 14, Steven Spinola, president of the Real Estate Board of New York, pulled aside David Axelrod, President Obama's closest adviser, to convey an urgent plea: move the 9/11 trial out of Manhattan," the *New York Times* reported on January 29, 2010.

I was not at all surprised to read that officials in New York City took David Axelrod aside and told him that the city could not allow the trial of Khalid Sheikh Mohammed and other 9-11 suspects to go ahead. I never expected that this trial would go ahead in anything resembling an open court. It is clear that a trial for the so-called "Mastermind of 9-11" cannot go ahead. The media discussion about the high cost of security is just a cover story. The FBI and the U.S. government do not want it to be exposed that a scapegoat has been used to push the fraudulent "War on Terror."

The Obama administration will not have an open 9-11 trial because it would expose the fraud that the person said to be Khalid Sheik Mohammed is not the terror mastermind of 9-11. The person said to be KSM is more likely a "feeble-minded" man named Ahmed Abdul Qudoos who has been scapegoated and made to fill in for the real KSM, who was killed in Pakistan a year after 9-11.

The U.S. government cannot hold an open trial in the United States with the false KSM because there are people in the United States who knew and remember the real KSM, such as his former teachers in North Carolina. As I wrote in 2007:

Furthermore, the real KSM was a person who had traveled and worked extensively across Asia and had lived in many foreign countries, from the United States to the Philippines to Bosnia. With this level of education and foreign travel, the real KSM would have a much greater command of the English language than what we find in the transcript.

There were no defense attorneys or members of the press allowed to the secret hearing in which the military tribunal heard the confession of the alleged architect of 9-11.

"The Detainee served as the head of the Al Qaida military committee and was Osama bin Laden's principal Al Qaida operative who directed the 11 September 2001 attacks in the United States," the statement said.

"I was responsible for the 9-11 operation, from A to Z," the detainee said through an interpreter, according to the transcript of the hearing. He also claimed responsibility for the 1993 bombing at the World Trade Center.

The detainee sat with an Arabic interpreter to his left and a U.S. military officer who was his official representative to his right.

"I not take the oath..." the detainee said in broken English about why he was not taking an oath in the court. "Just to explain for this one, does not mean I'm not saying that I'm lying. When I not take oath does not mean I'm lying."

"I understand," the tribunal president said.

But how can such meaningless gibberish coming from an unidentified detainee who has not taken an oath be seen by anyone as a credible confession?

No photographs accompanied the release of the KSM confession and there are very few photos of the person who is accused of being the terrorist mastermind of our time.

To see if the disheveled, hairy, and overweight person said to be Khalid Sheikh Mohammed resembled the mechanical engineering student that studied in Greensboro in the 1980s, I contacted the engineering faculty of North Carolina Agricultural and Technical University.

David E. Klett, a retired professor of thermodynamics, had the real KSM in several of his classes. Asked about the photos of the person said to be the terror mastermind, Klett said, "I did not recognize that person. I never saw that face before."

The Israeli newspaper *Ma'ariv* on Wednesday reported that Likud leader Benjamin Netanyahu told an audience at Bar Ilan university that the September 11, 2001, terror attacks had been beneficial for Israel.

"We are benefiting from one thing, and that is the attack on the Twin Towers and Pentagon, and the American struggle in Iraq," *Ma'ariv* quoted the former prime minister as saying. He reportedly added that these events "swung American public opinion in our favor."

"Netanyahu says 9-11 terror attacks good for Israel,"
Haaretz, April 16, 2008

Chapter X

Who Controls
Our Political Parties?

I spent several years in the Middle East and studied the history of Palestine and Zionism, i.e. Jewish nationalism. It is from this perspective that I approached the evidence of Israeli and Zionist involvement in 9-11. My investigation yielded a great deal of evidence of Israeli involvement in the false-flag terror attacks.

For journalists working in the controlled media, pursuing such investigations would be "career suicide," as many learned after 9-11. Most journalists, lawyers, and politicians are primarily interested in advancing their careers and learn to accept the yoke of their masters. Ambitious people put their self-interest first and agree to go along with lies and corruption rather than stand up for the truth. I've seen it many times.

I am not like that. During the past thirty years, I have witnessed first-hand the extremely brutal Israeli occupation of Palestine and seen how Zionists have subjugated an entire nation. I have seen how the population of the United States has been deceived by the Zionists who control its political system and media while thousands of Americans have been maimed or killed in their fraudulent wars in Afghanistan and Iraq.

American voters weren't given a choice about the on-going U.S. military intervention in the Middle East during the presidential elections of 2004 and 2008 as the leading candidates from both parties supported the wars. In 2008 both leading candidates supported the $700 billion "bail-out," which gave enormous sums of taxpayer money to private investment bankers and A.I.G., headed by the financial criminal Maurice R. Greenberg.

Unfortunately, it is usually the case that the presidential candidates are pro-war and pro-Israel. This is because both parties in the United States are financed and controlled by Zionists. Their control of our political parties compels candidates from both parties to support Israel, a foreign state based on a racist ideology of Jewish supremacy. What kind of patriotic American could support that?

"The Opinion that Prevails"

Jean-Jacques Rousseau wrote in *The Social Contract*: "It is therefore important, if the general will is to be properly ascertained, that there should be no partial society within the state, and that each citizen should decide according to his own opinion. When one of the associations is big enough to triumph over all the others the outcome is no longer the sum total of small differences, but a single difference, then there is no longer any general will, and the opinion that prevails is only a particular opinion."

Zionism is the "partial society" that triumphs over all the others in American politics today. In the United States, the pro-Israeli position is the only "opinion that prevails" in academia, the mass media, and the political parties with no consideration for the expense, injustice, and violence that it causes. American political support for Zionism has clearly been detrimental for the United States of America, yet the support continues without question. How does this happen?

Mossad Spied on Haider

Israel and the international Zionists control the political parties and news outlets not only in the United States, but in Europe as well, as the death of Austria's Jörg Haider revealed. Oddly, Haider, the leader of Austria's Freedom Party, had a Mossad agent named Peter Sichrovsky serving as "secretary-general" of the Austrian populist party. In 2005, *The Times* (UK) reported that Sichrovsky, the managing director of the party, had served as a spy for Israel's Mossad for five years. Three years later, after his party won parliamentary elections, Haider was suddenly killed in a very suspicious car accident.

"I wanted to help Israel and certainly did not do anything wrong," Sichrovsky said. "It's true, though, that I co-operated with Mossad until my withdrawal from politics in 2002." Sichrovsky admitted that he had spied for Mossad, a foreign intelligence agency, because he "wanted to help Israel." At the same time he maintained that he had done nothing wrong. This is exactly how many Jews feel about supporting Israel, even when their actions involve breaking the laws of the nations they reside in.

Facing a criminal investigation and charges of spying for a foreign power, Sichrovsky quickly fled to the United States where he began a new career as "a businessman concerned with military co-operation between Israel and China." Sichrovsky's career with Mossad evidently continued after he left Austria.

If Mossad infiltrates "third party" movements in small nations like Austria, imagine what they do to control the political parties in the United States. How much control does Israeli intelligence have over the major political parties in Britain and the United States? Let's look at the most obvious connections.

Mossad Controls Britain

The evidence indicates that Israeli intelligence has near complete control of the leading political parties in Britain and the United States. While the Zionist political controllers in London and Washington are well known to the owners of the mass media, discussion of the subject of Zionist or Israeli control of the parties is censored in the media outlets they control.

Specific examples of the pro-Israel bias in the media would include the media's unquestioning support of the 9-11 cover-up, the costly and disastrous wars in Iraq and Afghanistan, and the trillion dollar "bail-out." The complete lack of transparency in U.S. elections and the secretive private companies that run the electronic voting machines are censored subjects in the controlled press.

The Israeli-conceived fraud known as the "War on Terror" and the illegal wars in Iraq and Afghanistan have been designed and forced onto the American and British nations by Zionists who control the political systems of London, New York, and Washington. In Britain, the two political leaders who have promoted and supported the Zionist agenda and wars of aggression are Tony Blair and Gordon Brown. Their Zionist paymasters and handlers are not hard to discern, although they are never discussed in the media in such terms.

"Lord Cashpoint"

Michael Abraham Levy, or "Lord Levy," was known as "Lord Cashpoint" when he was the leading fundraiser for the Labour Party from 1994 to 2007. Described as "a long-standing friend of Tony Blair," Levy served as Blair's special envoy to the Middle East from 1998 until 2007, when he was replaced by Gordon Brown's appointee, Michael Williams.

Levy's son Daniel, an Israeli citizen since 1991, has held high-level positions in Israeli governments since 1995. While his father was bankrolling and managing Tony Blair, the younger Levy was a member of the Israeli team during the "Oslo 2" negotiations in the summer of 1995 under Prime Minister Yitzhak Rabin. He was also a member of the Israeli delegation to the Palestinian summit at Taba in January 2001.

The younger Levy served as senior policy adviser to former Israeli Minister of Justice, Yossi Beilin, from March 2000 to March 2001. Under Ehud Barak, Levy served as the prime minister's special adviser and head of the Jerusalem Affairs unit. The Levy link was obviously the connection that gave Israeli intelligence access to the head of the British government, Tony Blair.

"We Have to do Iraq"

Before the Anglo-American occupation of Iraq turned sour, Blair was fond of recalling what he, the first foreign leader to meet George W. Bush, told the newly installed president when they met in early 2001. "We have to do Iraq," was the first thing Blair told Bush, according to his own statements. Only by understanding that Blair and his New Labour Party were financed and controlled by Israeli interests can one understand how Blair was manipulated to support such a reckless and criminal scheme. Similar Zionist forces were at work on Bush.

When Tony Blair fell from power in June 2007, Gordon Brown, the Chancellor of the Exchequer, assumed the office of prime minister, upon the approval of Queen Elizabeth II. Prior to becoming prime minister, Brown had served ten years as Chancellor of the Exchequer, the minister responsible for economic and financial matters in Britain.

Prime Minister Brown, in turn, was bankrolled and controlled by Lord Ronald Cohen, who replaced the beleaguered and disgraced Lord Levy. The Egyptian-born Cohen was described as "Sir Ronald Cohen, the daddy of England's private equity industry and a bosom buddy of Prime Minister Gordon Brown."

In the British press Cohen was portrayed as a wealthy Jewish supporter of Brown and New Labour. Cohen's third wife, the Los Angeles-born Sharon Harel-Cohen, is usually described as a film producer whose father, Yossi Harel, commanded the Jewish refugee ship that became known as *Exodus* in 1947. Her Israeli nationality is seldom discussed.

What the controlled media doesn't tell us about Sharon Harel-Cohen is that she is an Israeli-American whose father was one of the founding chiefs of the Mossad and Israeli military intelligence until his death in April 2008. This means the daughter of one of the founders of Israeli intelligence is part of the team that controlled the British prime minister. This is how Mossad has controlled the political leadership of Britain since the 1990s and taken the United States and Britain into two costly and disastrous wars in the Middle East.

Sharon Ruth Harel was born in Los Angeles on March 6, 1952. Her mother, a "Julie Berez" married Mossad officer Joseph Hamburger (a.k.a. Yossi Harel) in 1950 while he was stationed in Los Angeles. Harel was, most likely, engaged in the illegal procurement of weapons, ships, planes, and military technology for the Israeli military. The reports that Harel, one of the highest Mossad agents, was studying at UCLA or M.I.T. are neither substantiated nor credible; this may have been his cover. Harel also had two sons.

The Mossad actually came into existence in the 1940s as the clandestine agency known as Ha'Mossad Le'Aliya Bet, the secret Zionist agency engaged in bringing Jewish refugees to British-occupied Palestine to swell the Jewish population prior to creating the "Jewish state." In 1946, Joseph Hamburger was sent on a secret mission to provide Mossad agents in Greece with gold to bribe European governments to facilitate the transit of Jews to Palestine, which was then illegal. Some Mossad tactics have not changed in the past sixty years; they still buy politicians with gold.

Joseph Hamburger (a.k.a. Yossi Harel) commanded four refugee ships and sailed to Israel with an estimated 25,000 immigrants during the period of the British Mandate. U.S. immigration records indicate that Mr. Hamburger used both his real name, Hamburger, and his Israeli name, Harel, during the 1950s, which is typical of Mossad agents.

His 2008 obituaries say that "Yosef" Hamburger was born, with a twin brother, in Jerusalem, British-occupied Palestine, in 1918. At the age of fifteen he joined the Haganah, the Zionist militia/terrorist group. Five years later he joined the Special Night Squad, an anti-Palestinian terrorist unit. In 1941, Harel joined the Palmach, the "strike force" of the Haganah before transferring to the Palyam, its naval unit.

During the 1948 Zionist war to conquer Palestine, Harel served as the liaison officer to the army's chief of staff, Yaakov Dori, and played an important role in coordinating the Zionist campaign. He was also the personal body guard for Israel's first president, Chaim Weizmann.

In 1954, Moshe Dayan, chief of staff of the Israeli Defense Forces, called Harel back to Israel to head Unit 131, a secret group that had agents in Arab countries. Harel's immediate task was to cover up the Lavon Affair, the Israeli false-flag terrorism plot designed to turn Britain and the United States against Egypt.

David Ben-Gurion, the first Israeli prime minister, assigned Harel to rebuild military intelligence from the ground up. Ben-Gurion, Dayan, and Shimon Peres were actually part of the group that supported the use of false-flag terrorism, such as the Lavon bombings, to achieve their goals. Given this context, Harel must have seen eye-to-eye with Ben-Gurion about deploying Israeli agents in foreign nations. Shiploads of Israelis were sent on missions to America and Europe in the 1950s, often disguised as students. Harel went on to pursue a successful business career, the *Telegraph* reported, "which served as a cover for his work for Israeli intelligence."

Like the Democrat "turncoat" Lewis M. Eisenberg, the head of finances for the Republican National Committee, Cohen changed political parties in order to support the Labour Party of Tony Blair. Cohen was a candidate in the Liberal party in the 1970s and only converted to Blair's New Labour in 1996. Since then he has reportedly given Labour an estimated $5 million and bankrolled Gordon Brown's career.

At their home in London the Cohens reportedly give lavish parties for the likes of the Rothschilds, the Rausing billionaires, and Cohen's old mentor, Sir Clive Sinclair. At their home in New York they entertain their friends Bill and Hillary Clinton. They also have a villa at Mougins, near Cannes.

"Cohen moved into Brown's orbit in 2000, when the chancellor appointed him chairman of a Treasury fund set up to encourage investment in deprived areas of the country. The next year he was rewarded with a knighthood," according to the *Times* 2005 profile entitled, "Sir Ronald Cohen: Midas with a mission - to make Gordon king."

Cohen began to replace Levy as Britain's liaison in the Middle East. In 2004, along with Blair and Brown, Cohen met Ehud Olmert, deputy to Israeli prime minister Ariel Sharon. In 2006, Cohen "started to take over the role of government emissary from Lord Levy by meeting Israeli leaders, including the prime minister, Ehud Olmert," the *Guardian* reported. As Brown replaced Blair, Cohen, the multimillionaire venture capitalist, replaced Levy as chief fundraiser for the ruling Labour party. About his connections to Israel, Cohen told the *Times*: "If you look at my history: born in Egypt, a refugee, married to the daughter of the commander of the *Exodus* who's an Israeli, there's an obvious connection between me and the region." Obvious, perhaps, but definitely not discussed in the media.

Cohen, who was called the prime minister's 'private banker', clearly had a great deal of influence over Gordon Brown. As the *Jewish Chronicle* wrote in their 2007 interview, "So what exactly is his relationship with Brown? There is a seven-second pause. 'I would classify myself as a friend of the Prime Minister, just as I was a friend of Tony Blair', he says carefully."

I pointed down the street, I said, "I lost people there." And he said, "I lost people there, too. Look, look, this is about 9-11 ... I put it in a folder named 9-11 ..." and it got pretty ugly from that point on. Basically he said that he needed to be sure that I would never mention Ptech again. And I said, "Here's the problem. I'm a senior consultant, I consult with a lot of people ... you may deny Ptech business here ... what happens to Citibank, what happens to Goldman Sachs, what happens to the rest?" He said, "That's not my problem." And I said, "That's why we have that hole in the ground up the street. It is everyone's problem."

Indira Singh, "The Story of Indira Singh", *Our World in Balance,* April 27, 2005

Chapter XI

Ptech and the Financial Crisis

Like 9-11, the financial crisis of 2008 did not simply fall out of the sky. Both were the results of decades of planning and preparation. President Clinton's denial of responsibility for the economic crisis notwithstanding, it was his special adviser, the Israeli dual-national Rahm Emanuel, who is credited for pushing the economically treasonous NAFTA bill through Congress. That a president from the supposedly pro-labor Democrat party would support a bill that eliminated the jobs of millions of working Americans as it devastated the U.S. manufacturing sector is something that the mainstream media has never addressed.

What America reaped in 2009 was the economic fallout from the "giant sucking sound" that the anti-NAFTA candidate Ross Perot had warned of during the presidential debates of 1992. Twenty years later no one is laughing about Perot's phrase that he used to describe what NAFTA and other free trade agreements would do to the American economy. Americans have suffered from the big lie about NAFTA and "free trade" with China. Ross Perot was right about how NAFTA and other "free-trade" policies would destroy America's prosperity by devastating our manufacturing sector.

Millions of U.S. jobs were exported as American companies moved their factories to Mexico and China as a result of the disastrous free trade policies enacted during the Clinton administrations. The "Made in America" label, a symbol of quality and pride, is seldom found on clothing, shoes, and other products in American stores. Original American products like blue jeans and Converse sneakers are no longer even made in the United States.

As an anti-NAFTA independent candidate, H. Ross Perot ran a valiant campaign to protect American jobs, the U.S. manufacturing sector, and our national prosperity. Bill Clinton, however, won the election and the American people lost much of their manufacturing sector, an essential part of the economy. The ever increasing trade deficits suffered since the early 1990's are the clearest evidence that America's wealth was sucked out of the nation at an incredible rate. Ross Perot was right: the U.S. dream could not be sustained solely by the service sector. I wonder if they still teach that lie in American universities. Perhaps they will rediscover the wisdom of the writings of the founding fathers, such as Alexander Hamilton on the importance of manufacturing and the economic causes of the American Revolution.

Behind such massive criminal hoaxes as the false-flag terror attacks of 9-11, the ongoing financial crises, and the government bailouts, are years of planning and preparation by high-level criminal organizations. Such immense crimes are designed to steal huge amounts of money, shape public opinion, and facilitate drastic changes in society and government. The so-called "War on Terror," the PATRIOT ACT, the U.S. Department of Homeland Security, and the trillion-dollar bailout and stimulus bills are all examples of such pre-planned responses. Fear is the primary tool used by the controlled media and corrupt politicians to force these pre-planned radical changes onto the skeptical and patriotic public.

The Tyranny of Lies

Maurice Greenberg, who is linked to the culprits of 9-11, is the head of the insurance company A.I.G., which eventually received more than $180 billion of U.S. taxpayer funds from the government bailout of 2008-2009. The first plane that struck the World Trade Center flew straight into the secure computer room of Marsh, a company run by his son Jeffrey Greenberg.

The Securities and Exchange Commission accused Maurice Greenberg of numerous improper accounting moves between 2000 and 2005. The false accounting amounted to more than $5 billion and resulted in A.I.G. paying more than $1 billion in fines. In August 2009 Greenberg was personally fined more than $130 million in a lawsuit filed on behalf of defrauded workers in Ohio.

While some of the key culprits behind the financial crisis of 2008 are known, for example Bernard Madoff and Maurice Greenberg, there has been no investigation by the mainstream media of the criminal networks they operate within. On the other hand, there has been a great deal of discussion by the media about the alleged Islamic network behind 9-11.

The government version of events, which has been promoted without question by the media, is that Al Qaida, a non-state entity supposedly headed by Osama Bin Laden, with the support of some state actors, such as Afghanistan, Pakistan, and Saudi Arabia, planned and carried out the 9-11 terror attacks for some reason that was never articulated by the perpetrators, or explained by the U.S. government.

On the day of 9-11, President George W. Bush told the world that Al Qaida had destroyed the World Trade Center and attacked the Pentagon because it hated America's democratic freedoms, as if that makes any sense. According to the claims made by the Bush administration and distributed by the controlled media, an anti-democratic Islamic faction from poor and undemocratic lands had committed the 9-11 terror atrocity in order to start a war between the Islamic world and the western democracies, headed by the United States.

Osama Bin Laden, however, said he had nothing to do with 9-11 and the discovery of super-thermite in the dust of the World Trade Center proves that the culprits behind the demolition of the Twin Towers and WTC 7 were high-tech wizards with access to nanotechnology - not Islamic fighters from Afghanistan.

Boiling Iron

Incredibly hot fires, hotter than the boiling point of iron, raged beneath the rubble of the World Trade Center for more than three months as the physical evidence of demolition was hastily being removed and destroyed with the connivance of the U.S. government, namely the criminal division of the Department of Justice headed by the Israeli-American Michael Chertoff. The Bush administration showed a callous disregard for the need to investigate the worst terror attack in U.S. history as it eagerly took up the gauntlet against Afghanistan, ruled by the Islamic Taliban. On October 5, 2001, the Taliban offered to try Bin Laden in an Afghan court if the United States provided "solid evidence" of his guilt, but the U.S. refused to provide any evidence and launched its invasion on October 7, 2001. Before the fires were extinguished at the World Trade Center, the pre-planned U.S. invasion of Afghanistan had already removed the Taliban from power.

The "War on Terror" is actually part of a long-planned Zionist strategy to dominate the Middle East. This strategy was first articulated by the extreme right-wing Israeli politician Benjamin Netan-yahu of the Likud party in 1980. This radical Zionist plan became U.S. policy in the aftermath of 9-11 and has been the rationale for at least five ongoing interventions in the region: Iraq, Afghanistan, Somalia, Pakistan, and Yemen.

At the beginning of his term President Obama ordered 17,000 more U.S. troops to Afghanistan, whence the terrorists of 9-11 sup-posedly came, at least according to the government's accepted myth about Bin Laden and his twenty hijackers. Obama's strategy to ex-pand and prolong this disastrous military campaign was extremely ill-advised. The Soviet Union had a land border with Afghanistan and more troops in the country, but still lost the war. What did Obama expect to win in Afghanistan?

Yet, the fundamental question remained unanswered: who really carried out 9-11? This is the key point where the official story diverges from the path of the evidence. The U.S. government, which confis-cated and destroyed tons of evidence from the crime scene, is holding the person alleged to be Khalid Sheikh Mohammed, the "mastermind of 9-11," but refuses to put him on trial in the United States. How very odd. At the same time, the grieving 9-11 relatives were denied a trial to determine who was responsible for the deaths of their loved ones.

Meanwhile, evidence of Israeli involvement in the events of 9-11 has been completely ignored by the government and media, as if it did not exist. I have examined and investigated these leads since Septem-ber 2001 and found that every line of inquiry leads to an Israeli or a Zionist. Such consistency validates the hypothesis that Israel was in-volved in carrying out 9-11 as a false-flag operation. My investigation has revealed a complex corporate and financial network in which high-level Zionists and Israeli intelligence agents have long operated in the United States. Within this network the connections of Zionists and Israelis to both 9-11 and the current financial crisis can clearly be seen.

While the huge U.S. government bailout was being considered and planned in the fall of 2008, I pointed out that some of the same individuals and entities, such as Maurice Greenberg of A.I.G., were deeply involved in both 9-11 and the financial crisis at the highest level. A.I.G., for example, a dodgy insurance company that has long engaged in fraudulent practices, received more than $180 billion of U.S. tax-payer funds. As I pointed out in my articles at the time, the key people behind the bailout, Ben Shalom Bernanke, the Chairman of the Federal Reserve, for example, are dedicated Zionists with histories of working with the Zionist criminal network.

In Bernanke's case, he began his career working for Alan Heller Schafer, the well-known Jewish criminal and political boss who ran a sprawling roadside gambling and drinking establishment called "South of the Border." Schafer was later convicted of rigging elections in South Carolina and sentenced to three and a half years in federal prison. As I concluded in my article about Bernanke's ties to Schafer, it is simply not credible that Bernanke, a student at Harvard, was unaware of Schafer's legendary criminality.

The so-called "mainstream media," news outlets such as the *New York Times, Chicago Tribune, Los Angeles Times,* CNN, and FOX News, however, will not investigate the connections of the Zionist corporate network with 9-11 or the financial crisis because they are part of the same network. This is how the Zionist-controlled media works: they shield Zionist criminals by blaming others. This is why CNN and FOX sought to smear me as an anti-Semite rather than discuss the evidence of 9-11.

The situation with the Zionist bankers and corrupt Israeli banks like Israel Discount Bank of New York is like that depicted in *The International*, the film about a corrupt bank which profits from Middle East weapons deals and war debt. As the Italian weapons dealer turned politician said: "It's not about the profits from the weapon deals; it's about control." Debt is the banker's instrument of control.

Indira Singh: Ptech Whistleblower

Enterprise software was used to provide real-time access and control of all data and information on the government computer networks on 9-11. Ptech and Mitre provided the unseen perpetrators of 9-11 with access to the crucial computer systems that failed. Ptech (or P-Tech) is also linked to some of the biggest investment banks involved in the financial crisis.

Shortly after 9-11 a woman named Indira Singh came forward with claims that a Massachusetts-based enterprise software company called Ptech had played a key role in the events of 9-11. In 2002, Singh was described in the Boston press as "a former Ptech consultant." Indira Singh began her career at First Boston in the mid-1970s when mortgage-based securities were first developed by Laurence D. Fink, now CEO of BlackRock.

Singh, formerly a risk architect and Information Technology (IT) professional with JP Morgan and a DARPA lab in Washington, D.C., certainly knew a great deal about Ptech and its spy software, which had reportedly been loaded onto the most critical computer networks in the U.S. government prior to 9-11. A front page article from the *Boston Globe* of December 7, 2002, entitled "FBI reportedly didn't act on Ptech tips" described Singh as "a former Ptech consultant," citing an interview she had done with WBZ-TV:

WBZ reported that a former Ptech consultant named Indira Singh came forward this past June. Singh said last night in an interview on WBZ that she told the FBI "in no uncertain terms" about the connection between Ptech and [Yasin al] Qadi. She said that weeks after talking to the Boston FBI, she was "shocked" and "frustrated" to learn that the FBI still had not alerted any of the government agencies using Ptech software that there were questions about the company's ties to suspected terrorist fund-raisers.

Indira Singh, the former Ptech consultant turned whistleblower, sought to put the blame on Arabs and the CIA. The essence of Singh's 9-11 comments was that the people behind Ptech were Arab Moslems tied to Saudi financiers of terrorism and a rogue element within the CIA, which included Vice President Dick Cheney.

Singh later did a series of interviews with Jamey A. Hecht, editor of From the Wilderness (FTW), a website that featured material written by Mike Ruppert. In these interviews Singh discussed Ptech's enterprise software, how it could have been used to manipulate data on critical government computer networks such as the FAA, NORAD, and U.S. Air Force, and who she thought was behind the company:

Hecht: You said at the 9-11 Citizens' Commission hearings, you mentioned – it's on page 139 of transcript - that Ptech was with Mitre Corporation in the basement of the FAA for two years prior to 9-11 and their specific job was to look at interoperability issues the FAA had with NORAD and the Air Force, in case of an emergency.

Singh: Yes, I have a good diagram for that…

Hecht: And that relationship had been going on mediated by Ptech for two years prior to 9-11. You elsewhere say that the Secret Service is among the government entities that had a contract with Ptech. Mike Ruppert's thesis in *Crossing the Rubicon*, as you know, is that the software that was running information between FAA and NORAD was superseded by a parallel subsuming version of itself that was being run by the Secret Service on state of the art parallel equipment in the PEOC with a nucleus of Secret Service personnel around Cheney.

Singh claimed that Ptech was connected to the CIA and Saudi millionaires. "Ptech had all the markings of a CIA front company," she said. "I think there is a CIA within the CIA. I think there is a Shadow CIA that does the Iran-Contra type of things. They get funding from illicit methods, and that the Saudis are in on it. They might have trained some operatives, and later it backfired - it was blowback within blowback, perhaps."

In one of the FTW articles about Ptech by Michael Kane, a list of three suspect groups is presented: the Muslim Brotherhood, Christian Cultists, and Nazis. Kane describes Ptech as "the Alpha dog" in a relationship with Mitre, but the ownership of Mitre is never discussed. Elsewhere, Vice President Dick Cheney is named as a suspect, depicted as the mastermind single-handedly running the whole show:

> Ptech was working with Mitre Corp. in the FAA and, according to Indira, Ptech was the Alpha dog in that relationship. Mitre has provided simulation and testing technologies for the Navy. They provide multiple FAA technologies and boast in their annual reports

that their two biggest clients are DOD and FAA. Mitre knew the FAA's technological enterprise inside and out, including any simulation-and-testing (war game) technology operated by the FAA.

This was the perfect marriage to ensure that the capacity to covertly intervene in FAA operations on 9-11 existed - in the middle of simulated war games. It is also the perfect marriage to ensure that the command and control of these capabilities was readily available to Dick Cheney via Secret Service Ptech software in the Presidential Emergency Operations Center, the bunker to which Cheney was "rushed" by the Secret Service. As already pointed out in Part 1 of this series, Ptech does what Total Information Awareness (TIA, the DARPA program to monitor all electronic transactions in real-time) is supposed to do. There are an undetermined number of other software programs in the hands of an undetermined number of corporations also capable of this. Again, enterprise architecture software is designed with the express purpose of knowing everything that is going on throughout the entirety of the "enterprise" in real-time.

In the case of Ptech software, installed on White House, Secret Service, Air Force and FAA systems (as well as most American military agencies), the enterprise included all of the real-time data of the above mentioned agencies.

Hecht, editor of the FTW website, described Ptech as a den of thieves and murderers in the introduction to "Ptech, 9-11, and USA-Saudi Terror" (2005):

The human side of Ptech is where the thievery and
murder come in: among the financiers and programmers of Ptech are apparent members of an international network of organized criminals involved in decades of narcotraffic, gunrunning, money laundering,
and terrorism. Their personal and professional connections reach up into the highest levels of the American government, and their activities are still underway.

But who are these financiers and programmers of Ptech? Who are the
"apparent members of an international network of organized criminals involved in decades of narcotraffic, gunrunning, money laundering, and terrorism?"

What Hecht, Kane, and Singh seem to have overlooked in their
investigation of Ptech was the conspicuous role played by Michael
Goff, a Zionist lawyer from Worcester, Massachusetts, who suddenly
left his law practice in 1994 to manage Ptech, a start-up company
headed by a Lebanese Muslim. How much sense does that make?
Not much, of course, unless one considers that Ptech was an Israeli-
controlled operation from the beginning.

Michael Goff was the first marketing and general manager of Ptech.
Goff wore many hats at the new company as Ptech's spy software found
its way onto the most critical networks of the U.S. government. Goff,
who was Ptech's first marketing manager, was also responsible for the
procurement of all software for a company that supposedly wrote enterprise software. He was also responsible for the hiring and training
of personnel. As I pointed out in my 2005 exposé about Ptech, Goff
went on to represent Guardium, an Israeli software company founded
and run by members of Israeli military intelligence.

Goff was certainly more than a young Jewish lawyer who wanted to help a Lebanese immigrant promote his enterprise software company. This is probably why Goff could not tell me the name of the agency which had placed him with Ptech. The agency was most likely a branch of Israeli military intelligence. In that case, how do the claims about Ptech made by Hecht and Singh fit in?

The evidence indicates that Ptech was disguised to look Arab-owned, but was actually run by Israeli intelligence. Goff was Israel's point man within the company and the person who hired the right people and through whom Israeli software became Ptech software. Goff appears to have been the conduit, the personal link through which malicious Israeli spyware was loaded onto U.S. government computers. Hecht, Ruppert, and Singh acted to pin the blame on Arabs and a nebulous cabal at the CIA in order to distract investigators from the Israeli connection to Ptech.

How else could it be that Singh, Hecht, and Kane saw only Arab terrorists and rogue CIA agents running Ptech without noticing Mike Goff, the Jewish lawyer from Worchester, who played so many key roles running Ptech from the beginning? How is it that Singh knows so much about Ptech but nothing about Michael Goff? His name was on Ptech documents, after all.

Although I discovered the Israeli connection to Ptech in March 2005, it was not something that was discussed by any other journalist in the mainstream or alternative media. It is possible that Singh knew nothing about Goff's role in building up Ptech in the mid-1990s. Israelis are, after all, generally seen as allies of the United States.

To better understand the connection between Ptech and Israeli military intelligence it may be helpful to read my articles about Ptech and Mitre. With the Israeli connection in mind, I recommend reading "The Story of Indira Singh" from an interview she did in April 2005. This is one of the most informative interviews she has done. It's worth reading for anyone interested in understanding 9-11 and the financial crisis. This interview contains interesting testimony about the downing of Flight 93 and the mysterious demolition of the forty-seven-story WTC 7, the third tower owned by Larry Silverstein to collapse on 9-11.

Singh's comments about Ptech and her work at JP Morgan shed some light on how Ptech enterprise software may have played a role in both 9-11 and the financial meltdown. I recommend reading the entire interview. To give an idea of what Singh discusses, I have provided some of the most interesting extracts below.

Extracts from "The Story of Indira Singh" from Our World in Balance, April 27, 2005:

> Indira Singh has been working on Wall Street since 1975. On 9-11 she was working as a senior consultant for JP Morgan Chase. She was tasked with developing a next-generation, operational, risk-blueprint which would pro-actively identify exposures, including money laundering, rogue trading, and illicit financing patterns. It was in this capacity nine months later [that] she became aware of the biggest threat to our country, a trans-nationally protected terrorist cartel that brought us 9-11. Indira Singh is a private pilot and a climber. Prior to 9-11, she volunteered as a civilian emergency medical technician, until she was injured at ground zero.

Singh: September 11th I was a senior consultant for JP Morgan
           Chase and Risk. I had cycled through several of their Risk
           areas as an enterprise architect, or an information archi-
           tect, technology architect... which basically means that
           you take a look at the entire enterprise and come up with a
           blueprint, make sure that all the systems, not just one sys-
           tem, but all the systems, the blueprints for all the systems
           that are developed to support the business, are in-line, in
           tune with the business goals and the business architecture
           and the business processes and where the business is go-
           ing. So it's pretty high-level, we call it the CXO level, or the
           Chief Information Officer, Chief Technology Officer lev-
           els and there are disciplines and methodologies and very
           esoteric software that's used to manage this. I did that at
           JP Morgan Chase and I also worked for a small company
           in Washington, D.C. that was doing some very innovative
           work regarding technology interoperability, they were
           developing some inference engines to think about how
           to put technology architectures together and I wanted to
           use that for my risk work, basically. ... We were seeking
           funding from In-Q-Tel, which was the CIA's information
           technology seeking arm, I had been spending pretty much
           every Friday, Thursday-Friday down in D.C. trying to get
           that project off the ground, and trying to get it funded...

Singh: Ptech is the one thread, the one golden thread you pull on,
           and all of this is unraveled. Because it goes into the cor-
           porations, it goes into these government entities, it goes
           into the terrorism financing entities... none of which have
           been taken to task... there are just so many questions

about what does this all mean? And as I investigated further, we found that the origins of Ptech were very interesting. Where did this company come from? Obviously, that is the first question. And how did they get to be so powerful? Who were the people, who were the organizations that brought them in. Who knew; who gave them the power? ...

Singh: BMI was identified as being involved with terror financing, but this is just not going to be, 'The Muslims Hate America!', that's not what it is, there is something else going on here, they're being used as a tool, just as the good people of the U.S. are being used, are being misled, and frightened and terrorized into, 'if we don't wage these horrific wars, our way of life will be over'. Who benefits? ...

Singh: The FBI. In fact, this has to be made very clear, there are some extraordinarily real patriotic Americans, and good people in the FBI, as has been said by Colleen Rowley, one of the FBI whistleblowers, there's a wall in the FBI. And this has been validated to me by various in Houston who are very close to the power bases and are pretty ticked off at what's happening in this country and are speaking out. As are many CIA agents who are very concerned that it has gone too far, as are many NSA agents who are concerned that it has gone too far, and FBI agents. So we have a lot of people who are speaking out, they have kept quiet too long, they're afraid, they are afraid of what's happening to this country . . .

Singh: Ari Fleischer spun it to find sugar that day. He said, 'There's nothing wrong. Nothing to see here, everything's fine.' So they did a token raid and that was basically it. But everything that I have done since that time has been for one reason and one reason only, that there may come a time, that people will find the trail to Ptech, and it won't be hidden or buried, I've kept it alive, whether they've renamed their company and moved on I want to keep the names, the details, everything alive, no matter what I have to do, so that, should there come a time for justice and accounting for 9-11, and for what's happening in the world today, it makes it easier for other people to unravel the truth...

Whatever you're political inclinations, this is wrong. This is criminal, this is murder, this is worldwide atrocity. And I have reached some very good people on the left and on the right, who are willing to speak out about Ptech. ...

Singh: It was possible that there was an alternate command and control system. Could you technically use Ptech software to do the surveillance and intervention? Well, gosh, yes, that's exactly what I was planning on using it for in one of the largest banks in the world. . . . .

Singh: The Towers came down, 3,000 people were killed, and what I know is the characters behind the funding of it, were totally in bed with characters in the U.S. And not only just for 9-11, but going on through our nation's history, and the big question is, "Why?" What are they up to?

Question: Could you describe the relationship of Ptech with the FAA? Ptech worked with the FAA for several years, didn't they?

Singh: It was a joint project between Ptech and Mitre, and they were looking at holes, basically in the FAA's interoperability, responding with other agencies, law enforcement, in the case of an emergency such as hijacking. So they were looking for... what people would do, how they would respond in case of an emergency, and find the holes, and make recommendations to fix it. Now, if anyone was in a position to know where the holes were, Ptech was. And that's exactly the point. If anybody was in a position to write software to take advantage of those holes, it would have been Ptech...

Singh: Now, with the FAA in particular, if something goes wrong, and there is an emergency with a particular flight, and the DOD needs to be notified, well that's a really major interoperability thing, a signal has to be sent in some way, shape or form, either mediated by a human in most cases, or automatically, or even if its mediated by a human something needs to be initiated on a separate computer to start a whole other sequence of events, interventions, scrambling a jet, notification up and downstream with many other organizations, such as NORAD, such as other terminal radar areas, such as local law enforcement, you name it. So, this all has to be blueprinted, mapped out, and that's where Enterprise Architecture comes in, you need some kind of blueprint to keep all of this together and that's what Ptech was so good at.

Question: Now was there a reference to Ptech having operated in the basement, out of the FAA?

Singh: Yes. Now, typically, because the scope of such projects are so overarching and so wide-ranging, when you are doing an enterprise architecture project, you pretty much have access to how anything in the organization is being done, where it's being done, on what systems, what the information is, and you pretty much have carte blanche. Now if it's a major project that spans several years, the team that comes in has literally access to almost anything they want because you're operating on a blueprint level, on a massive scale. So, yes, they were everywhere, and I was told that they were in places that required clearances, I was told they had log-on access to FAA flight control computers, I was told that they had passwords to many computers that you may not on the surface... let's say you... isolated part of a notification process that was mediated by a computer, and you wanted to investigate it further, then you typically get log-on access to that computer, and from that back upstream or downstream, so, who knows? In my experience, I could have access to almost anything I wanted to in JP Morgan Chase... and didn't, for the reason if anything went wrong, I didn't want to have the access. But if you were up to no good, as an enterprise architect, with such a mandate, you typically could have anything you wanted. Access to anything...

Singh: But there were four war games, four simulations going on the morning of 9-11, and I just want people to remember that the whole nature of what Mitre, they also developed software for intelligence, which includes the CIA, Mitre and Ptech would have, if they were going to test whether they had fixed these holes, would have probably run a simulation. I don't know that they did, but that's how we do things, but there were four of them going on. So was there room for confusion? I don't think these people were stupid, I think they were deliberately confused, if anything.

Question: Well we know very well that there was a simulation of the very event taking place during the event.

Singh: And I believe there is proof there was more than one. Just in case the first one didn't confuse people enough. So what does this say? I can be very objective about this and say, "Well, the terrorists knew that there were war games scheduled for this day and they took advantage of it and called 9-11 a particular day, however, we do know that 9-11 had been selected prior… ok, so maybe the war games were set many weeks prior for 9-11 …" and you can play this game over and over and over. Yes, it was the perfect day, and yes, you needed inside knowledge, and yes, Ptech with all its myriad associations would have had the inside knowledge, and yes, Ptech was a CIA front, and yes, Ptech was protected. . . .

Singh: Interestingly enough, I did not let people know that it was Ptech until maybe August, 2002 at ICH… we had pretty much moved on and uh, I accidentally let slip to one of my colleagues there that the name of the company that was being investigated was Ptech. And she was horrified… she said, "They're everywhere." And I said, "Yeah, fancy that. Wonder who put them there." . . .

Singh: Before Ptech was ever raided, before it ever became pub-
            lic, I took it all the way up to the top of the FBI. I took it
            everywhere. The reality of the situation is proven by the
            response I got there; more telling than the actual deed it-
            self. Their response to that is really what indicts them all.

Question: What was their response?

Singh: "Shut up and go away, or you will be killed," basically.

Question: Now, you got that response from all different levels in gov-
            ernment . . .

Singh: I got that response from JP Morgan. I got that response
            from Ptech. I got that warning from people within the
            FBI. Mostly the FBI . . .

Question: And what kind of response did you get from JP Morgan
            Chase, your employers at the time when you went to them
            with what you had found out about Ptech?

Singh: Well, they had told me that I should be killed for getting
            all this evidence . . . I was intimidated. I wrote a letter to my
            boss saying that I had been intimidated, and the person
            who had intimidated me, the 3rd highest ranking person
            in the bank, the General Auditor, so this has gone all the
            way up to the top, they were very aware of it, and that they
            were going to deny using Ptech at JP Morgan Chase. In fact
            they would even explicitly deny the URL to the website, so
            that no one could even look into them. Now the name has
            changed, so you wonder what is going on there, but, when
            he asked me, "Where did you get this from and that from?"
            I was basically thoroughly intimidated. They treated me

as though I was the bad guy. That's what happened. They treated me as if I was the bad guy for having dug up all of this stuff.

Question: And you were told by the Chief Auditor at JP Morgan Chase that the different individuals that you had gotten this information from should have been killed?

Singh: Yeah... I pointed down the street, I said, "I lost people there." And he said, "I lost people there, too. Look, look, this is about 9-11 ... I put it in a folder named 9-11 ..." and it got pretty ugly from that point on. Basically he said that, "He needed to be sure that I would never mention Ptech again." And I said, "Here's the problem. I'm a senior consultant, I consult with a lot of people ... you may deny Ptech business here... what happens to Citibank, what happens to Goldman-Sachs, what happens to the rest?" He said, "That's not my problem." And I said, "That's why we have that hole in the ground up the street. It is everyone's problem." ...

Singh: All of this stuff took money to fund. And it was funded through major financial crimes, money laundering, and looting, looting of the SNL's, looting of the banking system, what we're in the middle of now which is the looting of Social Security. And this is all being done, the looting of HUD, it's all being done systematically to keep the slush funds up for the game at play.

Question: Where do you think this is headed?

Singh: Not any place good for people. And it isn't just going to be America, it is going to be global.

U ltra-fine particles require extremely high temperatures, namely the boiling point of the metal.

Thomas Cahill, University of California at Davis, on the nanoparticles found in the smoke rising from the burning rubble of the World Trade Center

Chapter XII

Why Did Iron Boil
Beneath the Rubble?

In the late winter of 2006, we boarded the California Zephyr in Chicago's Union Station and headed west. After stopping in Denver to visit Ellen Mariani, a 9-11 widow, we got back on the train and traveled to Provo, Utah. After crossing the Rocky Mountains we arrived in Provo on a snowy morning. I had come to Provo to visit Professor Steven E. Jones, who was doing scientific research at Brigham Young University (BYU) about what had caused the Twin Towers to collapse on 9-11.

On the campus of the private Mormon university, surrounded by snow-capped peaks, Jones was teaching physics and carrying out research in the fields of metal-catalyzed fusion, solar energy, and archaeometry. As an archaeometrist, Jones applies physics to explain events in the past. After becoming aware of the unanswered questions of 9-11 in 2005, Jones focused his attention on the available data and evidence from the destruction of the World Trade Center.

The unexplained presence of large amounts of molten iron seen at the Twin Towers puzzled Jones and he had contacted me earlier to confirm my reports of molten metal from my articles of 2002. These were first-hand reports that came directly from two men involved in the removal of the rubble: Peter Tully of Tully Construction of Flushing, New York, and Mark Loizeaux of Controlled Demolition, Inc. of Phoenix, Maryland.

Tully told me in the summer of 2002 that he had seen pools of "literally molten steel" in the rubble. Mark Loizeaux confirmed Tully's report: "Yes, hot spots of molten steel in the basements," he said, "at the bottom of the elevator shafts of the main towers, down seven levels." The molten steel was found "three, four, and five weeks later, when the rubble was being removed," Loizeaux said. He also confirmed that molten steel was found at WTC 7, the 47-story tower which collapsed mysteriously in the late afternoon of 9-11.

In November 2005, Jones presented his ideas in a draft which later evolved into a 52-page scientific paper entitled "Why Indeed Did the WTC Buildings Collapse?" His paper began with an appeal for "a serious investigation of the hypothesis that WTC 7 and the Twin Towers were brought down through the use of pre-positioned cutter-charges." Jones presented photographic and scientific evidence that indicated that an alumino-thermic reaction using a form of Thermite had been used to cut the 47 massive core columns that held up each tower. The official version had not explained how these critical columns failed.

Thermite is a combination of finely ground aluminum and iron oxide (i.e. rust) that cuts through steel like a "warm knife through butter," Jones said, especially when mixed with 2 percent sulfur. The resulting eutectic combination, called Thermate, lowers the melting point of steel. Thermite was patented in Germany by Hans Gold-schmidt in the late 1800s. Extremely high temperatures are produced when the aluminum and iron oxide react. The reaction produces temperatures greater than 2,500 degrees Celsius (4,500 degrees F) as the ferric oxide is reduced to molten iron. Iron melts at 1,535 degrees C and boils at 2,862 degrees C (5,182 degrees F).

The heat-producing reaction causes the oxygen from the ferric oxide to bond with the aluminum, producing aluminum oxide, molten iron, and approximately 750 kilocalories per gram of Thermite. The aluminum oxide is a whitish smoke, which was observed in large amounts during the demolitions of the Twin Towers.

I attended a presentation of Jones' 9-11 research at BYU. Jones began with footage of the unexplained collapse of Larry Silverstein's WTC 7, at about 5:25 in the afternoon of 9-11. When Jones had been interviewed by Tucker Carlson of MSNBC, the producers refused to air the short video segment of the collapsing tower.

I was also invited to observe a Thermite reaction in Professor Jones' physics class. As a colleague combined the powdered rust and aluminum in a mounted ceramic flower pot, Jones filmed the reaction. A paper wick with magnesium ignited the sand-like mixture. The reaction was intense, nearly explosive, and white flames and pieces of metal flew out of the pot. From the bottom poured a white-hot liquid - pure molten iron. After a few seconds a glowing yellow-hot piece of iron was lifted with tongs and shown to the class.

Because Thermite does not require air, it can react underwater or in an oxygen-starved environment, which may explain the persistent hot spots that burned for weeks in the World Trade Center rubble completely unaffected by the continuous dousing from fire hoses. The scientific literature on Thermite says that the white-hot molten iron and slag it produces can itself prolong and extend the heating and incendiary action.

"As of 21 days after the attack, the fires were still burning and molten steel was still running," Leslie Robertson, structural engineer responsible for the design of the World Trade Center, said at the National Conference of Structural Engineers on October 5, 2001.

Footage taken by WABC-TV of the burning South Tower at 9:53 a.m., immediately before the building collapsed, shows large amounts of white-hot molten metal, presumably iron, pouring from the 81st floor of the east corner. While some have suggested that the molten metal seen falling was aluminum, this is challenged by the fact that molten aluminum appears silver-grey in daylight. The evidence indicates that the white-hot metal falling from the South Tower was molten iron and may have been produced by a large amount of Thermite. The amount of molten metal seen falling would indicate that tons of Thermite had been used on that floor. From the video footage it appears that several cubic meters of molten metal fell, which, if iron, would have weighed about 8.65 tons each.

"I consider the official FEMA, NIST, and 9-11 Commission reports," Jones writes, which claim "that fires plus impact damage alone caused complete collapses of all three buildings." He challenged the official explanation and provided evidence to support the controlled-demolition hypothesis, which, he said "is suggested by the available data, testable and falsifiable." Jones noted that the hypothesis that the towers were demolished by explosives "has not been analyzed in any of the reports funded by the U.S. government."

Ignoring the evidence of the controlled-demolition hypothesis, the FEMA-sponsored study of 2002 concluded, "The specifics of the fires in WTC 7 and how they caused the building to collapse remain unknown." Furthermore, the official report found that the fire-induced collapse hypothesis "has only a low probability of occurrence." "Further research, investigation, and analyses are needed to resolve this issue," the FEMA-funded engineers concluded.

"That is precisely the point," Jones said. "Further investigation and analyses are indeed needed, including serious consideration of the controlled-demolition hypothesis which is neglected in all of the government reports." The fact that the 9-11 Commission report does not even mention the collapse of WTC 7 "is a striking omission of data highly relevant to the question of what really happened on 9-11," he said.

Further investigation is what Jones was trying to get other scientists to do. One might have thought that the mainstream media would be interested in a highly-respected physicist answering questions about 9-11, but that has not been the case. The controlled media avoided Dr. Jones and his findings. Like a modern-day Galileo, Jones had exposed serious flaws in the official explanation of the collapses, "a myth," he said, "which has taken on religious proportions."

"There is a clear disconnect between what the official reports say happened and what actually happened," Jones said. "A scientific theory has to be falsifiable. It must be able to be tested and challenged. The data stands on its own. Where are the honest scientists?" Jones asked. "Take the blinders off and find out what happened."

The official 9-11 reports are what Jones calls "pathological science," in which investigators ignore all evidence that contradicts the conclusion they have been asked to prove. I contacted three scientists who support the official theory to ask if they would consider reviewing Jones' paper.

Thomas W. Eagar of MIT refused to even look at the paper and said there is no evidence of molten metal pouring from the South Tower. Challenged with the evidence, he hung up the phone.

Zdenek P. Bazant of Northwestern University submitted his fire-induced collapse theory to the American Society of Civil Engineers (ASCE) two days after 9-11, without examining any evidence. Asked if he would review Jones' paper, Bazant refused. "I have seen Jones' fiction before. If you want my private opinion, it is nothing but sensationalism," he said. "His purported refutation of my analysis is baseless." Asked to simply look at 5 photos in an email showing the cascading molten metal and core columns which appear to have been cut with Thermite, Bazant responded, "I do not have time."

Abolhassan Astaneh-Asl, an Iranian-born professor at Berkeley, who was a member of the FEMA-funded engineering team studying the collapses, also refused to look at Jones' paper, saying, "I will not be able to find time to review the material that you have sent me."

Professor Jones told me that he wanted to obtain samples of the dust that had been produced during the demolition of the Twin Towers. After a week in Provo, we got back on the California Zephyr and headed for the university town of Davis, California, where I had gone to college. My purpose in going to Davis was to interview Dr. Thomas A. Cahill, an expert on airborne aerosols and director of the DELTA Group at the University of California.

In the days after 9-11, when he saw the light bluish smoke rising from the rubble of the World Trade Center, Dr. Cahill knew the plumes contained large amounts of the very smallest particles, the extremely toxic ultra-fine particles less than 1 one-millionth of a meter in size, and smaller. Unlike the much larger dust particles from the destruction of the twin towers, these ultra-fine or nano-particles are particularly hazardous because of their extremely small size, which allows them to pass throughout the body and penetrate into the nucleus of the human cell.

In the end of September 2001, Robert Leifer, a colleague from the Department of Energy's Environmental Measurement Laboratory in New York City contacted Cahill and asked him to send one of the DELTA Group's air monitoring devices known as the 8-stage rotating drum impactor. By October 2, 2001, the Davis air monitoring unit was set up on the lab's roof at 201 Varick Street at the edge of the "exclusion zone," about one mile north of the smoking rubble of the World Trade Center. On top of the 12-story building, the Davis drum was at an elevation of about 150 feet above street level, but lower than most of the surrounding buildings. The exclusion zone was the area around Ground Zero which had no electricity as a result of the destruction of the power plant that had existed under WTC 7. Cahill's air sampling began on October 2, 2001, and continued until late December, when the last fires were finally extinguished.

"The EPA did nothing."

Asked why it took so long to begin a scientific evaluation of the air contamination that accompanied the destruction of the WTC, Dr. Cahill said he had assumed that there were scores of agencies and scientists monitoring the air quality in New York City after 9-11. "I assumed it was happening. I could not believe it was not," he said. "It [the Davis drum] was all by itself. The EPA did nothing."

When Cahill went to New York City in January 2002, rather than welcome his effort to evaluate the toxicity of the city's air, an official with the regional office of the Environmental Protection Agency (EPA) had but two questions for him: Who asked you to do it? Who's paying for it?

While Christine Todd Whitman, then administrator of the EPA, told New Yorkers that the air was safe to breathe in the days and weeks after 9-11, Cahill said there were enormous violations of standards that jeopardized the health of anyone exposed to the plumes coming from the rubble. Those most affected by the toxic smoke were the thousands of workers who labored on top of the rubble pile, he said.

The conditions were "brutal" for people working at Ground Zero without respirators and slightly less so for those working or living in adjacent buildings, Cahill, a professor emeritus of physics and atmospheric science, said. "It was like they were working inside the stack of an incinerator," he said. "The debris pile acted like a chemical factory. It cooked together the components of the buildings and their contents, including enormous numbers of computers, and gave off gases of toxic metals, acids and organics for at least 6 weeks," he said.

The DELTA Group's work revealed the presence of extremely small metallic aerosols in unprecedented amounts in the plumes coming from the burning WTC rubble. Most of the particles in these plumes were in the category of the smallest ultra-fine or nano-particles: from 0.26 to 0.09 microns. The extraordinarily high level of ultra-fine aerosols was one of the most unusual aspects of the data, Cahill said. "Ultra-fine particles require extremely high temperatures," Cahill said, "namely the boiling point of the metal."

While Cahill said he was not aware of evidence confirming the existence of molten metal in the rubble of the World Trade Center, his data showing high levels of ultra-fine particles in the smoke plume prove that incredibly intense hot spots, capable of boiling and vaporizing metals and other components from the debris, persisted beneath the rubble for weeks.

I reported in 2002 that pools of "literally molten steel" were seen in the basements of the collapsed twin towers and WTC 7 by contractors hired to remove the rubble. The official reports by NIST, FEMA, and the 9-11 Commission do not mention the large quantities of molten metal observed in the basement areas of WTC 7 and the Twin Towers.

The science library of U.C. Davis had a copy of the U.S. Geological Survey's "Particle Atlas of the World Trade Center Dust" from 2005, which contained two micrographs of tiny droplets of iron that had been found in large amounts in the dust. There was also a micrograph of a tear-drop-shaped silicate droplet. I photocopied the micrographs and much of the book, which I was glad to share with Dr. Jones when I returned to Provo.

"No explanation for the presence of the iron-rich and silicate spheres (which imply very high temperatures along with droplet formation) is given in the published USGS reports," Dr. Jones wrote in a 2008 scientific paper entitled "Extremely high temperatures during the World Trade Center destruction."

"The official reports do not adequately address the issue of molten metal found at the sites," Jones said, adding that this fact alone "provides compelling motivation for continued research on the WTC collapses."

The official version conspicuously fails to explain what caused these intense hot spots, which are clearly responsible for the ultra-fine particles found in the plumes and the pools of molten iron found in the basement. Cahill ruled out the gravitational potential energy of the towers' collapse being the cause of the super-intense hot spots saying their potential energy was only capable of raising the entire mass of debris a few degrees. So why was iron boiling in the rubble of the World Trade Center?

The use of large amounts of Thermite in the demolition of the World Trade Center would explain the extreme hot spots and large amounts of molten metal beneath the rubble. The 2005 government-funded (NIST) report on the World Trade Center said, based on the steel samples they had examined, there was no evidence of temperatures above 600 degrees C. This is, however, well below the temperature of the red-hot pieces of metal that were photographed being pulled from the rubble. It should be noted that by the time the government-funded study began, nearly all of the steel evidence from the World Trade Center had been cut into pieces shorter than 60 inches in length at a New Jersey junkyard and shipped to Asian steel mills where it was melted down.

M y opinion is, based on the videotapes, that after the airplanes hit the World Trade Center there were some explosive devices inside the buildings that caused the towers to collapse... It would be difficult for something from the plane to trigger an event like that.

Van Romero, explosion expert, "Explosives Planted In Towers, N.M. Tech Expert Says", *Albuquerque Journal,* September 11, 2001

B ased on these observations, we conclude that the red layer of the red/gray chips we have discovered in the WTC dust is active, unreacted thermitic material, incorporating nanotechnology, and is a highly energetic pyrotechnic or explosive material.

Dr. Steven E. Jones, "Active Thermitic Material Discovered in Dust from the 9/11 World Trade Center Catastrophe," March 2009

Chapter XIII

The Discovery of
Thermite in the Dust

One of the most significant developments in the search for the truth of 9-11 was the publication in March 2009 of a peer-reviewed scientific paper, written by nine scientists, about the discovery of "active thermitic material" in dust samples from the collapsed towers of the World Trade Center. A twenty-five-page scientific paper entitled "Active Thermitic Material Discovered in Dust from the 9-11 World Trade Center Catastrophe" presented scientific evidence that an extremely powerful form of super-thermite was used during the demolition of the Twin Towers.

The research paper written by an international team of nine scientists led by Dr. Steven E. Jones of Brigham Young University analyzes tiny red-gray chips of a highly-explosive thermitic material "characterized as nano-thermite or super-thermite." These chips were found in five different samples of dust from the collapsed towers.

The paper was published in the *Open Chemical Physics Journal* and marks a historic breakthrough in the scientific investigation of the explosive collapses of the Twin Towers, although it was not widely reported by the controlled media. If we had a truly free press in the United States this important discovery would have been front page news and a subject of discussion on every news program in the nation.

Super-thermite is a highly energetic form of thermite (iron oxide and aluminum) in which at least one component is in the extremely fine or nano-size range with particles 100 nanometers (1 nm = 1 billionth of a meter) or smaller, often combined with silicon and carbon. Super-thermite is an extremely powerful explosive that releases more energy per gram than any other conventional explosive used in demolition. Furthermore, the chips found in the dust were an extremely powerful form of super-thermite.

Two of the chips tested released more energy by mass (kJ/g) than HMX, TNT, TATB explosives or normal thermite. The chips released between 50 to 100 percent more energy than the four conventional explosives. One of the chips released twice as much energy per gram than Xerogel, a similar super-thermite nanocomposite. The chips in the dust from the World Trade Center all ignited at 430 degrees C, 100 degrees lower than the ignition temperature for Xerogel.

The Jones paper proves that the official explanation for the destruction of the Twin Towers is false. The findings presented in the paper are especially important for 9-11 truth seekers. We now have solid evidence of the super-thermite that was used to demolish the Twin Towers, which means that critics of the official version can no longer be dismissed as "conspiracy theorists."

The discovery of the active thermitic material in the dust from the World Trade Center is crucial to understanding what really happened on 9-11. This scientific discovery reveals that sophisticated demolition explosives had been applied to interior surfaces of the Twin Towers long before the two planes struck. Although we already had evidence that the towers were demolished with thermitic explosives, this is the first time we have actual fragments of the explosive that was used to pulverize the concrete floors of the buildings.

This crucial discovery was not front-page news in the United States because our cherished "free press" is actually very tightly controlled. But the truth cannot be so easily dismissed. Americans are now in the uncomfortable and conflicted position where they have verifiable scientific evidence that proves that their government is complicit in the criminal cover-up of what really happened on 9-11.

The evidence that Professor Jones and his team examined was in the form of very small fragments found in five different samples of dust from the pulverized Twin Towers. In each sample they found small chips of a coating that was composed of two layers, a red layer and a gray layer. The gray layer consisted mostly of iron oxide, while the red layer contained iron, oxygen, aluminum, silicon, and carbon — all the components of super-thermite.

The analysis and testing of the red and gray chips revealed that the super-thermite composite ignited at the surprisingly low temperature of 430 degrees Celsius and caused an explosive reaction which resulted in iron spheroids, exactly like thermite does. In other words, the heat-producing explosive reaction created temperatures hotter than 1538 degrees Celsius, the melting point of iron.

The paper concludes:

> The small size of the iron oxide particles qualifies the material to be characterized as nanothermite or super-thermite...Based on these observations, we conclude that the red layer of the red/gray chips we have

discovered in the WTC dust is active, unreacted thermitic material, incorporating nanotechnology, and is a highly energetic pyrotechnic or explosive material.

How did Super-Thermite get into the World Trade Center?

Super-thermite, which has been fabricated at the Lawrence Livermore National Laboratory and other labs, can be sprayed or even painted onto surfaces, effectively forming an energetic or even explosive paint, the study pointed out. "The sol-gel process is very amenable to dip-, spin-, and spray-coating technologies to coat surfaces," scientists from Lawrence Livermore wrote in a 2002 paper entitled "Energetic nanocomposites with sol-gel chemistry: Synthesis, safety, and characterization."

"The red chips we found in the WTC dust conform to their description of 'thin films' of 'hybrid inorganic/organic energetic nanocomposite'," the Jones paper says. "Indeed, the descriptive terms 'energetic coating' and 'nice adherent film' fit very well with our observations of the red-chips which survived the WTC destruction."

The published documentation of evidence of super-thermite in the dust of the World Trade Center has taken the 9-11 truth movement to a new level. If Osama Bin Laden and Al Qaida did not spray super-thermite in the Twin Towers, who did?

It is now evident that a sophisticated form of super-thermite had been applied to large sections of the World Trade Center. It may have been applied as a spray coating inside the wire ducts that ran through the floors or to the undersides of the floor pans under the guise of fire-proofing or some other form of building maintenance. Super-thermite is safe to handle and only becomes dangerous when it is dry.

We need to find out who manufactured the nanocomposite thermite and who applied the explosive coating inside the buildings. This certainly must have been a task that involved a team of men working for weeks, if not months, and their presence must have been observed by security and other personnel involved in maintaining the buildings. Finding the source of the super-thermite and identifying the people who applied it to the Twin Towers will reveal the true culprits of 9-11.

Several years ago, I contacted Burton Fried, president of LVI Services, Inc., a demolition company that reportedly had done extensive "asbestos abatement" work in the twin towers. I considered LVI's work in the twin towers as suspicious because the company is primarily known for asbestos abatement and preparing structures for demolition. LVI has also done millions of dollars of research and development for the U.S. Department of Defense. In 2000, for example, FedSpending. org shows that LVI Group, Inc. received $3.25 million worth of contracts with the U.S. Army, of which nearly $3 million was for "Applied Research and Exploratory Development." It should be noted that the military is the main user and developer of super-thermite.

LVI has also worked closely with Controlled Demolition Inc. on large demolition projects. LVI's role in these projects is reportedly to prepare the structure for demolition prior to the placement of charges. LVI advertises that it sets up "turn-key" demolition projects. Is this the kind of work LVI did at the World Trade Center? Burton Fried denied having done the extensive "asbestos abatement" work in the towers as reported in *Engineering News-Record* on September 13, 2001. Debra Rubin, one of the journalists who wrote the piece, confirmed that the source of this information had been LVI. Fried's quick reaction, "I didn't do it," increased my suspicions.

What happens now depends on what the people do with this important information and evidence about what really destroyed the Twin Towers on 9-11: The three buildings that collapsed were not brought down by the fires caused by the burning fuel of two airliners. They were demolished with pre-planted explosives, including large amounts of an extremely potent form of super-thermite, which had been applied to surfaces of the building in the weeks or months prior to 9-11. Osama Bin Laden and his gang of twenty Arabs certainly did not spray super-thermite throughout the towers of World Trade Center in the weeks and months before 9-11. So who did?

What we have to do as concerned citizens with moral courage is to spread this information and ask our local news media to publish information about this crucial discovery. We have to bring this discovery to the attention of our local politicians, representatives, and senators in the U.S. Congress. We have to endeavor to have this matter discussed in the media and the halls of power. It is time for us to stand up against those who have hijacked the truth about 9-11.

The world will not be the same from today on. It's an attack against our whole civilization. I don't know who is responsible. I believe we will know in twelve hours. If it is a kind of Bin Laden organization, and even if it's something else, I believe that this is the time to deploy globally concerted effort led by the United States, the U.K., Europe and Russia against all sources of terror. The same kind of struggle that our forefathers launched against the piracy on the high seas… It's time to launch an operational concrete war against terror.

Ehud Barak on BBC World television, September 11, 2001

Chapter XIV

Ehud Barak and 9-11

Within minutes of the explosive demolitions of the Twin Towers on 9-11, the Israeli politician and military leader Ehud Barak was in the London studio of the BBC World television network ready to provide a plausible and political explanation to the world. During the interview, before any evidence of culpability was found, Barak called for a "War on Terror" and U.S. military intervention in Afghanistan. Barak, the former commander of the Sayeret Matkal, the covert operation force under the Directorate of Military Intelligence, is suspected of being one of the real masterminds of 9-11. His appearance on BBC World is a textbook example of how false-flag terrorism is supposed to work. The perpetrator is the first one to assign blame by pointing his finger at his enemy in order to shape public opinion, which is the real purpose of such atrocities.

Ehud Barak (formerly Brug) was born at Kibbutz Mishmar Hasharon on February 12, 1942. He enlisted in the Israeli Army at age 17, became a career army officer, and helped to found and lead the elite Sayeret Matkal covert operations commando unit. After serving as head of Israeli Intelligence and Central Command during the 1980s, Barak was appointed IDF Chief of Staff in 1991. Barak was Israel's minister of defense during Israel's assault on the Gaza Strip in 2008-2009. Based on the report of the U.N. Fact Finding Mission on the Gaza Conflict, written by Justice Richard Goldstone, Barak is legally responsible for a host of war crimes committed during that aggression. The government of the United States, as a state that has ratified the Geneva Conventions, is obliged to arrest Ehud Barak based on the evidence and findings presented in the Goldstone report.

Socrates' observation that unpunished criminals become worse is the story of modern Israel. The most serious criminals of the Zionist state have never been punished in any meaningful way by the international community. The *laissez faire* attitude regarding Israeli war criminals has enabled the most unscrupulous and ruthless criminals to rise to the top of the Israeli government, where they sit today. The criminal audacity of Israel's leaders, however, is not sustainable for the long term because their rampant criminality endangers the Zionist state and its citizens.

It should be noted that the Israeli prime minister at the time of the attacks was Ariel Sharon, a Zionist extremist and terrorist who espoused the position that all Jews, including American Jews, should live in Israel. Sharon had a dream that one million American Jews would emigrate to Israel, while in reality more Israelis have chosen to live in America. Was 9-11 designed to compel American Jews to move to Israel?

Ehud Barak was prime minister of Israel from July 1999 until March 7, 2001, when he was replaced by Ariel Sharon. I attended an event at the University of Illinois in Chicago where both Barak, then prime minister, and Sharon were involved shortly before the Israeli election that brought Sharon to power. The fact that Barak and Sharon had travelled together to Chicago illustrated the fakeness of their rivalry.

Previous positions held by Barak include Head of Defense Planning and Budgeting, Head of the Israeli Intelligence Community, Chief of the General Staff of the Israel Defense Forces (IDF), Minister of the Interior in Prime Minister Yitzhak Rabin's cabinet, Minister of Foreign Affairs in the Shimon Peres cabinet, and Labor Party Chairman. If the Israeli military is involved in 9-11, as Dr. Alan Sabrosky says and which the evidence indicates, Ehud Barak certainly knows all about it.

When Sharon assumed power in March 2001, Barak came to America. He supposedly came to the United States to work as a special advisor for Electronic Data Systems and as a partner with SCP Partners, a Mossad-run private equity company focused on "security-related" work - but this was merely his cover. His real assignment, in my opinion, was to oversee the preparation for the terror attacks of 9-11. As a partner with SCP Partners, Barak was well placed to supervise the false-flag terror operation. The complex false-flag terror attacks of 9-11 required that the mastermind of the operation be in the country to manage the critical details.

One of the key aspects of 9-11 that Barak needed to arrange was the production and application of an advanced form of super-thermite, an extremely powerful explosive produced using nanotechnology. In 2001, SCP Partners happened to have a suitable company in their portfolio, a private company called Metallurg Holdings, Inc., which has its office in Wayne, Pennsylvania. Today, SCP has another company called Advanced Metallurgical Group, N.V. (AMG) in its portfolio. AMG and Metallurg actually share the same phone number and address at 435 Devon Park Drive in Wayne. SCP Private Equity Partners L.P. and its management company named Safeguard

International, which controls the metallurgical subsidiaries, are also based at this address. AMG/Safeguard International have several subsidiaries, including one that specializes in the production of atomized aluminum, a component of super-thermite, and others which manufacture specialized coatings of nano-composites.

SCP Partners, where Ehud Barak worked from 2001 until 2007, clearly had the capability in 2001 to produce nano-composite explosives like the super-thermite that was evidently used to pulverize the World Trade Center on 9-11. There are very few companies or countries in the world that had the capability to manufacture super-thermite in 2001, but Ehud Barak and his SCP Partners did have that capability. Osama Bin Laden and Al Qaida, on the other hand, did not and could not have had anything to do with the super-thermite found in the dust of the pulverized Twin Towers. With the discovery of large amounts of super-thermite in the dust of the World Trade Center the government version has been exposed as a pack of lies designed to start a preplanned war of aggression against Afghanistan. Ehud Barak was actually the first person to call for the U.S. to invade Afghanistan, something he did only hours after the attacks on BBC World television.

Rafi Eitan, the octogenarian Mossadnik who ran a spy operation against the United States using Jonathan Pollard, fled to Israel after Pollard was caught in 1985. Eitan was then offered the position as head of state-owned Israel Chemicals Corporation, which also has production and manufacturing facilities in the United States. In 1978, when Israeli intelligence began planning the false-flag terror operation of 9-11, according to the documented comments of the Mossad chief Isser Harel, Eitan was serving as Menachem Begin's "advisor on terrorism". This is probably the real reason that Rafi Eitan remained in the Israeli security cabinet until 2009. He is one of the architects of 9-11.

Rafi Eitan was also involved in the 1968 theft and illegal smuggling of nearly 600 pounds of plutonium from a plant in Pennsylvania to Israel for the production of nuclear weapons. As the *Pittsburgh Tribune* reported in a series of articles about the stolen plutonium, Eitan is the key suspect:

> Four other Israelis visited NUMEC on Sept. 10, 1968, and met with Shapiro [then-NUMEC President Zalman M. Shapiro, a staunch supporter of Israel] to "discuss thermoelectric devices (unclassified)," according to a Sept. 12, 1968, letter from Bruce D. Rice, NUMEC security manager, to Harry R. Walsh, director of AEC security and property management, seeking AEC approval for the visit.
>
> The four visitors were: Avraham Hermoni, Ephraim Beigon, Abraham Bendor and Raphael (or, Rafael) Eitan.
>
> In their 1991 book, "Dangerous Liaison," Andrew and Leslie Cockburn wrote, "At the time of his visit to Apollo in 1968, Eitan was acting as an agent for Mossad on special assignment to LAKAM ... a shadowy intelligence agency ... born in the 1950s with the express purpose of acquiring nuclear technology by any means."
>
> Soon after the men's visit, 587 pounds of weapons-grade uranium reportedly went missing from NUMEC, according to Udall's papers.

In a recent article entitled "America's Loose Nukes in Israel," Grant Smith wrote: "To date, all of the uranium-diversion masterminds, financiers, and beneficiaries have escaped criminal prosecution, even as U.S. taxpayers fund a nuclear waste cleanup at the (now defunct) NUMEC Apollo facility."

Eitan's unscrupulous character can be seen in a comment he made to the wife and lawyer for Jonathan Pollard, the captured spy he had managed:

> Eitan told us the only thing he regrets about the Pollard affair is that he did not 'finish the job' before leaving the States. We asked him what he meant by this. Eitan replied, "If I had been at the embassy when Pollard came to seek asylum, I would have put a bullet through his head. There would have been no Pollard affair."
> —Esther Pollard, *Maariv*, March 30, 2006

At SCP Partners Barak worked closely with another Mossadnik named Eitan - Yaron I. Eitan. Although Yaron Eitan looks very much like Rafi Eitan, the relationship between the two Eitans is not known. Rafi Eitan was actually born Raphael Hantman in Mandate Palestine to Noah Hantman from Minsk, Byelorussia. Rafi reportedly has three children, named Yael, Sharon, and Yuval.

For more than three months, structural steel from the World Trade Center has been and continues to be cut up and sold for scrap. Crucial evidence that could answer many questions about high-rise building design practices and performance under fire conditions is on the slow boat to China, perhaps never to be seen again in America until you buy your next car. ... The destruction and removal of evidence must stop immediately.

Bill Manning, "Selling Out the Investigation", *Fire Engineering*, January 2002

Chapter XV

The Destruction of the Evidence

The explosive demolitions of the Twin Towers pulverized the concrete floors and contents of the towers leaving nothing but steel and dust. "The concrete was literally pulverized; all you're left with is steel and dust," said Robert Kelman of Hugo Neu about the rubble of the World Trade Center.

The dust was found to contain large amounts of molten iron and a sophisticated form of thermite made using nanotechnology. Molten iron is one of the products of a thermite reaction. Because the remaining steel would reveal how the Twin Towers were destroyed, the architects of terror had set up a secure network to destroy this crucial evidence before it could be examined.

A Decade of Deception and War

The terror atrocity of 9-11 is a wicked criminal deception that is not meant to be solved, which is why sincere efforts to solve the crime, like mine, have encountered such vicious opposition. 9-11 is a textbook example of an elaborate criminal deceit known as "false-flag terrorism" in which the perpetrators designed the crime and spent years preparing the atrocity with the intention that a targeted group, in this case Osama Bin Laden and his nebulous band of Islamic fighters, Al Qaida, would be wrongly blamed.

In an act of false-flag terrorism, placing the blame on the targeted entity is the primary motive for the crime. For an act of false-flag terrorism to succeed it is essential that crucial evidence be removed and destroyed to protect the fraud, and the criminals behind it, from being exposed. The destruction of the evidence and the promotion of the deception are intrinsic parts of the crime. The people behind the destruction of the 9-11 evidence are partners in crime with the terrorists who planned and executed the attacks.

The main purpose of the 9-11 terror spectacle was to shock and scare the nation to swing public opinion behind supporting the pre-planned Zionist fraud known as the "War on Terror" and the U.S.-led invasion and occupation of Afghanistan. In the aftermath of the terror atrocity the unproven assertion that Al Qaida was behind the attacks became political dogma, the unchallengeable "party line" of both parties – and the controlled press. Although there were clearly a number of serious problems with the explanation that Al Qaida was behind the attacks, such as the unexplained explosive demolitions of the three towers at the World Trade Center, these issues were never discussed in the mainstream media. By ignoring the many unanswered questions about 9-11 the masters of the media sought to marginalize those who pointed out the glaring problems with the "politically correct" explanation that blamed Osama Bin Laden and Al Qaida.

Shock and Awe

The real masterminds of 9-11 designed the attacks to be a shocking spectacle of terror that would profoundly affect the American psyche and change the general perception of the Middle East. In order to scare the public and subjugate reason to fear, the architects of terror employed the psychological warfare tactic known as "shock and awe." The explosions that accompanied the aircraft crashing into the towers and the apocalyptic scenes of the buildings' collapses were meant to create frightening images of "Islamic terrorism" to be seared into the consciousness of every American.

The attacks had to be seen as being the work of Arab Muslim terrorists in order for the terror deception to succeed and achieve the desired effect on public opinion. It was essential that the blame be put on the targeted scapegoat as quickly as possible to preclude any serious doubts or questions being raised about who was behind the atrocity. Getting the interpretation desired by the terror masterminds to the global public required having "terrorism experts" such as Ehud Barak, the Israeli commando leader and defense minister, ready in a BBC television studio in London immediately after the attacks to present a plausible explanation blaming Osama Bin Laden and Al Qaida - and calling for U.S. intervention in Afghanistan. The Israeli military chief's interpretation, the first to accuse Osama Bin Laden, was later bolstered by bits of incriminating evidence such as the pristine passport of an alleged Arab hijacker "found" near the rubble of the World Trade Center and a terrorist handbook on how to hijack airplanes supposedly left behind in one of the terrorists' rental cars.

Although the government collected all the evidence from the 9-11 crime scenes, including confiscated video tapes, black boxes, pieces of the aircraft, and human remains, it has never presented any evidence to identify the aircraft or support its assertion that Al Qaida was responsible for the attacks. It was, therefore, based on nothing more than fabricated evidence that President George W. Bush invaded Afghanistan in October 2001.

If the government had real evidence that would conclusively prove its case for waging war, why has it not presented the evidence in a federal court after 10 years? The only logical explanation for this failure is that the government does not have the solid evidence to support its allegations. Vice President Dick Cheney admitted as much in an interview with Tony Snow on March 29, 2006. "We've never made the case, or argued the case that somehow Osama Bin Laden was directly involved in 9-11. That evidence has never been forthcoming," Cheney said. While it is said that Cheney made a slip of the tongue, the fact remains that not a single piece of evidence linking Osama Bin Laden to 9-11 has ever been presented.

If the attacks were truly carried out by Osama Bin Laden and Al Qaida there would be no reason to hide any of the evidence because it should serve to corroborate and confirm the official version. If, on the other hand, 9-11 was a false-flag terror deception it would be absolutely imperative for the perpetrators to confiscate and destroy any evidence that could disprove their false interpretation of events and expose the fraud.

This is exactly what happened when, for example, agents of the Federal Bureau of Investigation (FBI) confiscated video recordings from privately-owned cameras overlooking the Pentagon. These video tapes have never been shown to the public. Likewise, the FBI collected many numbered aircraft parts which could identify the specific plane they came from, yet none of these parts has ever been presented to support the official version. The failure of the government to use the evidence in its possession to prove its version suggests that the aircraft used in the 9-11 attacks were not the planes that are said to have been involved.

Understanding that 9-11 was an act of false-flag terrorism is the first step in comprehending the nature of the crime and identifying the real perpetrators. This is not an easy task because it requires thinking counter-intuitively about the crime and looking at it from a completely different angle than how it has been explained by the government and controlled media. This is very difficult for people who place a great deal of trust in what the government and media say. It also means understanding that the criminal cover-up and destruction of evidence continued long after the attacks.

Finding those responsible for the destruction of the evidence requires investigating a most unlikely set of suspects, including current and former officials of the U.S. government, law enforcement, and military, and ascribing to them criminal behavior quite unlike what one would expect of such people. This means recognizing that the highest officials in the Department of Justice, for example, whose obligation it was to investigate the crime and prosecute those responsible, actually oversaw the confiscation and destruction of crucial evidence.

A proper criminal investigation has to begin with the evidence. Any inquiry that does not examine and consider all the evidence is not an investigation, but a fraud. Rather than a federal investigation of 9-11, there was a "non-investigation" that allowed crucial evidence, such as the structural steel from the World Trade Center, to be destroyed before it could be examined. Instead of solving the crime and bringing those responsible to justice, people in positions of power participated in a criminal conspiracy to destroy the evidence and obstruct justice.

One of the clearest indications that 9-11 was an act of false-flag terrorism is that during the first ten years after the attacks not a single victim's lawsuit went to trial, although peripheral "terrorist" cases that did not require proving the official version were tried. Likewise, although the government claims to have Khalid Sheikh Mohammed, the alleged

"Mastermind of 9-11" in detention, in April 2011 the Obama administration abruptly reneged on its promise to try the 9-11 suspects in an open court and announced that the accused terrorists would be processed in a closed military tribunal in Guantánamo, Cuba.

If the government had evidence that could prove the veracity of its charges, why has it obstructed justice and refused to let a single 9-11 lawsuit go to trial? For years after the attacks government officials defended the concealment of the evidence saying that pending lawsuits required such secrecy, but after ten years there still had not been a trial to determine who was really responsible for the attacks and with all the wrongful death cases settled out of court there is virtually no hope there ever will be.

Alvin K. Hellerstein, the federal judge in Manhattan who handled the 9-11 litigation, effectively blocked any trial for the relatives that would have addressed the question of culpability for the terror attacks that changed America – and the world. In a judicial war of attrition against the families of the victims the court forced all of the 9-11 families to accept out-of-court settlements.

The Invasion of Afghanistan

The Bush administration's explanation that Osama Bin Laden and Al Qaida were responsible for the 9-11 atrocity led directly to the U.S. invasion of Afghanistan on October 7, 2001. The invasion was authorized by a joint resolution of the U.S. Congress on September 14, 2001, opposed by only one representative. The war resolution, known as "The Authorization for Use of Military Force Against Terrorists", granted President Bush the authority to use all "necessary and appropriate force" against those who he determined "planned, authorized, committed or aided" the attacks, or who harbored said persons or groups. Although the U.S. has been at war in Afghanistan since October 2001, it has never actually proven that Al Qaida was responsible for the attacks.

The controlled media and government officials who promoted the unproven version that Al Qaida carried out the attacks are all part of the 9-11 deception. Cognizant that the government and media were deceiving the public about what really happened on 9-11, I pursued my quest to identify the real perpetrators of the terror spectacle that brought us the "War on Terror" and a decade of deception and war.

Destroying the Evidence

According to the U.S. indictment against the alleged terrorists, there were 2,976 "murder victims" on 9-11, of whom about 93 percent were murdered at the World Trade Center. This includes the 147 people said to have been on the two airliners that struck the buildings, plus the 2,605 victims trapped in the towers when they were demolished. This makes the demolition of the Twin Towers the largest case of mass murder in U.S. history, but that's not how it was handled by the authorities of the federal government or New York City.

What is most appalling about the 9-11 case is how the most crucial evidence from the crime scene was confiscated and destroyed before it could be properly examined. While it was quite clear to many people including explosion experts like Van Romero that the steel-framed Twin Towers did not collapse due to burning jet fuel, this unproven explanation was accepted without question by the officials responsible for the criminal investigation. While the Federal Bureau of Investigation was supposedly investigating the crime, it was actually allowing the steel from the World Trade Center to be cut up into small pieces and exported to Asian smelters before it could be examined.

The officials who oversaw the investigation at the World Trade Center certainly knew it was wrong to dispose of evidence from the crime scene before it had been properly examined. The fact that the highest officials at the Department of Justice and the FBI allowed the structural steel to be destroyed without been examined indicates that a high-level criminal conspiracy was at work to prevent it from becoming forensic evidence. The conspiracy to destroy the steel is an intrinsic part of the 9-11 crime that was essential to prevent the discovery of who and what had caused the murderous demolition of the towers.

The spectacular explosive demolitions that pulverized the 220 concrete floors of the Twin Towers from the top down were evidently accomplished using an extremely powerful form of "super thermite". A sophisticated bi-layered coating of super thermite had evidently been applied to surfaces inside the towers, perhaps in the ducts running through the concrete floors or on the undersides of the floor pans. When the explosive thermitic coating was detonated it pulverized the 4-inch thick concrete floors and the steel pans that held them. The intense heat released by the alumino-thermic reaction melted the steel pans, creating billions of tiny molten iron droplets that fell like burning hail from the apocalyptic clouds that rolled across lower Manhattan on 9-11.

The abundance of iron-rich spheroids in the dust of the destroyed towers is not explained in the U.S. Geological Survey's published study or by the government-funded research that concluded that burning jet fuel caused the towers to collapse. A fire of burning jet fuel does not produce temperatures anywhere near the melting point of steel and cannot explain the extremely large amount of molten iron found in the dust and rubble.

The discovery of fragments of unexploded super thermite in the dust of the World Trade Center by Dr. Steven E. Jones, on the other hand, explains both the pulverization of the concrete floors and the abundance of molten iron droplets in the dust. Conventional thermite cutter charges were apparently also used to slice the massive core columns that held up the towers. Numerous eyewitnesses, including a reporter from the BBC, reported powerful explosions at the base of the towers long before the collapses occurred. None of this evidence of explosions, even from reporters on the scene, was taken into account by the government or the controlled media.

Steel is said to have a memory because when it is exposed to explosions or extreme heat its structure is affected. Because explosions and thermite leave permanent telltale signs on steel, the real masterminds of 9-11 had arranged a network in advance to manage the quick recovery and hasty destruction of the steel from the World Trade Center – before it could be examined by experts.

The Gang from Asia House

Mindful of the evidence of Israeli involvement in the terror attacks and cognizant of the hypothesis that 9-11 was an elaborate false-flag deception carried out by Israeli military intelligence and Zionist agents in high places, I pursued my investigation. Having found Israeli nationals or dedicated Zionists at every key point of the 9-11 matrix, I expected to find Zionist agents involved in the criminal destruction of the steel from the World Trade Center. When I discovered that the scrapyard that managed the destruction of most of the steel had employed a team of metal traders sent by a high-level agent of the Mossad to dispose of the steel by sending it to Asian smelters, I was not surprised because it was consistent with what I had expected.

In January 1999 the Business Wire reported that two scrap iron traders who worked for Marc Rich and his renamed company, Glencore AG, were being sent to New York to create an international trading division at Hugo Neu Schnitzer East, the scrap metal company who managed the destruction of the lion's share of the steel from the World Trade Center. Marc Rich and his lieutenant Ivan Glasenberg, CEO of Glencore International, are both Israeli citizens with close ties to the Mossad. The head of the Marc Rich Foundation in Israel is a former Mossad operative named Avner Azulay (sometimes spelled Azoulai).

The Marc Rich Foundation in Israel is run by Azulay working out of Shaul Eisenberg's Asia House in Tel Aviv. Eisenberg was the owner of Israel Corp., Israel Aircraft Industries, ZIM shipping, ATASCO, and hundreds of Mossad ventures in Asia, including Atwell Security, the company that obtained the security contract for the World Trade Center in the 1980s. (See "The Planes of 9-11")

Shaul Eisenberg left Germany in 1939 and moved to the Far East, making his primary bases of operation Japanese-occupied Shanghai and Japan itself. In Shanghai, Eisenberg, along with Imperial Japanese military intelligence, formed units of future Jewish terrorist groups - the Irgun and the Shanghai Betar. The Irgun and Betar gangs used the knowledge gained from the Japanese in their terror campaign against British and Arab forces in Palestine following World War II.

Eventually, Irgun and Betar veterans would create the Likud Party, which is now headed by Benjamin Netanyahu, an extreme right-winger. After the war, Eisenberg began selling iron and steel scrap. Married to a Japanese woman who converted to Judaism, Eisenberg established the Israel Corporation, a huge holding company, which, during the 1970s, began to secretly export Israeli military equipment and weapons to China. Under a Panama-based company called United Development, Inc., Eisenberg began exporting weapons to Central America's most insidious dictatorships, including that of Anastasio Somoza in Nicaragua. Eisenberg's vast holdings eventually included Israel Aircraft Industries and Zim Israel Navigation Company.

Azulay was a Mossad operative in Lebanon during Israel's invasion in 1982. In Lebanon, Azulay worked closely with Ariel Sharon, the Minister of Defense who carried out the murderous invasion. The prime minister at the time was Menachem Begin, the former head of the terrorist Irgun group, which later became the Likud party.

The two New Jersey junkyards who handled most of the steel from the World Trade Center were the final links in a secure network arranged by the Zionist masterminds behind 9-11 to destroy the crucial evidence. The highest agent in the network was Michael Chertoff, the Assistant Attorney General in charge of the Criminal Division of the U.S. Department of Justice. The FBI has special investigative jurisdiction in crimes of terrorism, and Chertoff, an Israeli national and son of a Mossad agent, was the senior official who oversaw the FBI investigation and the collection of evidence.

Because it was Chertoff's responsibility to oversee the gathering of the evidence from the crime scenes of 9-11, I asked him if he had authorized the destruction of the steel. Chertoff wrote back saying, "No." Asked if he knew who had, Chertoff said, "No idea." If the criminal destruction of the evidence from the World Trade Center were to be prosecuted as it should be, Chertoff should be investigated for criminal negligence because it was his responsibility to oversee the proper collection and protection of evidence in order to prosecute those behind 9-11.

Chertoff's failure to protect the steel evidence allowed officials of New York City to oversee the removal and disposal of evidence from the crime scene. As head of the criminal division of the Department of Justice, Chertoff had authority over the FBI investigation. Under the guise of the "clean-up" of the rubble, Chertoff allowed the control of the crucial steel evidence to devolve upon an agency of the city of New York headed by an official appointed by Mayor Rudy Giuliani.

Richard J. Sheirer, then commissioner of Giuliani's Office of Emergency Management (OEM), was the local official who was given complete authority over the "clean-up" at the World Trade Center. As *New York* magazine of October 15, 2001, reported:

> Since September 11, Sheirer has taken charge of the biggest clean-up effort in American history, coordinating 100 federal, state, and local agencies, including FEMA. He's become, in effect, the CEO of a company with thousands of workers and a budget that could run up to $40 billion — or, if you prefer, the mayor of the hot zone . . . "OEM is in charge," says Mike Byrne, deputy federal coordinating officer of FEMA for this incident. "Sheirer gives the marching orders. So far, we're blown away by OEM's performance."

Sheirer delegated the handling of the steel to an agency under his command, the Department of Design and Construction (DDC), headed by Kenneth Holden. When Holden gave his statement to the 9-11 Commission on April 1, 2003, he said that he had received "verbal permission" to send the steel to scrap yards in New Jersey, but failed to name the person who had authorized the removal. Seeing that Richard Sheirer of the OEM was in charge of the clean-up and giving "marching orders" to the DDC, it is logical to assume that it was Sheirer who authorized the removal of the steel to the two junkyards in New Jersey, Hugo Neu and Metal Management Northeast, where it was cut into small pieces, mixed with other scrap, and shipped to Asian steel companies.

Hugo Neu and Metal Management Northeast were the final links in the closed system that was set up by the terror masterminds to ensure the secure destruction of the steel evidence from the World Trade Center. In three easy steps from the FBI to the junkyard, the control of the crucial steel evidence passed from one Zionist-controlled agency to the next until it was destroyed in the smelters of Asian steel companies.

Hugo Neu

Hugo Neu "played a pivotal role as the principal recycler of steel from the World Trade Center," the company says about its role in the destruction of the steel. Robert A. Kelman, then senior vice president and general manager of Hugo Neu, told the Associated Press in 2002 that his company had handled 250,000 tons of trade center scrap and had shipped it to 11 countries, including Malaysia, China, South Korea, and Japan.

Each of the towers contained about 78,000 tons of recyclable steel. Frank Lombardi, chief engineer for the Port Authority of New York and New Jersey, which built the World Trade Center and owned six of the seven buildings (except Larry Silverstein's WTC 7), said the rubble contained an estimated 285,000 tons of steel. This would mean that Hugo Neu processed about 88 percent of the steel from the World Trade Center.

Less than a month after 9-11, James Glanz of the *New York Times* reported how Kelman's company was hastily cutting up the steel, destroying the crucial evidence that could reveal how the World Trade Center had been demolished:

> When it reached the Port Authority pier, the Kathleen dropped off the loaded barge, picked up one of three waiting empty barges and immediately headed back to Pier 6 in Manhattan. A second tug would pick up the steel and tow it to one of two scrap recyclers, either Metal Management of Newark or Hugo Neu Schnitzer East.
>
> The docks at Hugo Neu Schnitzer East, in the Claremont Channel in Jersey City, reveal the next leg of the journey. With a clear view of the altered skyline of Manhattan, a grappler on steel treads lifts beams out of another blue sanitation barge and adds it to a pile of wreckage that already stretches some 600 feet, reaching 30 or 40 feet high in places...
>
> A few steps from the grappler, a team of men with torches were already cutting beams into pieces five or six feet long. It is in that form that the material will be sent to steelmakers who will melt it down in huge ovens to make new products.
>
> Kelman said Hugo Neu had a work force of nearly one hundred people working on the scrap metal from

the World Trade Center, including 25 workers assigned to girder cutting, working around the clock in
twelve-hour shifts. Kelman told the AP that the steel
from the Twin Towers was sliced into pieces with
industrial guillotines or blow torches and thrown in
with other scrap before being shipped to smelters in
Asia. Alan Ratner, president of Metal Management
Northeast, the second junkyard processing the steel,
said his firm had 40 to 60 people working on the job.

The people at Hugo Neu and Metal Management Northeast were obviously engaged in a hasty effort to cut up the steel, mix it with other
scrap, and export it to distant Asian smelters. The real purpose behind
this effort was to prevent the steel from being properly examined and
becoming evidence that could expose the real cause of the explosive
demolition that claimed nearly 2,800 lives. The crucial roles played
by Hugo Neu and Metal Management in the recycling of the steel did
not happen by accident but were part of a well-organized plan to ensure the destruction of the evidence from the World Trade Center.

Having contacted the key players involved in the destruction of
the steel, I have not found one that is willing to discuss the subject. I
have, therefore, relied primarily on press articles and other information in the public domain to try to piece together the arrangement by
which this critical part of the 9-11 cover-up was carried out.

Mossad Creates the Network

Knowing there would be a huge amount of structural steel remaining after the explosive demolition of the Twin Towers, the terror masterminds put in place a network to manage the destruction of the steel, the solid evidence that could expose their crime. One scrap metal dealer, Hugo Neu Schnitzer East of Jersey City, already had the contract with New York City to recycle steel from the Fresh Kills dump on Staten Island, where the first truckloads of steel from the World Trade Center were taken. Hugo Neu reportedly processed nearly 90 percent of the steel from the rubble by cutting it up into pieces shorter than 60 inches, mixing it with other scrap, and sending it to Asian steel mills.

The second generation German-Jewish scrapyard was certainly well prepared to handle the massive job. In August 2001, Hugo Neu was engaged in a private-public project to dredge the narrow, two-mile Claremont Channel that ships used to reach its yard. The channel, which was only 10 feet deep in places, was dredged to a depth of 34 feet. Because the dredging was done to improve shipping for Hugo Neu, the company paid $24 million while the New Jersey Office of Maritime Resources paid $20.5 million. The dredging allowed larger ships to load at Hugo Neu's Claremont facility, which is exactly what was required to export the 9-11 steel on ocean-going vessels to Asia.

To broker the deals with Asian mills Hugo Neu had created a global trading division in 1999, headed by two veteran ferrous metal traders from Marc Rich and Glencore AG in Switzerland. But why would Hugo Neu invest $24 million in dredging the channel and create a global trading division when scrap iron prices were at the lowest levels in 50 years?

As the Business Wire reported from New York in January 1999:

NEW YORK—(BUSINESS WIRE)—Jan. 19, 1999—Hugo Neu Corporation and Schnitzer Steel Industries, Inc., who jointly own and operate an extensive network of scrap metal collection, processing and recycling facilities throughout the United States, announced today the formation of a new jointly owned international trading venture.

The new venture, known as Hugo Neu Schnitzer Global Trade LLC, will build on the years of experience and expertise of Hugo Neu and Schnitzer in the international ferrous scrap metal markets and their long-term industry leadership in scrap metal processing and recycling operations. The principal officers of this venture will be Nathan K. Fruchter and Jehuda Saar, formerly co-managers of the ferrous scrap department of Glencore AG in Europe, who bring extensive experience and commodity trading know-how with them. Combined with the processing, recycling and trading capabilities of Hugo Neu and Schnitzer, Hugo Neu Schnitzer Global Trade will offer an unparalleled array of services and a broader scrap supply to a large base of overseas and domestic customers.

The new trading venture will maintain executive offices in New York and will purchase scrap and other commodities from suppliers in Eastern and Western Europe, Australia, South Africa and other foreign

countries for sale to steel mills and foundries around
the world.

January 1999 seems like an odd time for Hugo Neu to have created
a global trading division in ferrous scrap metal considering that the
price of scrap iron had plunged 50 percent and was at its lowest point
in 50 years – between $70-80 per ton. Having fallen from $150 per
ton in late 1998, the price of scrap steel remained very low from 2001
through 2003, exactly the period when the steel from the World Trade
Center was exported to Asian mills halfway around the world. With
shipping costs running about $25 per ton, the cost of shipping steel to
Asia devoured most of the dealer's profit margin. As Robert Kelman
of Hugo Neu told the *Record* of New Jersey in November 2001, "I'm
hoping I net $5 a ton, but I don't know."

The two recyclers who bought the steel from the World Trade
Center were taking on a huge amount of steel in the most depressed
scrap market of their time. Was there a hidden partner directing the
destruction of the steel? Why didn't Hugo Neu simply sell the high
quality steel from the World Trade Center to U.S. mills and save
money on the cost of shipping? It seems that there must have been
a hidden imperative behind the decision to sell the steel to distant
Asian steel mills.

If Hugo Neu's role in exporting the steel to Asia was part of the
9-11 cover up, the "principal officers" of Hugo Neu Schnitzer Global
Trade would have been part of the conspiracy. This is how Jehuda
Saar and Nathan K. Fruchter describe their history with Hugo Neu:

> After spending their early professional careers with
> the Marc Rich Group both in the US and the UK,

the principals of Idoru Trading Corp, Nathan K. Fruchter and Jehuda Saar, took over the Ferrous Scrap division at Glencore in Europe in 1994. They ran the division until 1999 when they were recruited by then US scrap giants Schnitzer Steel and Hugo Neu Corp. to set up their new international division, Hugo Neu Schnitzer Global Trade LLC (HNSGT).

In 2001 the two left HNSGT and created a new ferrous scrap division, Idoru LLC, for the Midland Group, combining their extensive experience in global ferrous scrap trade with Midland's steel expertise in Ukraine and the CIS. By 2005 the Midland Group completed their spin-off of the scrap division, and Idoru Trading was born.

It is not known when Saar and Fruchter actually left Hugo Neu Global Trading and went to work for the Midland Group, founded by two Russian Jews, Alex Shnaider and Eduard Shifrin. Fruchter told me that he had been fired from Hugo Neu in January 2000, which is certainly not true because a November 2000 article in the *International Herald Tribune* describes Nathan Fruchter as "vice president of the international trading division of Hugo Neu Corporation in Manhattan." It was obvious that Fruchter did not want to tell me when he actually left Hugo Neu, but why would he want to conceal that?

It seems very likely that Fruchter and Saar had Zionist partners working on both ends of their deals. That is to say that the deals concerning the crucial steel evidence from the World Trade Center were probably done within a closed trading network of Zionist agents, with Alex Shnaider, for example, an Israeli who migrated to Israel from the Ukraine when he was 4 years old. Like Marc Rich, Shnaider's Midland Group also has an office in Hong Kong. From their early days with Marc Rich and Glencore, on to Hugo Neu and the Midland Group, Saar and Fruchter have always worked for companies closely tied to Israel and the Mossad. In 2006, the Belgian Jew Jehuda Saar emigrated from Teaneck, New Jersey, to Israel with his family. His mission in the United States was evidently finished.

The Zionist Junkyards

If the scrapyards that handled the steel from the World Trade Center were part of a Zionist conspiracy we would expect to find that the junkyards themselves were Zionist-owned operations. This would be consistent with the thesis that 9-11 is a conspiracy in which the key players are all dedicated partisans of the state of Israel. The junkyards would need to be under Zionist control in order to facilitate the secure destruction of the steel. This is exactly what we find with Hugo Neu Schnitzer East and Metal Management Northeast, the two junkyards that processed the steel from the World Trade Center.

Hugo Neu was a Jewish immigrant from Cologne who headed Associated Metals and Minerals Corp. (AMMC) in New York with two other German Jewish immigrants, Dr. Meno Lissauer and his brother-in-law, Walter M. Rothschild. The Hugo Neu company was started in 1947 and is still run by the tightly knit Neu family. The chairman and chief executive, John L. Neu, is the son of the founder, and Robert Kelman, the general manager, is his brother-in-law. Hugo Neu's vice president in charge of environmental and public affairs is Wendy K. Neu, Neu's wife and Kelman's sister. The father of Robert and Wendy was Captain Peter B. Kelman, a Hugo Neu business associate for nearly 40 years before his death in April 2005. The Kelman family managed the shipping part of the Hugo Neu business. Captain Kelman headed a firm of marine surveyors, Peter B. Kelman & Sons, Hugo Neu's principal marine surveyor in its export business.

Hugo Neu's Zionist character can be seen by its investment in an Israeli venture capital fund called the Agua-Agro Fund, which is managed by an Israeli named Nir Belzer. Belzer also happens to be the senior manager and co-founder of Israel's Millennium Materials Technologies Funds with a man named Oren Gafri. Gafri's biographical sketch says he served as an executive of the Israeli Aircraft Industries Ltd (IAI), Bedek Division, as the Manager of Materials and Process, in charge of the Chemical, Metallurgical, Composite and Non Destructive Testing (NDT) facilities, Labs and R&D from 1979 to 1989. The key connections linking IAI, Bedek, ATASCO, and Shaul Eisenberg with 9-11 are discussed in "The Planes of 9-11."

Gafri trained at Israel's Nuclear Research Center (Dimona) in the Negev Desert, where explosive coatings using nanotechnology are developed. Gafri is a specialist in energetic nano-composite coatings exactly like the one that was found in the dust of the World Trade Center. For the junkyard that destroyed most of the steel from the Twin Towers to be invested with an Israeli fund manager who develops such coatings is noteworthy, to say the least.

Metal Management & CIBC World Markets

Metal Management Northeast (MMNE) of Newark was the other junkyard that handled a large amount of steel from the World Trade Center. This scrapyard facility had been a family-owned business, formerly known as Naporano Iron & Metal Co. (and NIMCO Shredding Co.), before being acquired by Metal Management, Inc. of Chicago in July 1998. In March 2001, six months before 9-11, Metal Management, Inc. announced that Alan D. Ratner had replaced Andrew J. Naporano as president of MMNE. Although he had sold his family business, Naporano remained at the company through 2001 and acted as "the consultant" to the Department of Design and Construction on the removal of the steel.

With the fall of the price of scrap steel, the junkyard industry faced financial pressures in the late 1990s. Burdened by its acquisitions in a depressed market, Metal Management Inc. filed Chapter 11 bankruptcy in November 2000. Daniel W. Dienst, a managing director with CIBC World Markets, was hired to turn the company around and became a director of Metal Management in June 2001. CIBC World Markets was also known as CIBC Oppenheimer, which became a subsidiary of the Canadian Imperial Bank of Commerce after CIBC acquired New York-based Oppenheimer & Co. in 1997. When Dienst later became chairman of the board for Metal Management Inc. in April 2003 he was still a managing director at CIBC World Markets, where he remained until January 2004. Today, after a merger with Sims Group, Dienst is Group CEO of Sims Metal Management, Ltd. The Hugo Neu Corporation has also merged with the Australia-based Sims Group. The two companies created a joint venture corporation in 2005 known as Sims Hugo Neu Company. The merger created a new division, Hugo Neu Recycling.

At CIBC World Markets, Dienst worked under David Jonathan Kassie, chairman and CEO, and Lior Bregman, the Israeli who was managing director of CIBC World Markets and its predecessor Oppenheimer & Co., from 1988 to 2001. In May 2001, the *Jerusalem Post* reported that CIBC was the No. 1 underwriter in Israel and had underwritten more than $4.5 billion worth of merger and acquisitions transactions during the previous five years in Israel. "CIBC Oppenheimer has been the driving force behind investment in Israel since the early 1990s," Kassie said. In 2001, CIBC was also providing research for almost 100 Israeli companies, mainly hi-tech firms, the *Post* reported.

Kassie, a devoted Zionist, has participated in the Maccabiah Games in Israel. He is also involved in the major Zionist organizations in Canada and the United States, and is a director of the Shoah Foundation. Under his leadership, CIBC World Markets invested in an Israeli venture capital fund called the Genesis Funds, where Lior Bregman was a partner. Bregman, as managing director of equity research at CIBC Oppenheimer, is well known to the Israeli high-tech community. With a background as a military analyst, he coordinated communications equipment activity.

Kassie, Bregman, and Dienst were key players on the team of Zionists behind the takeover of Metal Management Inc. in 2000-2001. When the crucial steel evidence was removed from the World Trade Center and taken to the junkyards of Metal Management Northeast and Hugo Neu Schnitzer East it was being taken to companies that were controlled by dedicated partisans of the state of Israel.

A plot of this magnitude and audacity could only have been conceived under faultless cover and down to the smallest detail.

Ian Fleming, *Thunderball* (1961)

Chapter XVI

Making Sense of the 9-11 Cover-Up

The preceding chapter explains how the structural steel from the Twin Towers, crucial evidence of the murderous demolitions, was destroyed by a network of Zionist agents before it could be examined. From Michael Chertoff, the senior official responsible for investigating and prosecuting the crimes of 9-11, to the Mossad-controlled traders and owners of the New Jersey junkyards that managed its destruction, the steel passed from one Zionist agent to another until it was completely destroyed in the furnaces of Asian steel mills. What does this fundamental part of the 9-11 cover-up tell us about who is really behind the crime? If Osama Bin Laden and 19 Arab hijackers truly brought down the World Trade Center, why was a network of Israeli intelligence agents engaged in a concerted effort to destroy the evidence?

Common sense tells us that Israeli intelligence did not mastermind the hasty destruction of the steel from the World Trade Center because Osama Bin Laden was responsible for the explosive demolitions of the Twin Towers and Larry Silverstein's WTC 7. Rather, Zionist agents destroyed the evidence to protect the lie that Arab terrorists were responsible for the deaths of nearly 3,000 people on 9-11. The physical evidence of the towers was hastily destroyed by a network of Zionist agents because it could expose the real perpetrators. Indeed, the fact that a Zionist network had been established to manage the destruction of the evidence confirms the hypothesis that 9-11 was a false-flag terror atrocity carried out by Israeli intelligence and their agents in the U.S. government.

The intensely hot pile of rubble at the World Trade Center was the scene of a mass murder in which 2,752 people were killed. Dust and steel were virtually all that remained after the explosive demolitions destroyed the towers and the people within them. "The concrete was literally pulverized; all you're left with is steel and dust," said Robert A. Kelman, general manager of Hugo Neu Schnitzer East, the Jersey City junkyard that managed the destruction of the largest part of the steel from the World Trade Center.

The unexplained explosive demolitions of the 110-story towers directly caused the deaths of hundreds of people, but the cause of the unprecedented demolitions was certainly not known to the FBI investigation team at the remains of the World Trade Center. One of the first objects of any proper criminal investigation should have been to determine exactly what had caused the explosive demolitions of the towers. The federal investigation should have started with a thorough forensic examination of the dust, the steel, and anything else that remained of the Twin Towers. To allow the remaining structural steel to be destroyed without being examined was clearly a grave breach of duty by the officials at the Department of Justice and their investigative agency, the Federal Bureau of Investigation.

The hasty destruction of the unexamined steel from the World Trade Center could not have occurred had the FBI not allowed it to happen. The highest officials at the Department of Justice were clearly part of the conspiracy to conceal the truth about 9-11 by allowing the crucial evidence from the World Trade Center to be destroyed without having it examined and documented by steel experts, scientists, and engineers.

The Zionist Cover-Up

The facts indicate that the 9-11 cover-up is a Zionist operation in which partisans of the state of Israel have played all the key roles. If the attacks of 9-11 were truly acts of Muslim Arab terrorists there would be no reason for Zionists to manage the destruction of the evidence. The terror plot to destroy the World Trade Center had been planned for more than 20 years and was being discussed by senior Israeli intelligence figures in 1980, as we know from published comments of Michael D. Evans, an American Zionist who poses as a Christian missionary. Evans was told by the former Mossad chief Isser Harel of the plan to bomb the World Trade Center in 1980, when Osama Bin Laden was about 23 years old. (See "America the Target: 9-11 and Israel's History of False Flag Terrorism")

This indicates that Israeli intelligence began planning and preparing the false-flag terror attacks of 9-11 in the late 1970s when the notorious terrorist chief Menachem Begin and his Likud party came to power in Israel. Begin had created the Likud party in 1973 from the membership of the Irgun, the Zionist terror group he headed in Palestine in the 1940s. The false-flag terror plan for 9-11 required having high-level Zionist agents connected to the Mossad occupying positions from which they could directly control the cover up.

Putting the agents into the key positions was arranged by controlling the presidential appointments of judges and officials at the

Department of Justice. Such political appointments are greatly facilitated by having Mossad agents in the inner corridors of power. Rahm Emanuel, for example, the son of an Israeli terrorist who worked closely with Menachem Begin, was the key Mossad insider in the Clinton White House where, for example, he single-handedly pushed the disastrous NAFTA bill through Congress. Emanuel later became the first chief of staff for President Obama and mayor of Chicago.

How the Cover-Up Worked

There are three fundamental fields that need to be controlled in a cover-up like 9-11: the investigation, the interpretation, and the prosecution and related litigation.

The investigation involves the detective work supposedly done by the FBI and includes the collection and analysis of the evidence. Interpretation is how the events are explained to the public by the government and controlled media. Prosecution and litigation use the courts to assign blame for the crime and responsibility for the losses. In the 9-11 cover up we find high-level Zionist agents in the key positions of all three fields.

Zionist control over the political interpretation of 9-11 can be readily seen in how the Bush administration and the controlled media accepted without question the unproven explanation blaming Osama Bin Laden and Al Qaida. This explanation was exactly what the architects of terror wanted the world to believe and was first articulated by Ehud Barak, the former Israeli commando leader and prime minister, on BBC World television minutes after the demolitions of the Twin Towers. Barak openly called for the United States to begin the "War on Terror" by invading Afghanistan.

Through their media networks (e.g. FOX News, CNN, CBS, *New York Times*, etc.) the Zionist interpretation of 9-11 was pushed relentlessly on the gullible American public. No other possible explanation was even discussed and people who held dissenting points of view were ignored, slandered, and attacked, as I was by the ADL, FOX News, CNN, *The Chicago Tribune*, and finally a three-man squad of undercover police in Hoffman Estates, Illinois.

Zionist control of the media was essential in shaping public opinion about 9-11 and directing the anger and blame at Osama Bin Laden and Al Qaida. The controlled politicians dutifully parroted the media version, which quickly became the "party line" of both parties. Dissent was quashed. Politicians, academics, and journalists who expressed doubts or raised questions about what really happened were treated like pariahs and removed from their positions.

The Zionist control of the cover up is also seen very clearly in the investigation and prosecution fields. Michael Chertoff, as Assistant Attorney General in charge of the criminal division of the Department of Justice, was directly responsible for the federal prosecution of the terrorists behind 9-11 and for overseeing the investigation by the FBI. Chertoff, an orthodox Jew, is an Israeli citizen by virtue of the fact that he is the son of an Israeli, Livia Eisen, who happened to be one of the first Mossad agents. Had the FBI collected and examined the steel and dust from the Twin Towers, questions would have been raised by the discovery of evidence of explosives and thermite. Rather than deal with the evidence, Chertoff simply allowed Zionist officials working under Mayor Rudy Giuliani to "clean up" the crime scene by destroying the steel evidence through specially prepared junkyards in New Jersey.

As the federal official responsible for the criminal prosecution, Chertoff had control over access to the evidence. Through a newly created agency, the Transportation Security Administration (TSA) and a special category of evidence known as Sensitive Security Information (SSI), Chertoff retained his control over the 9-11 evidence after he became the secretary of the Department of Homeland Security in 2005. The key role that Chertoff played in the 9-11 cover-up is solely due to the fact that he, like Rahm Emanuel, is a high-level Zionist partisan from a family with a long and close connection to Israeli intelligence.

Alvin K. Hellerstein is the other hand of the Zionist-controlled cover-up in the judicial field in which access to the evidence is crucial. Hellerstein is a U.S. district judge in Manhattan, appointed to the federal bench by President Bill Clinton in 1998. Judge Hellerstein presided over all 9-11 tort litigation and criminal cases related to the terror attacks and prevented a 9-11 trial from ever taking place. Hellerstein's judicial war of attrition against the victims' families resulted in all of them being forced to accept out-of-court settlements.

Judge Hellerstein's son, Joseph, lives in Israel and works for an Israeli law firm that represents the parent company of one of the defendants in the 9-11 tort litigation, Mossad's "security" company International Consultants for Targeted Security (ICTS NV). ICTS owns Huntleigh USA, the airport security company responsible for screening the passengers that boarded the planes on 9-11. The fact that Hellerstein is a Zionist with a close family connection to one of the defendants should have disqualified him from managing the 9-11 litigation, but it didn't. This glaring conflict of interest was ignored by the media.

The impropriety of Judge Hellerstein's glaring conflict of interest in the 9-11 litigation has been completely ignored by the media. Hellerstein and Chertoff both facilitated the 9-11 cover up and obstructed justice for the families of the victims with their improper conduct. Brazen and shameless, they are confident their misdeeds will be ignored and that they will be remain protected and supported by the larger Zionist network that controls the U.S. government.

As German intelligence experts told me in 2001, 9-11 was a sophisticated operation that required years of planning and the fixed structure of a state intelligence agency. It was, they said, far beyond the capabilities of a loosely structured group like Al Qaida. Such a false-flag terror operation consists of three levels, Andreas von Bülow said: the architectural, managerial, and working levels. The architectural level designs the terrorism primarily to affect public opinion while the managerial level manages the execution of the crime and the cover up. The working level, von Bülow said, is actually part of the deception. While Hellerstein and Chertoff are probably not architectural level planners of the terror attacks, they are certainly dedicated Zionist managers of the 9-11 cover up.

The reason for Hellerstein and Chertoff to be confident in the face of their blatant misconduct is obvious. In spite of the serious nature of their crimes to facilitate the 9-11 cover up, these two Zionist agents of deception have not suffered any penalties under the law or faced a single word of criticism from the media for the glaring improprieties they committed as federal employees. Where is the watchful eye of the government? Why do Hellerstein and Chertoff act as if they are above the law? Where is the free press, the watchdog of a properly functioning democratic state? Is this not evidence of a conspiracy?

The false-flag terror atrocity of 9-11 changed more than public opinion. The 9-11 deception that has been foisted on the nation has changed the fundamental relationship between the U.S. government and the American people. The proper role of government is to alleviate the suffering of the people, not increase it. The Declaration of Independence states that governments are instituted among men in order to secure their unalienable rights, namely life, liberty, and the pursuit of happiness, and that "whenever any Form of Government becomes destructive of these ends, it is the Right of the People to alter or to abolish it."

The deception of 9-11 was used to instill fear in the population in order to usher in the fraudulent "War on Terror." To submit to the 9-11 deception is to subject ourselves and our nation to an open-ended agenda of war. The Zionist fraud known as the "War on Terror" began with the false-flag terror attacks of 9-11, which led directly to illegal wars of aggression in the Middle East and a greatly enlarged police-state apparatus in the United States. We have certainly not seen the end of it.

The disastrous and costly wars in Afghanistan and Iraq have done immense damage to our nation and others, wasting more than $1.6 trillion and ruining countless lives. Believing the lies about 9-11 has made helpless victims of millions of people, such as those who have gone to war in Afghanistan and Iraq thinking they were defending their nation from terrorists. The only way to liberate ourselves and our nations from continued enslavement to this criminal deception is to understand how it was imposed on us and who is behind it.

Liberation from the deception can only happen when individuals choose to reject fear and examine the facts with a truly open mind. The personal choice to examine the evidence, embrace the facts, and conquer fear is the most important decision we can make as free men.

As my patriotic duty to my nation and as a service to mankind, I am sharing my insights and the fruits of my research about the 9-11 deception in the hope that by understanding how this evil deception was planned and executed we can liberate ourselves from it and secure a more just and peaceful world for our children.

B e not deceived; God is not mocked: for whatsoever a man soweth, that shall he also reap.

Galatians 6:7

Selected Sources

9-11 Encyclopedia, "Maurice Greenberg," www.911review.org

ABC News, "Terror Hits the Towers: How Government Officials Reacted to 9-11 Attacks," September 14, 2002

ABC News, "The White Van: Were Israelis Detained on Sept. 11 Spies?" June 22, 2002

Ashkenazi, Eli, "Commander of legendary Jewish immigrant ship Exodus dies at 90," *Haaretz,* April 26, 2008

Babcock, Charles R., "Israeli Firm Loses N.Y. Airport Award – Official Involved in Killings of Hijackers," *Washington Post,* April 12, 1987

Barbash, Fred; Lescaze, Lee; Elizur, Yuval; "Ugandan Plane Deal Believed Key to Israeli Spy Operation," *Washington Post,* September 11, 1978

Bardach, Ann Louise, "The Last Tycoon," *Los Angeles Magazine,* April 2000

Bar Zohar, Michael, *Ben Gurion, A Biography,* Delacorte, New York, 1978

BBC World, "Ehud Barak interview," September 11, 2001

Bennet, James, "A Day of Terror: The Israelis," *New York Times,* September 12, 2001

Bennet, James, "Spilled Blood is Seen as Bond That Draws 2 Nations Closer," *New York Times,* September 12, 2001

Berger, Sharon, "CIBC acquires Israeli brokerage firm," *Jerusalem Post,* May 2, 2001

Biography of Ehud Barak, Zionism-Israel.com

Boyes, Roger, "Mossad spied on far-right Austrian," *The Times* (U.K.), June 2, 2005

SOLVING 9-11

"Civil Justice, Military Injustice," *New York Times*, October 5, 2010

Coleman-Lochner, Lauren, "Jersey City, N.J., Steel Recycler Works on Remains of World Trade Center," *The Record*, Hackensack, N.J., November 2, 2001

"Computer Expert Used Firm to Feed Israel Technology," *Washington Post*, October 31, 1986

Cowen, Lauren; Long, James; "CIA Proprietary Kept Arizona Air Park Humming," *The Oregonian*, August 22, 1988

Crewdson, John, "Special Report: New revelations in attack on American spy ship," *Chicago Tribune*, October 2, 2007

Delevan, Richard, "Welcome to the Art of Electronic Warfare," *Irish Times*, October 5, 2001

Emigh, Jacqueline, "GPS on the Job in Massive World Trade Center Clean-Up," SecuritySolutions.com, July 1, 2002

Evans, Michael D., "Is America in Bible Prophecy?" Deborah Caldwell interview, Beliefnet.com, August 2004

Frantz, Douglas, "A Midlife Crisis at Kroll Associates," *New York Times*, September 1, 1994

Goshko, John M., "Israel Got U.S.-Made Devices," *Washington Post*, May 14, 1985

Goshko, "U.S. Asks to Inspect Israeli Atom Sites to Verify Use of Restricted Device," *Washington Post*, May 15, 1985

Goshko, "L.A. Man Indicted in Export of Potential Nuclear Bomb Component to Israel," *Washington Post*, May 17, 1985

Griscom, Amanda, "Man Behind the Mayor," *New York*, October 15, 2001

Guttman, Nathan, "Israelis at center of ecstasy drug trade", *Haaretz*, 6 April 2003

Harrit, Niels H. et al, "Active Thermitic Material Discovered in Dust from the 9-11 World Trade Center Catastrophe," *The Open Chemical Physics Journal*, Vol. 2, 2009, with Jeffrey Farrer, Steven E. Jones, Kevin R. Ryan, Frank M. Legge, Daniel Farnsworth, Gregg Roberts, James R. Gourley, Bradley R. Larsen

Hecht, Jamey, "Ptech, 9-11, and USA-Saudi Terror," From the Wilderness, 2005

Hernandez, Javier C., "Holder, High Achiever Poised to Scale New Heights," *New York Times*, November 30, 2008

Holtappels, Dr. Peter and Hummel, Capt. Werner, "The Diving Investigation," *The Group of German Experts* Estonia *Investigation Report*, 1999

Holtappels and Hummel, "Safety Organisation," especially 7.3.4, "Training and Drills" and the summary of the RITS Exercise on *Estonia* on February 2, 1994

Israel Venture Capital, www.ivc-online.com

J7: The July 7th Truth Campaign, "Peter Power Dorset Police Suspension & the DPP File," julyseventh.co.uk, February 7, 2008

J7: The July 7th Truth Campaign, "The 7/7 Terror Rehearsal," julyseventh.co.uk

James, George, "Ex-Koch Deputy Favored As Head of Port Authority," *New York Times*, August 2, 1990

Joffe, Lawrence, Obituary: "Mordechai Hod: Israeli air force mastermind behind the six day war," *Guardian* (UK), July 2, 2003

Johnson, Jim, "N.J. duo tackles NYC metal mass," *Waste News*, 2001

Kapeliouk, Amnon, "Begin and the 'Beasts'," *New Statesman*, June 25, 1982

Kaplan, Kenneth, "The Colombia Connection," *Jerusalem Post*, September 1, 1989

Khaleel, Kaasem, *Wrongly Blamed: The Real Facts Behind 9-11 & the London Bombings*, Knowledge House Publishers, 2007

Le Carré, John, *The Little Drummer Girl*, Hodder & Stoughten Ltd., London, 1984

Leppard, David and Robert Winnett, "Brown picks tycoon to back power bid," *Sunday Times*, January 16, 2005

Lima, Paolo, "Five men detained as suspected conspirators," *Bergen Record*, September 12, 2001

Longstreth, Andrew, "Making History With Obama," *The American Lawyer*, June 5, 2008

Lueck, Thomas J., "Port Authority Powerhouse: Stephen Berger," *New York Times*, August 2, 1987

Manning, Bill, "Selling Out the Investigation," *Fire Engineering Magazine*, January 2002

Martin, Douglas, "Yossi Harel," *New York Times*, May 1, 2008

Martinson, Jane, "Sir Ronald Cohen," *Guardian*, July 7, 2006

May, Capt. Eric H., "False Flag Prospects, 2008 - Top Three US Target Cities," www.thepriceofliberty.org, February 25, 2008

McArthur, Shirl, "A Conservative Estimate of Total Direct U.S. Aid to Israel: $108 Billion," *Washington Report on Middle East Affairs*, Washington, D.C., July 2006

Melman, Yossi, "Israeli communications said to prove IAF knew Liberty was U.S. ship," *Haaretz*, October 4, 2007

Mendelson, Udi, U.S. Aviation Technology documents archived at: http://web.archive.org/web/20041206032229/http://us-aviation-technology.com/bplan325.pdf

MITRE Technical Report, "FAA Data Registry (FDR) Concepts of Use and Implementation," www.mitre.org, September 2000

MITRE Working Note, "Adapting Information Engineering for the National Airspace System and Its Application to Flight Planning," www.mitre.org, September 1999

"Mossad spied on Austria's Haidar," United Press International, June 2, 2005

National Commission on Terrorist Attacks Upon the United States, 9-11 Commission Staff Statement No. 17, June 17, 2004

NATO Press Release (94)82, "Exercise Cooperative Venture 94," September 16, 1994, http://www.nato.int/docu/pr/1994/p94-082.htm

Netanyahu, Benjamin, *International Terrorism: Challenge and Response*, Transaction Publishers, New Jersey, 1982

Netanyahu, Benjamin, *Terrorism: How the West Can Win*, Farrar, Straus and Giroux, New York, 1986

O'Meara, Kelly Patricia, "A Historical Whitewash?" *Insight, Washington Times*, December 22, 2003

Ostrovsky, Victor, and Hoy, Claire, *By Way of Deception: The making and unmaking of a Mossad Officer*, St. Martin's Press, 1990

O'Sullivan, Arieh, "GSS Agent 'Proud' To Have Murdered Terrorists," *Jerusalem Post*, July 24, 1996

Perliger, Arie and Weinberg, Leonard, "Jewish Self Defense and Terrorist Groups Prior to the Establishment of the State of Israel," *Totalitarian Movements & Political Religions*, Vol. 4, No. 3 (2003) pp. 91-118

Piller, Charles, "Electric power grids vulnerable to hackers," *Los Angeles Times*, August 20, 2001

Prince-Gibson, Eetta, "Reflective truth," *Jerusalem Post* (Editor-in-Chief), July 27, 2006

"Profile: Sir Ronald Cohen," *Sunday Times*, January 23, 2005

Ranalli, Ralph, "FBI reportedly didn't act on Ptech tips," *Boston Globe*, December 7, 2002

Rokach, Livia, *Israel's Sacred Terrorism*, AAUG Press, Belmont, Mass., 1980

Rowan, David, "Interview: Sir Ronald Cohen," *Jewish Chronicle*, September 22, 2007

Rubin, Debra, and Richard Korman and Gary Tulacz, "Industry Firms Pitch in for World Trade Cleanup While Others Account for Employees in Doomed Buildings," *Engineering News-Record*, September 13, 2001

Sachar, Howard M., *A History of Israel from the Rise of Zionism to Our Time History of Israel*, Knopf, New York, 1976 (3rd Edition, 2007)

Schmidt, Olivier, "The Sinking of the *Kursk* and 'Retired' US Navy Spy Edmond Pope," *The Intelligence Files: Today's Secrets, Tomorrow's Scandals*, 2005

Seely, Hart, "Untold Stories: 'We were suddenly no kidding under attack'," *Post-Standard*, Syracuse, NY, January 20, 2002

Shahzad, Syed Saleem, "A Chilling Inheritance of Terror," *Asia Times*, October 30, 2002

Shahzad, Syed Saleem, "Khalid: 'A Test for U.S. Credibility," *Asia Times*, March 6, 2003

Singh, Indira, "Ground Zero 911, Blueprint for Terror, Part Two," Pacifica radio, July 20, 2005

Singh, Indira, 9-11 Citizens' Commission, New York City, September 9, 2004

Singh, Indira, "The Story of Indira Singh," *Our World In Balance*, ourworldinbalance.blogspot.com, April 27, 2005

Smith, Grant, "America's Loose Nukes in Israel," *Antiwar.com*, April 14, 2010

Smyth, David, Associated Press, "Americans Rebut Israeli Version of 1967 Attack on U.S. Ship," *Lexington Herald-Leader* (KY), October 29, 1984

Suroor, Hasan, "Celebrating Terror, Israeli-style," *The Hindu* (Madras, India), July 24, 2006

"Suspicious Activities Involving Israeli Art Students at DEA Facilities," U.S. Drug Enforcement Administration, Office of Security Programs, 2001

Thomas, Mary Ann and Ramesh Santanam, "Government Agencies Investigated Missing Uranium, NUMEC," *Pittsburgh Tribune-Review*, August 25, 2002

"U.S. Drops Plan for a 9-11 Trial in New York City," *New York Times*, January 29, 2010

Vladimirsky, Dr. Irena, "Jews of Harbin," Beit Hatfutsot, Israel, bh.org.il

Von Bülow, Andreas, "Former Top German Minister Rejects Official Story of 911 Attacks," *Tagesspiegel*, January 13, 2002

Washington Post, "Page Airways Denies Operating Amin's Airplane," March 4, 1977

Wilson, Drew, *The Hole*, Diggory Press, Cornwall, UK, 2006

Wisconsin Project on Nuclear Arms Control, "Israeli Nuclear Program Pioneered by Shimon Peres," *The Risk Report*, Vol. 2 No. 4, July-August 1996

Yinon, Oded, "A Strategy for Israel in the Nineteen Eighties," *The Zionist Plan for the Middle East*, ed. Israel Shahak, AAUG Press, Belmont, Mass., 1982

"Yossi Harel" (obituary), *The Times*, April 30, 2008

CHRISTOPHER BOLLYN is an investigative journalist and writer. After finishing high school in Schaumburg, Illinois, he sojourned in Europe and the Middle East before studying languages, history, and journalism at the University of California at Davis and Santa Cruz. He earned a degree in history with the focus on the Israeli occupation of Palestine. After the first Gulf War he led an international team of photojournalists on a trip through the West Bank and Gaza Strip. He has written in-depth articles about the Middle East, electronic vote fraud, the dangers of depleted uranium, and the history and geo-political background of the terror attacks of 9-11. He has been invited to speak at numerous 9-11 events across Europe and the United States.

The author speaking to the Citizens' Grand Jury on the Crimes of 9-11 in Los Angeles, California, on October 23, 2004.

CPSIA information can be obtained
at www.ICGtesting.com
Printed in the USA
FFHW02n1922290918
48604856-52575FF